Spring Boot 2.0 P

Build production-grade reactive applications and microservices with Spring Boot

Mohamed Shazin Sadakath

BIRMINGHAM - MUMBAI

Spring Boot 2.0 Projects

Copyright © 2018 Packt Publishing

All rights reserved. No part of this book may be reproduced, stored in a retrieval system, or transmitted in any form or by any means, without the prior written permission of the publisher, except in the case of brief quotations embedded in critical articles or reviews.

Every effort has been made in the preparation of this book to ensure the accuracy of the information presented. However, the information contained in this book is sold without warranty, either express or implied. Neither the author, nor Packt Publishing or its dealers and distributors, will be held liable for any damages caused or alleged to have been caused directly or indirectly by this book.

Packt Publishing has endeavored to provide trademark information about all of the companies and products mentioned in this book by the appropriate use of capitals. However, Packt Publishing cannot guarantee the accuracy of this information.

Commissioning Editor: Richa Tripathi
Acquisition Editor: Sandeep Mishra
Content Development Editor: Tiksha Sarang
Technical Editor: Supriya Thabe
Copy Editor: Safis Editing
Project Coordinator: Prajakta Naik
Proofreader: Safis Editing
Indexer: Rekha Nair
Graphics: Jisha Chirayil
Production Coordinator: Aparna Bhagat

First published: July 2018

Production reference: 1260718

Published by Packt Publishing Ltd.
Livery Place
35 Livery Street
Birmingham
B3 2PB, UK.

ISBN 978-1-78913-615-9

www.packtpub.com

To my parents, for going through tough times in order to give me a good education and manners, and to my wife, Nadhiya, for being my loving partner throughout our life journey together.

mapt.io

Mapt is an online digital library that gives you full access to over 5,000 books and videos, as well as industry leading tools to help you plan your personal development and advance your career. For more information, please visit our website.

Why subscribe?

- Spend less time learning and more time coding with practical eBooks and Videos from over 4,000 industry professionals

- Improve your learning with Skill Plans built especially for you

- Get a free eBook or video every month

- Mapt is fully searchable

- Copy and paste, print, and bookmark content

PacktPub.com

Did you know that Packt offers eBook versions of every book published, with PDF and ePub files available? You can upgrade to the eBook version at www.PacktPub.com, and as a print book customer, you are entitled to a discount on the eBook copy. Get in touch with us at service@packtpub.com for more details.

At www.PacktPub.com, you can also read a collection of free technical articles, sign up for a range of free newsletters, and receive exclusive discounts and offers on Packt books and eBooks.

Contributors

About the author

Mohamed Shazin Sadakath is an experienced software engineer with over 9 years of software development experience in J2SE-, J2EE-, and Spring-based applications. He is a BSc (Hons) software engineering graduate, having achieved first class honors. He has worked in different domains, ranging from telecommunications to real estate. In his spare time, he contributes to open source projects, such as Spring Security, and writes technical articles for blogs. He is a Stack Overflow Moderator and loves answering Java-related questions.

> *I would like to thank my loving wife, Nadhiya, for her help and encouragement while writing this book. I would like to thank Gunith Devasurendra for the technical reviewing of this book. I would also like to thank Sudharshan Selvenayagam and Manoj Senevirathne for their assistance while writing this book.*

About the reviewers

Gunith Eranda Devasurendra is a senior software engineer with 10 years, professional development experience, specializing in Java. Born in Sri Lanka, he became interested in programming as he considers elegant programming and design to be an art form. Gunith has a master's in computer science awarded by the University of Colombo. He is a speaker and a trainer on technical topics including Spring, and Git. He is also an advocate of FOSS. Gunith also helps out in the Stack Overflow community.

> *To Lord Buddha. To my parents for raising me and giving me an education so that I could contribute to this book. To my wife, Vimanga, for her love and helping me on so many levels so that I can contribute. To my son Sasen for his love. To Shazin, the author, for nominating me and trusting me. To all my teachers and friends who taught me things.*

Biharck Araújo has been working as a principal software architect and lead programmer for the past 15 years. He is passionate about technology and academic research. He has been working with JavaEE technology for web projects that demand high-security standards in terms of information transmission for companies across different sectors. He has extensive experience in activities regarding software architecture. He works in bioinformatics using technology in life's favor.

Packt is searching for authors like you

If you're interested in becoming an author for Packt, please visit authors.packtpub.com and apply today. We have worked with thousands of developers and tech professionals, just like you, to help them share their insight with the global tech community. You can make a general application, apply for a specific hot topic that we are recruiting an author for, or submit your own idea.

Table of Contents

Preface — 1
Chapter 1: Introduction — 7
  Technical requirements — 7
  Generating Spring Boot Projects — 8
    Opening the generated project with IntelliJ — 9
    Opening the generated project with STS — 11
  Getting started with Spring Boot — 13
    Learning about Spring Boot — 13
      Anatomy of a Spring Boot application — 14
      Supporting the Spring Framework ecosystem in Spring Boot — 16
  Changes since Spring Boot 1.x — 17
    Registering a Spring Bean using ApplicationContextInitializer — 18
    Configuration property binding — 19
      New property binding API — 20
      Property origin — 21
      Tightened rules for governing relaxed property binding — 21
      Environment variables with indices — 22
      Direct binding of property type java.time.Duration in the ISO-8601 form — 22
    Custom endpoints for Spring Boot Actuator using annotations — 22
      Exposing a custom Spring Boot Actuator endpoint — 23
      Extending a custom endpoint with a specialized implementation for the web — 24
      Connecting to a custom endpoint using monitoring and management tools — 24
    Custom metrics using Micrometer — 26
    Custom health indicator — 27
    Using the HTTP/2 protocol — 28
    Securing applications with Spring Security — 31
  The next milestone — 32
  Migration — 33
    Using the correct JDK and JVM — 33
      Running on Java 9 — 33
        Tackling JAXBException — 33
        Using the correct AspectJ version — 34
        Being aware of limitations on Apache Cassandra drivers — 34
        Being aware of issues with the Maven Surefire Plugin — 34
    Using the upgraded Spring Framework 5.0 — 34
      Modified CORS support behavior — 35
      Removed packages, classes, and methods — 35
      Dropped support for frameworks — 35
    Using the updated configuration properties — 36
    Using the changed servlet-specific server properties — 36
    Using the modified template engine extension handling — 36

Using the changed actuator configuration properties	37
Using the changed actuator base path	37
Using the renamed actuator endpoints	37
Using the changed Embedded Container Configuration	38
Using the changed default behavior for path mapping	38
Using the changed default dispatcher types for the servlet filter	39
Using the modified transitive dependency to spring-boot-web-starter	39
Using the changed default proxying strategy	40
Using the modified configuration location strategy	40
Using the changed Jackson/JSON support	40
Using the changed Spring Boot Actuator security	40
Using the changed HikariCP default connection pool for JPA	41
Using the changed default database initialization strategy	41
Using the changed database schema creation strategy	41
Using the changed testing support	42
Using the revised Spring Security	42
Using the changed default security auto-configuration strategy	42
Spring Security OAuth2 is migrated to Spring Security core	42
Using the AuthenticationManager bean	42
Understanding removed features	43
Summary	**43**
Questions	**44**
Further reading	**44**
Chapter 2: Building a Basic Web Application	**45**
Technical requirements	**45**
Getting started	**46**
Web application architecture	46
Workflow of Spring Web MVC	47
Requirements for our web application	49
The use case diagram	49
Using Spring Data JPA for persistence	**50**
Understanding the Java Persistence API (JPA)	50
Understanding Spring Data JPA	51
Class diagram for the domain model	51
Implementation of the domain model using JPA annotations	52
Setting up dependencies and configuration	52
Implementing the domain model	54
Implementation of Spring Data JPA repositories	56
Testing Spring Data JPA repositories	56
Using Spring Boot Devtools for database visualization	59
Using Services to encapsulate business logic	61
Testing Services	62
Using Spring Thymeleaf for the view	**65**
Understanding template engines	65
Spring Thymeleaf	66

UI design for the Retro Board	66
UI implementation for the Retro Board using Spring Thymeleaf	67
Using Spring Web MVC with servlet 3.x for the controller	**69**
Implementation of Controllers annotations	70
Testing controllers	71
Using Spring Security for authentication and authorization	**74**
Demonstrating the Retro Board	**77**
Summary	**79**
Questions	**79**
Further reading	**80**
Chapter 3: Building a Simple Blog Management System	**81**
Technical requirements	**81**
Getting started	**82**
Web application architecture	82
Workflow of Spring WebFlux	83
Requirements of the Bloggest system	83
The use case diagram	84
Using Spring Data Elasticsearch for persistence	**85**
Understanding Elasticsearch	85
Understanding Spring Data Elasticsearch	86
Class diagram for the domain model	86
Implementation of the domain model using Spring Data Elasticsearch annotations	87
Setting up dependencies and configuration classes	87
Implementing the domain model	88
Implementation of Spring Data Elasticsearch repositories	89
Using Apache FreeMarker for the view	**90**
Understanding template engines	90
Apache FreeMarker	91
UI design for Bloggest	92
UI implementation for Bloggest using Apache FreeMarker	94
Implementing a common layout using Apache FreeMarker	95
Implementing a List Articles page	98
Implementing a Create Article page	101
Implementing a Show Article page	103
Implementing an error page	105
Using Spring WebFlux for controller	**106**
Implementation of controllers	106
Implementation of ControllerAdvice	110
Using Spring Security for authentication and authorization	**111**
Demonstrating Bloggest	**114**
Summary	**122**
Questions	**123**
Further reading	**123**

Chapter 4: Introduction to Kotlin — 125
  Technical requirements — 125
  Getting started with Kotlin — 126
    Default imports — 126
    Basic data types — 127
      Numeric data types — 127
      Learning numeric literals — 127
      Numeric representation — 128
      Numeric operations — 128
      String literals — 129
    The syntax for Kotlin code — 129
      The Kotlin packages — 129
      String interpolation — 130
      Functions in Kotlin — 130
      Variables in Kotlin — 131
      Conditional statements — 131
        The if statement — 131
        The when statement — 132
      Type checking and automatic casting — 132
      Nullable values and compile-time null safety — 132
      The for loop — 133
        The for loop with an array — 133
        The for loop with a collection — 133
        The for loop with a value range — 134
      The while loop — 134
  Object-oriented programming with Kotlin — 135
    Learning about visibility modifiers — 135
    Classes in Kotlin — 136
      Abstract classes — 136
      Concrete classes — 137
    The concept of interfaces in Kotlin — 137
    Learning about extensions — 138
    Generic types in Kotlin — 139
    Enums in Kotlin — 139
    Objects in Kotlin — 140
      Object expressions — 140
      Object declarations — 140
      Companion objects — 141
  Advanced programming with Kotlin — 141
    Functions — 142
      Infix notation in functions — 142
      Local functions in Kotlin — 142
      Default arguments in functions — 143
      Named arguments in functions — 143
      Generics in functions — 144
      Variable number of arguments (vararg) in functions — 144
  Summary — 144
  Questions — 145

| Further reading | 145 |

Chapter 5: Building a Reactive Movie Rating API Using Kotlin — 147
- Technical requirements — 147
- Getting started — 148
  - REST architecture — 148
  - Requirements of REST architecture — 149
    - The use case diagram — 150
- Using Spring Data MongoDB for persistence — 150
  - Understanding MongoDB — 151
  - Understanding Spring Data MongoDB — 151
  - Class diagram for the domain model — 152
  - Implementation of the domain model using Spring Data MongoDB annotations — 153
    - Setting up dependencies and configuration — 153
    - Implementing the domain model — 153
  - Implementing of Spring Data MongoDB repositories — 155
  - Using a service to encapsulate business logic — 155
  - Testing Services — 157
- Using Spring WebFlux for controllers — 161
  - Implementation of controllers — 162
  - Testing controllers — 163
- Using Spring Security for basic authorization — 166
- Demonstrating Moviee — 168
  - Integration testing — 168
  - Demonstrating the use of Postman — 171
    - Accessing the List Movies endpoint — 171
    - Accessing the Get Movie endpoint — 172
    - Accessing the Get Movie endpoint with an invalid Movie ID — 173
    - Accessing the Rate Movie endpoint — 174
- Summary — 175
- Questions — 175
- Further reading — 176

Chapter 6: Building an API with Reactive Microservices — 177
- Technical requirements — 178
- Getting started — 178
  - Microservices architecture — 178
  - The requirements of microservices architecture — 180
    - The use case diagram — 181
    - The project structure to develop microservices — 182
- Using Spring Data Redis for persistence — 183
  - Understanding Redis — 183
  - Understanding Spring Data Redis — 183
  - Class diagram for the domain model — 184
  - Implementation of domain model using Spring Data Redis annotations — 185

[v]

Setting up dependencies and configuration	185
Implementing the domain model	185
Implementation of Spring Data Redis repositories	187
Using a Service to encapsulate business logic	187
Using Spring WebFlux for a controller	**193**
Implementation of controllers	194
Using asynchronous data transfer for cross-microservice communication	**197**
Asynchronous data transfer using Redis	197
Using Docker to support microservices	**199**
Understanding Docker	199
Using Maven to build Docker images	200
Building a system of microservices with Docker	202
Deploying microservices with Docker	206
Demonstrating Saber	**207**
Submitting to the Register Taxi endpoint	207
Submitting location to update Taxi Location endpoint	209
Submitting to Update Taxi Status endpoint	210
Accessing the Get Taxi Status endpoint	211
Accessing the GET available Taxis endpoint	212
Submitting to Book Taxi endpoint	213
Submitting to Accept Taxi Booking endpoint	214
Submitting to cancel Taxi Booking endpoint	215
Accessing Taxi Bookings endpoint	216
Summary	**217**
Questions	**217**
Further reading	**218**
Chapter 7: Building a Twitter Clone with Spring Boot	**219**
Technical requirements	**219**
Getting started	**220**
Beginning with the Tweety architecture	220
Tweety requirements	221
The use case diagram	221
Using Spring Data JPA for persistence	**222**
Class diagram for the domain model	222
Implementation of the domain model using Spring Data JPA annotations	223
Setting up dependencies and configuration	223
Implementing the domain model	224
Implementing Spring Data JPA repositories	226
Caveat for going reactive with blocking JDBC	226
Using Service to encapsulate business logic	227
Using Angular 5 for the frontend	**229**
Getting started with Angular 5 application development	229
Generating Angular services	230
Generating the users service	231

Generating Angular page components	233
Generating the Tweets Add page	235
Generating the User Profile page	237
Using Spring Web Flux for the REST controller	238
Implementing controllers	239
Enabling Angular frontend access to controllers	241
Using Spring Security for authentication and authorization	242
Understanding OAuth2	242
Setting up dependencies and configuration	243
Configuring the Resource Server	244
Configuring the Authorization Server	244
Configuring web security	245
Using an Angular service for OAuth2 authentication and authorization	246
Demonstrating Tweety	249
Accessing the login page	250
Accessing the List Tweets page	251
Accessing the Send Tweet page	251
Accessing the User Profile page	252
Summary	253
Questions	254
Further reading	254
Chapter 8: Introducing Spring Boot 2.0 Asynchronous	255
Technical requirements	255
Getting started	256
Synchronous applications	256
Asynchronous applications	257
The requirement of asynchronous applications	257
The use case diagram	258
The architecture of an image resizing application	259
Using Spring Kafka for communication	259
Understanding Apache Kafka	260
Setting up dependencies and configuration	261
Configuration for the Image Resize Request Producer	261
Configuration for Image Resize Request Consumer	264
Starting Spring Boot applications in a non-web mode	265
Using Quartz for scheduling	266
Understanding Quartz	266
Setting up dependencies and configuration	266
Configuration for Quartz scheduling	266
Demonstrating Image Resizer	268
Building all dependencies	268
Running Apache Kafka	268
Running Apache ZooKeeper on Windows	268
Running Apache Kafka on Linux/Unix	269
Running Apache Kafka on Windows	269

Table of Contents

Running Image Resize Request Consumer	269
Running Image Resize Request Producer	269
Summary	272
Questions	272
Further reading	273
Chapter 9: Building an Asynchronous Email Formatter	275
Technical requirements	275
Getting started	276
Why Email Formatter is useful	276
The use case diagram	277
The architecture of the Email Formatter application	278
Using Spring Data JPA for persistence	278
Class diagram for the domain model	279
Implementation of the domain model using JPA annotations	279
Setting up dependencies and the configuration class	279
Implementing the domain model	280
Implementation of Spring Data JPA repositories	281
Using Services to encapsulate business logic	281
Using Apache FreeMarker for templates	283
Using Spring Kafka for communication	285
Setting up dependencies and the configuration class	286
Configuration for User Registration	286
Configuration for the Email Formatter consumer	288
Configuring Java Mail	290
Using Spring Web MVC for the REST controller	291
Implementation of controller annotations	291
Using Spring Security for authentication and authorization	292
Demonstrating Email Formatter	293
Building all dependencies	293
Running Apache Kafka	294
Running Apache ZooKeeper on Windows	294
Running Apache Kafka on Linux/Unix	294
Running Apache Kafka on Windows	294
Running SMTP server	295
Running the Email Formatter consumer	296
Running the User Registration microservice	296
Summary	300
Questions	301
Further reading	301
Assessments	303
Other Books You May Enjoy	311
Index	315

Preface

This book is about Spring Boot 2.0 hands-on development for beginners, intermediate, and expert-level software developers. The purpose of this book is to increase the practical knowledge of the readers by going through the practical uses of the features introduced in Spring Boot 2.0.

This book covers vast topics with example applications so that it is much easier to grasp and use in real-life projects.

Who this book is for

This book is for anyone interested in developing applications using the Spring Framework, and specifically, Spring Boot 2. The readers may have prior experience of Spring Boot, but it is not compulsory, as even beginners can benefit from the content of this book.

This book expects the readers to have some level of understanding of software development using Java.

What this book covers

Chapter 1, *Introduction*, outlines the Spring Boot 2.0 application development framework and compares its features with the previous version of Spring Boot. It also talks about configuration property changes, API changes, platform changes, and more in Spring Boot 2.0. Furthermore, it explains how to migrate from the previous version of Spring Boot application to Spring Boot 2.0 application.

Chapter 2, *Building a Basic Web Application*, begins with the practical side of developing a basic web application using the Spring Boot 2.0 Framework. It also talks about Spring Data JPA persistence, Spring Thymeleaf view, and Spring WebFlux controllers.

Chapter 3, *Building a Simple Blog Management System*, presents the practical side of developing a simple blog management system using the Spring Boot 2.0 framework. It also talks about Spring Data Elasticsearch for persistence, Apache FreeMarker view, and Spring WebFlux controllers.

Preface

Chapter 4, *Introduction to Kotlin*, introduces the programming language Kotlin by comparing it with Java programming language side by side. It will help to get started with Kotlin programming, subsequently moving into advanced topics in Kotlin such as OOP and other features.

Chapter 5, *Building a Reactive Movie Rating API Using Kotlin*, discusses reactive movie rating API development using Kotlin programming language with Spring Boot 2.0. It talks about Spring Data MongoDB persistence, Spring WebFlux controllers, and Spring Security authentication and authorization.

Chapter 6, *Building an API with Reactive Microservices*, explains reactive microservices development using Spring Boot 2.0. It also talks about Spring Data Redis persistence, Spring Web Flux controllers, Asynchronous data transfer among microservices, and Docker deployment of microservices.

Chapter 7, *Building a Twitter Clone with Spring Boot*, covers Angular application acting as a client for Spring Boot 2.0 REST API. It also talks about Spring Data JPA persistence, Angular 5 frontend, Spring Web Flux controllers, and Spring Security OAuth2 authentication and authorization.

Chapter 8, *Introducing Spring Boot 2.0 Asynchronous*, Quartz Scheduler introduces asynchronous application development using Spring Boot 2.0. It also talks about Apache Kafka as a message broker that enables decoupled, asynchronous communication between applications.

Chapter 9, *Building an Asynchronous Email Formatter*, explains details of how to build an Asynchronous Email Formatter, using Spring Boot 2 as the backend development framework and Apache Kafka as a message queue. It will also explain how to use JPA as the persistence layer, which is a widely used data source. It will use Apache FreeMarker to create the email templates and show how to use placeholders to provide dynamic data to email templates.

To get the most out of this book

You need knowledge of the following:

1. The Java programming language
2. Spring Framework
3. Web application concepts

The following tools will be used throughout chapters:

1. Java Development Kit 8+
2. Maven 3
3. IntelliJ IDEA or Spring Tool Suite

Download the example code files

You can download the example code files for this book from your account at www.packtpub.com. If you purchased this book elsewhere, you can visit www.packtpub.com/support and register to have the files emailed directly to you.

You can download the code files by following these steps:

1. Log in or register at www.packtpub.com.
2. Select the **SUPPORT** tab.
3. Click on **Code Downloads & Errata**.
4. Enter the name of the book in the **Search** box and follow the onscreen instructions.

Once the file is downloaded, please make sure that you unzip or extract the folder using the latest version of:

- WinRAR/7-Zip for Windows
- Zipeg/iZip/UnRarX for Mac
- 7-Zip/PeaZip for Linux

The code bundle for the book is also hosted on GitHub at https://github.com/PacktPublishing/Spring-Boot-2.0-Projects-Fundamentals-of-Spring-Boot-2.0. In case there's an update to the code, it will be updated on the existing GitHub repository.

We also have other code bundles from our rich catalog of books and videos available at https://github.com/PacktPublishing/. Check them out!

Preface

Conventions used

There are a number of text conventions used throughout this book.

`CodeInText`: Indicates code words in text, database table names, folder names, filenames, file extensions, pathnames, dummy URLs, user input, and Twitter handles. Here is an example: "An `ApplicationStartedEvent` will be sent right after the application context is refreshed but before any command-line runners run."

A block of code is set as follows:

```
public class Address {
    private String number;
    private String street;
    private String city;
    private String country;
    private String zipCode;
    // Getters, Setters, Equals, Hashcode
}
```

Any command-line input or output is written as follows:

```
$ jconsole
```

Bold: Indicates a new term, an important word, or words that you see onscreen. For example, words in menus or dialog boxes appear in the text like this. Here is an example: "Select **File** | **Open** from the menu bar."

Warnings or important notes appear like this.

Tips and tricks appear like this.

Get in touch

Feedback from our readers is always welcome.

General feedback: Email `feedback@packtpub.com` and mention the book title in the subject of your message. If you have questions about any aspect of this book, please email us at `questions@packtpub.com`.

Errata: Although we have taken every care to ensure the accuracy of our content, mistakes do happen. If you have found a mistake in this book, we would be grateful if you would report this to us. Please visit `www.packtpub.com/submit-errata`, selecting your book, clicking on the Errata Submission Form link, and entering the details.

Piracy: If you come across any illegal copies of our works in any form on the Internet, we would be grateful if you would provide us with the location address or website name. Please contact us at `copyright@packtpub.com` with a link to the material.

If you are interested in becoming an author: If there is a topic that you have expertise in and you are interested in either writing or contributing to a book, please visit `authors.packtpub.com`.

Reviews

Please leave a review. Once you have read and used this book, why not leave a review on the site that you purchased it from? Potential readers can then see and use your unbiased opinion to make purchase decisions, we at Packt can understand what you think about our products, and our authors can see your feedback on their book. Thank you!

For more information about Packt, please visit `packtpub.com`.

Introduction

This chapter will introduce the reader to Spring Boot and explain how it stands out from other competing frameworks. It will begin by explaining how to get started developing applications using Spring Boot. Also, it will explain about Spring Boot 1.x and the improvements introduced in Spring Boot 2.0. Furthermore, it will walk through the most noticeable features and/or improvements of Spring Boot 2.0. Continuing on, it will explain progress with Spring Boot 2.0 and supply tips on migration from the older versions to Spring Boot 2.0.

This chapter covers the following topics:

- Understanding Spring Boot
- Generating Spring Boot Projects
- Getting started with Spring Boot
- Changes since Spring Boot 1.x
- The next milestone
- Migration

Technical requirements

Technical requirements for this chapter are as follows:

- To install **Java Development Kit (JDK)** 8, it can be downloaded from its official page at `http://www.oracle.com/technetwork/java/javase/downloads/jdk8-downloads-2133151.html`
- To install Maven 3, download it from its official page at `https://maven.apache.org/download.cgi`

Introduction

- To install IntelliJ IDEA, download it from its official page at `https://www.jetbrains.com/idea/download/`
- To install **Spring Tool Suite (STS)**, download it from its official page at `https://spring.io/tools`

Generating Spring Boot Projects

In this book, we will be using `http://start.spring.io`, which is a convenient tool for generating Spring Projects with the required dependencies to get started. This tool supports multiple Spring Boot versions, programming languages (**Java**, **Groovy**, **Kotlin**), project types (**Maven**, **Gradle**), and dependencies. Learning to use this tool will help readers to get started quickly with Spring Projects. The following is a screenshot of the tool to help us get familiarized with it:

This tool allows the selection of a Project type (**Maven Project**, **Gradle Project**), programming language (**Java, Groovy, Kotlin**), Spring Boot version (**2.0.***, **1.5.***), project artifact group, artifact name, and project dependencies. After selecting the correct options, click on **Generate Project** will download a ZIP file of the project.

Chapter 1

The ZIP file needs to be extracted first before being used. The extracted ZIP file will have the following structure:

```
<Project Name>/
├── src/
├── pom.xml
├── mvnw
└── mvnw.bat
```

Opening the generated project with IntelliJ

To open the generated project with IntelliJ, we perform the following steps:

1. Open IntelliJ IDE.
2. Select **File** | **Open** from the menu bar as shown in the following screenshot:

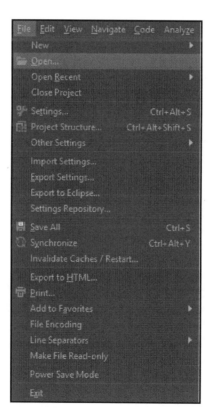

Introduction

3. Navigate to the location where the extracted project is and click on **OK** after selecting the project, shown as follows:

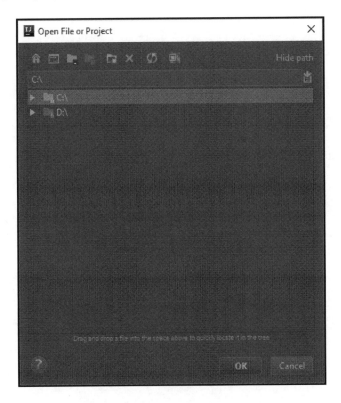

4. The IDE will show the opened project.

Opening the generated project with STS

To open the generated project the Spring Tool Suite, we perform the following steps:

1. Open STS.
2. Select **File | Open Projects from File System...** from the menu bar, as shown in the following screenshot:

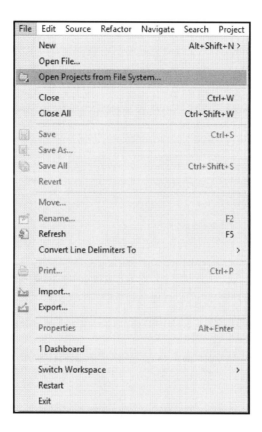

Introduction

3. From the dialog box that launched, click on the **Directory...** button:

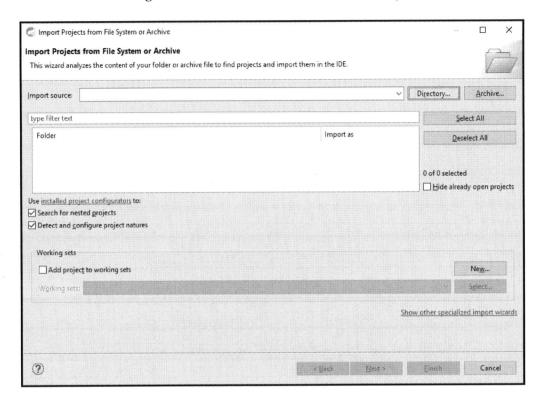

4. Navigate to the extracted project location and Click on **OK** after selecting the project:

5. Finally, click on **Finish** on the import projects dialog box.
6. The IDE will show the opened project.

The source code for this chapter can be found at `https://github.com/PacktPublishing/Spring-Boot-2.0-Projects-Fundamentals-of-Spring-Boot-2.0`, in the `Chapter01` directory.

Getting started with Spring Boot

This section will enable readers to get started with Spring Boot by explaining its features in detail. Furthermore, it will help you get started with Spring Boot application development by explaining the bare-bones of a Spring Boot application. Furthermore, it will explain the Spring Framework ecosystem and how it can be used in the Spring Boot application to harness the power of time-tested, industry-standard databases, messaging systems, and so on.

Learning about Spring Boot

Spring Boot is an application development framework for the **Java virtual machine** (**JVM**) that enables users to write stand-alone, production-grade, flexible, and extensible Spring-based applications with minimum code and configurations. This follows the **Rapid application development** (**RAD**) paradigm where the focus is on writing business logic that matters. With the introduction of cloud-based hosting services and microservice architectures, Spring Boot has been further elevated into a must-know technology platform. The following are some of its features:

- **Standalone**: A Spring Boot application is self-contained and easily deployable. It can start with its own embedded Tomcat, Jetty, Undertow web container, or as a console application from a just standard file such as **Java Archive** (**JAR**) or **Web Archive** (**WAR**). An example of this would be an application that has `spring-boot-starter-web` as a dependency, which when run will by default inside an embedded Tomcat web container.
- **Production-grade**: A Spring Boot application enables most of the features required for production, such as monitoring, connection pools, externalized configurations, and so on, out of the box, and ships with industry-standard, time-tested, and proven third-party applications such as Tomcat.

- **Flexible**: A Spring Boot application will have most of its settings auto-configured with default settings based on the dependencies available in the classpath of the application. But the auto-configuration will step back whenever a custom configuration is made. An example for this would be when a Spring Boot application finds a MySQL JDBC driver in the classpath; it auto-configures DataSource, which connects to the host localhost and port `3306`, as those will be the settings for a MySQL Server with a default installation.
- **Extensible**: A Spring Boot application will have most core functionalities implemented out of the box, but also has a lot of **Service Provider Interfaces (SPI)**, which are used by third-party developers to implement or modify functionality. An example of this would be when a requirement arises for a custom endpoint in Spring Boot Actuator; extending and overriding the `AbstractEndpoint.invoke` method in a Spring Bean will expose it as a new endpoint under Spring Boot Actuator.

Spring Boot does not do any code generation and does not require any XML files to be configured in order to run. Spring Boot is ideal for on-premise and cloud-based deployments with a quick boot-up time and a good memory footprint. The uniqueness of Spring Boot comes from its ecosystem of Spring modules, which covers security, data persistence, batch processing, and so on and from the highly active, competent community of developers who keep on improving the Spring Boot Framework.

Anatomy of a Spring Boot application

The anatomy of a Spring Boot application will be that it will be inheriting from a `spring-boot-starter-parent` project that will in return have all the common dependencies available for a Spring Boot application. Apart from this, there will be one or more `spring-boot-starter` POM such as `spring-boot-starter-web`, `spring-boot-starter-jpa`, and so on. The following example excerpt from `pom.xml` shows the basic dependencies of a Spring Boot application:

```
<parent>
   <groupId>org.springframework.boot</groupId>
   <artifactId>spring-boot-starter-parent</artifactId>
   <version>1.5.9.RELEASE</version>
   <relativePath/> <!-- lookup parent from repository -->
</parent>

<dependencies>
   <dependency>
      <groupId>org.springframework.boot</groupId>
      <artifactId>spring-boot-starter</artifactId>
```

```
        </dependency>
        ...
</dependencies>
```

The minimum bootstrapping point of a Spring Boot application will be a class with a `main` method that will be annotated with a `@SpringBootApplication` annotation along with the `main` method body, which calls the `SpringApplication.run` static method, for which a configuration class (a class with `@Configuration` annotation—the `@SpringBootApplication` annotation transitively has one) needs to be passed, along with a String array of arguments. The following code shows the minimum bootstrapping point of a Spring Boot application:

```java
import org.springframework.boot.ApplicationRunner;
import org.springframework.boot.SpringApplication;
import org.springframework.boot.autoconfigure.SpringBootApplication;
import org.springframework.context.annotation.Bean;

@SpringBootApplication
public class SpringBootIntroApplication {

    public static void main(String[] args) {
        SpringApplication.run(SpringBootIntroApplication.class, args);
    }

    @Bean
    public ApplicationRunner applicationRunner() {
        return args -> {
            System.out.println("Hello, World!");
        };
    }
}
```

By running the preceding class, a Spring Boot application can be provisioned and executed. There are several ways to run a Spring Boot application; some of them are mentioned here:

- Running the Spring Boot application `main` class using an IDE.
- Building a JAR or WAR file using the following Maven command and then running:

    ```
    $ mvn clean install
    $ java -jar target/<package-name>.[jar|war]
    ```

- Run this using the Spring Boot Maven plugin:

    ```
    $ mvn clean spring-boot:run
    ```

Introduction

The `@SpringBootApplication` annotation comprises of `@EnableAutoConfiguration` and `@ComponentScan` annotations that do the heavy lifting of auto-configuring the Spring Boot application with the default settings and scanning the packages for any Spring-specific components such as services, components, repositories, and so on.

Supporting the Spring Framework ecosystem in Spring Boot

What made the Spring Boot application development framework stand out from other competing alternatives is the fact that it has a lot of supporting frameworks for easing development, with starter dependencies that cover industry-standard, enterprise-grade methodologies and tools such as Web MVC, JPA, MongoDB, Elasticsearch, Redis, and many more.

This makes Spring Boot a unique solution for day-to-day programming needs. By including a starter dependency, a Spring Boot application will have all the necessary dependencies and auto-configurations included in the application without any developer intervention.

This makes the life of a developer easy and enables us to focus on the business logic of the application instead of configurations and dependency management. At the time of writing, there are more than thirty of these starters available to be used in a Spring Boot application. The complete list can be found at `https://github.com/spring-projects/spring-boot/tree/master/spring-boot-project/spring-boot-starters`.

Spring Boot is a powerful framework as it has a very gradual learning curve and is built on the basis of the ability to write applications that just run with minimal effort. Having said that, Spring Boot should not be mistaken for a silver-bullet solution for all problems. In the areas of memory utilization, optimization, latency reduction, and many more, work may be needed, so developer commitment and effort are still required. But all in all, Spring Boot can be considered as a very good solution as it enables users to develop a **minimum viable product** (**MVP**) that is production-ready within maybe a couple of days or hours.

Changes since Spring Boot 1.x

The last released version of Spring Boot 1.x was 1.5.10.RELEASE, after which Spring Boot 2.0 was released in early 2018. As Spring Boot 2.0 is a major release it has JVM level, platform level, **application programming interface (API)** level, and dependencies level changes, which must be taken into account when developing applications with Spring Boot 2.0.

The major changes from Spring Boot 1.x to Spring Boot 2.0 are listed as follows:

- **Java 8 is the baseline and Java 9 is supported**: This means the minimum JVM version on which a Spring Boot 2.0 application can be run is now Java 8 because the framework is modified to use many features introduced in Java 8. Furthermore, Spring Boot 2.0 is fully supported to run on Java 9, which means all the dependency JARs shipped will have module descriptors to support the Java 9 module system.
- **Third-party libraries upgraded**: Spring Boot 2.0 requires Spring Framework 5.0 along with Tomcat 8.5, Flyway 5, Hibernate 5.2, and Thymeleaf 3.
- **Reactive Spring supported**: Supports the development of functional, non-blocking, and asynchronous applications out of the box. Reactive Spring will be explained and used extensively in upcoming chapters.
- **Micrometer Framework introduced for metrics**: Uses Micrometer instead of its own API for metrics. A micrometer is a third-party framework that allows dimensional metrics.
- **Spring Boot Actuator changed**: Spring Boot Actuator endpoints are now placed inside the context path `/actuator` instead of being mapped directly to `root`, to avoid path collisions. Additionally, a new set of endpoint annotations have been introduced to write custom endpoints for Spring Boot Actuator.
- **Configuration property binding**: Improved relaxed binding of properties, property origins, converter support, and a new Binder API.
- **Kotlin language supported**: Supports Kotlin, a new concise and interoperable programming language introduced by IDEA. Kotlin will be explained in detail in `Chapter 04`, *Introduction to Kotlin*.
- **HikariCP shipped out of the box instead of Tomcat Connection Pool**: HikariCP is the most efficient, high-performing database connection pool available for the JVM and it is shipped by default with Spring Boot 2.0.

Introduction

- **A new way to dynamically register Spring Bean with** `ApplicationContextInitializer`: Adds to previous methods of registering a Spring Bean by providing the means to define it in an XML file, annotate `@Bean` on a method that returns an object, annotate with `@Component`, `@Service`, `@Repository` annotations, and so on. Spring Framework 5 has introduced `ApplicationContextInitializer`, which can do dynamic registering.
- **HTTP/2 supports out of the box**: HTTP/2 is the latest version of the widely used **Hypertext Transfer Protocol (HTTP)**, which has a lot of performance gains when compared to older versions.
- **Newly added event** `ApplicationStartedEvent`: An `ApplicationStartedEvent` will be sent right after the application context is refreshed but before any command line runners run. `ApplicationReadyEvent` will, however, be sent right after the application context is refreshed and any command-line runners run. This means the application is in a ready state to accept and process requests.

These are the most notable changes, but there are so many more, as with any major release. Other changes can be seen in the Spring Boot 2.0 release notes, found at `https://github.com/spring-projects/spring-boot/wiki/Spring-Boot-2.0-Release-Notes`.

Let's have a look at some of the notable features of Spring Boot 2.0 with some hands-on examples.

Registering a Spring Bean using ApplicationContextInitializer

Spring Boot allows Builder to create customized Spring Boot application bootstrapping with a tool called `SpringApplicationBuilder`. This can be used as follows to customize the Spring Boot application and register a Spring Bean dynamically:

```
public static void main(String[] args) {
   new SpringApplicationBuilder(SpringBoot2IntroApplication.class)
         .bannerMode(Banner.Mode.OFF)
         .initializers((GenericApplicationContext
           genericApplicationContext) -> {
             genericApplicationContext.registerBean
             ("internet",
              InternetHealthIndicator.class);
                })
```

```
            .run(args);
    }
```

In this code, a new instance of `SpringApplicationBuilder` is instantiated with a configuration class. By invoking the `bannerMode(Banner.Mode.OFF)` method, the banner shown in the console at the Spring Boot Bootstrap is switched off.

By invoking the `initializers()` method with a lambda function (learn about lambda functions in the reference documentation at https://docs.oracle.com/javase/tutorial/java/javaOO/lambdaexpressions.html) for `ApplicationContextInitializer`, the `GenericApplicationContext.registerBean` method is used to register a Spring Bean called `internet` and with class type `InternetHealthIndicator`.

Configuration property binding

Configuration properties are a great feature of Spring Boot for reading properties with type safety. This section will explain the concept with the following `DemoApplicationProperties` class file:

```
@ConfigurationProperties(prefix = "demo")
public class DemoApplicationProperties {

    private Integer number;

    private String username;

    private String telephoneNumber;

    private List<String> emailAddresses =
    Arrays.asList("shazin@techtalks.lk");

    private String firstName;

    private String lastName;

    private Duration workingTime;

    // Getters and Setters
}
```

The `application.yml` has the following configuration properties:

```
demo:
  number: 10
  user-Name: shazin
  firstName: Shazin
  lAsTNamE: Sadakath
  telephone_number: "0094777329939"
  workingTime: 8h
  EMAILADDRESSES:
    - shazin.sadakath@gmail.com
    - shazin.swe@gmail.com
  addresses:
    - number: "B 22 2/3"
      city: Colombo
      street: "Ramya Place"
      country: "Sri Lanka"
      zipCode: "01000"
    - number: "123"
      city: Kandy
      street: "Dalada Weediya"
      country: "Sri Lanka"
      zipCode: "01332"
```

For configuration properties, an `application.properties` file also can be used over an `application.yml` file. Lately, YML files are becoming famous among developers because they can provide a structure with indentations, the ability to use collections, and so on. Spring Boot supports both at the moment.

New property binding API

Spring Boot 2.0 introduces a new binding API for configuration properties. The most notable change in Spring Boot 2.0 related to configuration property binding is the introduction of a new binding API with the following `Address` **Plain Old Java Object (POJO)**:

```
public class Address {
    private String number;
    private String street;
    private String city;
    private String country;
    private String zipCode;
    // Getters, Setters, Equals, Hashcode
}
```

The following `Binder` fluent API can be used to map properties directly into the `Address` POJO.

This code can be written inside any initializing code such as `CommandLineRunner`, `ApplicationRunner`, and so on. In the application this code is available inside the `SpringBoot2IntroApplication.runner` method:

```
List<Address> addresses = Binder.get(environment)
    .bind("demo.addresses", Bindable.listOf(Address.class))
    .orElseThrow(IllegalStateException::new);
```

The preceding code will create a `Binder` instance from the given `Environment` instance and bind the property for a list of `Address` classes. If it fails to bind the property then it will throw `IllegalStateException`.

Property origin

Another notable addition to configuration property binding is exposing the origins of a property. This is a useful feature because many developers have struggled in the past because they had configured the wrong file and ran an application to just see unexpected results. Now, the `origin` of a property is shown along with the file, line number, and column number:

```
"demo.user-Name": {
   "value":"shazin",
   "origin":"class path resource [application.yml]:5:14"
}
```

Tightened rules for governing relaxed property binding

Relaxed property binding rules have the following changes:

1. Kebab-case format (lower-case, hyphen-separated) must be used for prefixes. Examples of this are `demo` and `demo-config`.
2. Property names can use kebab-case, camel-case, or snake-case. Examples of this are `user-Name`, `firstName`, and `telephone_number`.
3. The upper case underscore format that is usually used for environment variables should be followed, where the underscore should only be used to separate parts of the key. The upper case underscore format is usually used for environment variables. The underscore is used to separate parts of the key. An example of this would be `DEMO_ENV_1`.

Introduction

The complete set of rules for relaxed bindings can be seen in the Spring Boot documentation at `https://docs.spring.io/spring-boot/docs/current/reference/html/boot-features-external-config.html#boot-features-external-config-relaxed-binding`.

Environment variables with indices

Furthermore, environment variables with indices can be mapped to names with array syntax and indices, shown as follows:

```
DEMO_ENV_1 = demo.env[1]
DEMO_ENV_1_2 = demo.env[1][2]
```

So, the `DEMO_ENV_1` environment variable can be read in the application as follows:

```
System.out.printf("Demo Env 1 : %s\n",
environment.getProperty("demo.env[1]"));
```

Direct binding of property type java.time.Duration in the ISO-8601 form

Another notable change is the ability to specify time duration in days (d), hours (h), minutes (m), seconds (s), milliseconds (ms), and nanoseconds (ns), which will be correctly mapped to a `java.time.Duration` object in the configuration property. In the example `workingTime: 8h`, the property will be mapped to the `java.time.Duration` `workingTime` property correctly. Values such as `8m`, `8s`, `8d` can also be specified to define duration.

Custom endpoints for Spring Boot Actuator using annotations

In Spring Boot 1.x, in order to write a custom endpoint for Spring Boot Actuator, `AbstractEndpoint` had to be extended and its `invoke` method has been overridden with custom logic. Spring Boot Actuator is a production-ready feature for monitoring and managing a Spring Boot application using HTTP endpoints or JMX. Auditing metrics such as health could also be gathered using this feature. Finally, it had to be injected into the Spring Context as a Bean. This endpoint was technologically agnostic, in the sense that it could be invoked using JMX as well as with web requests.

If a custom behavior was required for a particular technology, such as JMX or the web, then `AbstractEndpointMvcAdapter` or `EndpointMBean` had to be extended respectively and had to be injected as a Spring Bean. This is cumbersome, and Spring Boot 2.0 has introduced technology-specific annotations such as `@Endpoint`, `@WebEndpoint`, and `@JmxEndpoint`; technology-independent operation annotations such as `@ReadOperation`, `@WriteOperation`, and `@DeleteOperation`; and technology-specific extension annotations such as `@EndpointWebExtension` and `@EndpointJmxExtension`, to ease this process.

By default, only the /info and /health endpoints are exposed. The `management.endpoints.web.exposure.include=*` property must be set to expose other endpoints, including custom ones.

Exposing a custom Spring Boot Actuator endpoint

The `@ReadOperation` annotation will expose the Getter for the custom endpoint and the `@WriteOperation` will expose the Setter for the custom endpoint. The endpoint will be mapped under the http://<host>:<port>/actuator/custom URL (the default host is localhost, and the default port is 8080 unless configured otherwise) and also exposed as a JMX Management bean:

```
@Component
@Endpoint(id = "custom")
public class CustomEndpoint {

    private final static Logger LOGGER =
      LoggerFactory.getLogger(CustomEndpoint.class);

    @ReadOperation
    public String get() {
        return "Custom Endpoint";
    }

    @WriteOperation
    public void set(String message) {
        LOGGER.info("Custom Endpoint Message {}", message);
    }
}
```

Extending a custom endpoint with a specialized implementation for the web

The following extension class, which uses `@EndpointWebExtension` to extend `CustomEndpoint` for custom behavior for web technology and for JMX technology, will not be changed:

```
@Component
@EndpointWebExtension(endpoint = CustomEndpoint.class)
public class CustomEndpointWebExtension {
    ...

    @ReadOperation
    public WebEndpointResponse<String> getWeb() {
        ...
        return new WebEndpointResponse<>("Custom Web
          Extension Hello, World!", 200);
    }
}
```

The `@EndpointWebExtension` annotation will make the `CustomEndpointWebExtension` a web extension for `CustomEndpoint` with its endpoint property. The method with the `@ReadOperation` annotation will be the overridden `Getter`.

Accessing `http://<host>:<port>/actuator/custom` (the default host is `localhost`, and the default port is `8080` unless configured otherwise) and a URL using a browser will prompt for the username (specify `sysuser`) and password (specify `password`) and when logged in will return the following:

```
Custom Web Extension Hello, World!
```

Connecting to a custom endpoint using monitoring and management tools

Running the Spring Boot application with the following VM arguments will enable it to be connected using `jconsole` remotely, and the exposed `CustomEndpoint` JMX Bean can be accessed using monitoring and management tools such as `jconsole`, which is shipped with the JDK installation:

```
-Djavax.management.builder.initial=
-Dcom.sun.management.jmxremote
-Dcom.sun.management.jmxremote.port=8855
-Dcom.sun.management.jmxremote.authenticate=false
-Dcom.sun.management.jmxremote.ssl=false
```

Chapter 1

Run `jconsole` with the following command:

```
$ jconsole
```

Making a remote process connected with it to `<host>:8855` will list all the **MBeans** from the Spring Boot application under **MBeans** tab. When the `Custom.get` operation is executed from `jconsole` it will show the return from `CustomEndpoint.get` as expected, as shown in the following screenshot:

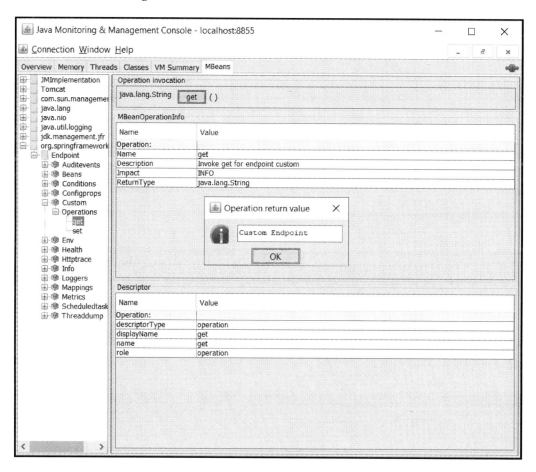

Custom metrics using Micrometer

With the introduction of Micrometer to Spring Boot Actuator in Spring Boot 2.0, metrics can be customized easily. The following code snippet from `CustomEndpointWebExtension` shows how to make use of `io.micrometer.core.instrument.MeterRegistry` to maintain a counter with the name `custom.endpoint.calls`, which will be incremented every time `CustomEndpointWebExtension` is invoked:

```
public static final String CUSTOM_ENDPOINT_CALLS =
"custom.endpoint.calls";

private final MeterRegistry meterRegistry;

public CustomEndpointWebExtension(MeterRegistry meterRegistry) {
    this.meterRegistry = meterRegistry;
}

@ReadOperation
public WebEndpointResponse<String> getWeb() {
    meterRegistry.counter(CUSTOM_ENDPOINT_CALLS).increment();
    return new WebEndpointResponse<>("Custom Web Extension Hello, World!", 200);
}
```

The preceding code injects `MeterRegistry` from the Micrometer Framework, which is used to create and retrieve a counter named `custom.endpoint.calls` and increment it during each read operation of the custom web endpoint extension.

This metric will be available under the `http://<host>:<port>/actuator/metrics/custom.endpoint.calls` URL, which will show a result similar to the following:

```
{
    "name":"custom.endpoint.calls",
    "measurements":[
        {
            "statistic":"COUNT",
            "value":3.0
        }
    ],
    "availableTags":[ ]
}
```

Custom health indicator

Spring Boot Actuator's health endpoint is really helpful for checking the status of Spring Boot application and dependent systems such as databases, message queues, and so on. Spring Boot ships out of the box with many standard `HealthIndicator` implementations such as `DiskSpaceHealthIndicator`, `DataSourceHealthIndicator`, and `MailHealthIndicator`, which can all be used in Spring Boot applications with Spring Boot Actuator. Furthermore, custom health indicators can also be implemented if required:

```java
public class InternetHealthIndicator implements HealthIndicator {

    private static final Logger LOGGER =
LoggerFactory.getLogger(InternetHealthIndicator.class);

    public static final String UNIVERAL_INTERNET_CONNECTIVITY_CHECKING_URL = "https://www.google.com";

    private final RestTemplate restTemplate;

    public InternetHealthIndicator(RestTemplateBuilder restTemplateBuilder) {
        this.restTemplate = restTemplateBuilder.build();
    }

    @Override
    public Health health() {
        try {
            ResponseEntity<String> response =
restTemplate.getForEntity(UNIVERAL_INTERNET_CONNECTIVITY_CHECKING_URL, String.class);
            LOGGER.info("Internet Health Response Code {}",
                response.getStatusCode());
            if (response.getStatusCode().is2xxSuccessful()) {
                return Health.up().build();
            }
        } catch (Exception e) {
            LOGGER.error("Error occurred while checking
                internet connectivity", e);
            return Health.down(e).build();
        }

        return Health.down().build();
    }
}
```

Introduction

The preceding `InternetHealthIndicator` is intended to show the status of internet connectivity from within Spring Boot applications to the outside world. It will send a request to www.google.com to check whether it sends a successful HTTP response code, and based on that the health status of this indicator will be set to up or down. This was injected as a Spring Bean using an `ApplicationContextInitializer` earlier. Invoking the `http://<host>:<port>/actuator/health` URL will return the internet status as in the following:

```
{
    "status":"UP",
    "details":{
        "internet":{
            "status":"UP"
        },
        "diskSpace":{
            "status":"UP",
            "details":{
                "total":399268376576,
                "free":232285409280,
                "threshold":10485760
            }
        }
    }
}
```

Using the HTTP/2 protocol

HTTP was invented by Tim Berners-Lee in 1989 while he was working at CERN. It was designed as a way to share scientific findings among coworkers and is almost three decades old. When HTTP was invented, it was never intended to be the backbone of today's low-latency, high-traffic web, used by millions if not billions of people. So HTTP 1-and HTTP 1.1-based web applications had to have a lot of workarounds to cater to the high demands of the modern web. The following are some of those workarounds:

- Concurrent resources are download by the browser since HTTP 1.x can download only one resource at a time, and Domain Sharding is used to tackle limitations on the maximum number of connections per domain
- Combining multiple resources such as CSS/Javascript files together with complex server-side logic and downloading them all in one go
- Multiple image sprites in a single resource to reduce the number of image file downloads
- Inlining static resources in an HTML file itself

But HTTP/2 is designed from the ground up to tackle these pain points. Compared to HTTP 1.x, HTTP/2 doesn't use text to communicate between the client and server. It uses binary data frames, which makes it much more efficient and reduces the text-to-binary and binary-to-text conversion overhead in the servers. Furthermore, it has the following features introduced:

- **HTTP/2 multiplexing**: This multiplexing feature allows opening one connection to a server and downloading multiple resources using that connection:

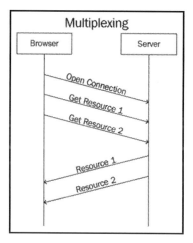

- **HTTP/2 push**: This will send resources to clients even before resources are requested:

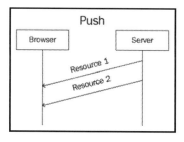

- **HTTP/2 header compression**: Eliminates the repeating of the same headers across multiple requests by maintaining an HTTP header table, thus reducing request bandwidth

Introduction

Spring Boot 2 supports HTTP/2 out of the box for server Undertow, and, with minor dependencies at `https://docs.spring.io/spring-boot/docs/2.0.x-SNAPSHOT/reference/htmlsingle/#howto-configure-http2`, also supports Tomcat and Jetty servers. But Spring Boot 2 doesn't support the clear text version of HTTP/2, so **Secure Socket Layer (SSL)** is a must. It requires the following dependencies in `pom.xml`:

```xml
<dependencies>
  <dependency>
     <groupId>org.springframework.boot</groupId>
     <artifactId>spring-boot-starter-web</artifactId>
     <exclusions>
        <exclusion>
           <groupId>org.springframework.boot</groupId>
           <artifactId>spring-boot-starter-tomcat</artifactId>
        </exclusion>
     </exclusions>
  </dependency>

  <dependency>
     <groupId>org.springframework.boot</groupId>
     <artifactId>spring-boot-starter-undertow</artifactId>
  </dependency>
  ...
</dependencies>
```

The configuration properties in `application.yml` configure both SSL and HTTP/2:

```yaml
server:
 port: 8443
   ssl:
     key-store: keystore.p12
     key-store-password: sslcert123
     keyStoreType: PKCS12
     keyAlias: sslcert

 http2:
    enabled: true
```

In this configuration SSL `key-store`, `key-store-password`, `keyStoreType`, and `keyAlias` are configured along with the port for HTTPs. The key was generated using `keytool`, which is a utility shipped with the JDK release with the following command, and fills in the necessary details when prompted by the utility tool:

```
$ keytool -genkey -alias sslcert -storetype PKCS12 -keyalg RSA -keysize 2048 -keystore keystore.p12 -validity 3650
```

This key-store is not recommended for production as it is not generated by a Trusted Certificate Authority. A proper SSL Certificate must be used in production.

Now when the `https://<localhost>:8443/actuator/custom` URL is accessed it will be served over HTTP/2.

Securing applications with Spring Security

Spring Boot 2.0 has introduced updated support for Spring Security with Spring Framework 5.0 and Reactive support for Spring Security, providing simplified default configurations and ease of customization for Spring Security. As opposed to having multiple auto-configurations for Spring Security, Spring Boot 2.0 has introduced a single behavior that can be overridden easily and can be customized easily with a `WebSecurityConfigurerAdapter` such as the following:

```
@Configuration
public class SecurityConfig extends WebSecurityConfigurerAdapter {

  @Override
  protected void configure(HttpSecurity http) throws Exception {
  http.httpBasic().and()
  .authorizeRequests()
  .requestMatchers(EndpointRequest.to("info", "health")).permitAll()
  .requestMatchers(EndpointRequest.toAnyEndpoint()).hasRole("SYSTEM")
  .antMatchers("/**").hasRole("USER");

  }

  @Override
  protected void configure(AuthenticationManagerBuilder auth) throws Exception {
  auth.inMemoryAuthentication()
  .passwordEncoder(new MessageDigestPasswordEncoder("SHA-256"))
  .withUser("user")
 .password("5e884898da28047151d0e56f8dc6292773603d0d6aabbdd62a11ef721d1542d8")
  .roles("USER")
  .and()
  .withUser("sysuser")
 .password("5e884898da28047151d0e56f8dc6292773603d0d6aabbdd62a11ef721d1542d8")
  .roles("SYSTEM");
```

Introduction

```
    }

}
```

One thing to note here is the introduction of the `EndpointRequest` helper class, which makes it easier to protect endpoints.

The next milestone

Spring Boot is a highly active project with contributors from all around the World. At the time of writing, the Spring Boot 2.1.0 milestone is set and is under active development. The following are some of the features proposed for that Spring Boot minor-version release:

- **Support for embedding Tomcat 9**: Tomcat 9 has introduced a lot of features, but Spring Boot 2.0 still only supports up to Tomcat 8 by default. With this support, Spring Boot 2.0 will be able to offer features such as Servlet 4.0 API, JSP 2.4, WebSocket 2.0, and so on.
- **Auto-configuration of JettyMetrics**: Micrometer has metrics support for Jetty, which is planned to be included in the next release of Spring Boot 2.0.
- **Support for embedding Undertow 2.0**: Undertow 2.0 has a lot of features, such as Servlet 4.0, but is not yet supported by Spring Boot 2.0.
- **Support for Hibernate 5.3.0 and JPA 2.2**: Hibernate 5.3.0 and JPA 2.2 are the latest releases for the persistence layer, which needs to be incorporated into Spring Boot 2.0.
- **Actuator endpoint for listing and clearing cache**: The actuator endpoint is intended to return caches per context and provides a `delete` operation to clear the cache.
- **Allowing `@ConfigurationProperties` binding on interfaces**: At the moment only a class can be used to bind properties from a configuration properties file with a `@ConfigurationProperties` annotation. This feature will allow interfaces with methods with property names to be mapped to their corresponding property.
- **Having consistent auto-configuration behavior for default connection of data sources**: Currently, behavior for default connection auto-configurations differs from data sources as such as MongoDB, Couchbase, and so on. This proposed change will make it consistent.

However, these enhancements and features are still under active evaluation and debate and can be further improved or reduced based on the collective decisions of the Spring Boot developer community.

Migration

Spring Boot 2.0 is a major release; it will require care when migrating from Spring Boot 1.x, as a lot has changed. Migration is unavoidable, as existing applications require the use of new features and enhancements available in the latest Spring Boot 2.0 release. The official migration guide can be read at `https://github.com/spring-projects/spring-boot/wiki/Spring-Boot-2.0-Migration-Guide` and in this section, the most notable migration tips will be discussed.

Using the correct JDK and JVM

Spring Boot 2.0 doesn't support Java 6 or Java 7, which are still widely used in many production environments. So the first thing that needs to be done is to upgrade both development environments and runtime environments to at least Java 8 or above.

Running on Java 9

Since Java 9 was a major release and has one of the most complex enhancement modifications made to Java since its inception (the modular system), special care needs to be taken when running the Spring Boot 2.0 application on it. The following tips will help you get started.

Tackling JAXBException

The following exception can be expected as soon as a Spring Boot 2.0 application is run on Java 9:

```
java.lang.NoClassDefFoundError: javax/xml/bind/JAXBException
```

Introduction

This is because Hibernate requires JAXB, which is not shipped by default in Java 9. The following dependency needs to be added in `pom.xml` to include it:

```
<dependency>
    <groupId>javax.xml.bind</groupId>
    <artifactId>jaxb-api</artifactId>
    <version>2.3.0</version>
</dependency>
```

Instead, you can add the `java.xml.bind` module to Java 9 directly to get rid of this exception.

Using the correct AspectJ version

Java 9 requires AspectJ version 1.9 (currently in Release Candidate version) if JDK weaving of classes is required. Spring Boot 2.0, however, can work with the lower version 1.8 that is shipped by default.

Being aware of limitations on Apache Cassandra drivers

Apache Cassandra drivers that run on Spring Boot 2.0 are not fully supported by Java 9 at the time of writing this book, so if a Spring Boot 2.0 application uses these then it must be properly tested. The issue can be followed at https://github.com/spring-projects/spring-boot/issues/10453 for more updates.

Being aware of issues with the Maven Surefire Plugin

Maven Surefire Plugin version 2.20.1 has re-introduced a bug that was fixed on other Java versions and only raised when running tests on Java 9. In order to fix this, the Maven Surefire Plugin has to be downgraded to 2.20.0 or the `java.se.ee` module needs to be excluded from the runtime while running tests.

Using the upgraded Spring Framework 5.0

Spring Boot 2.0 by default uses and supports Spring Framework 5.0. Thus, any change to it will affect migration to Spring Boot 2.0. Some notable changes are explained in the following topics.

Modified CORS support behavior

The `@CrossOrigin` annotations property `allowCredentials` now has the default value `false`. This means that it needs to be explicitly set if cookies or authentication are required.

Removed packages, classes, and methods

The following packages, classes, and methods are no longer supported in the Spring Framework 5.0 release:

- The `beans.factory.access` package, including the class `SpringBeanAutowiringInterceptor`.
- The `jdbc.support.nativejdbc` package, which is replaced by JDBC 4 implementation.
- The `mock.staticmock` package, with which `AnnotationDrivenStaticEntityMockingControl` is no longer supported.
- The `web.views.tiles2` package, with the minimum version requirement for tiles being version 3.
- The `orm.hibernate3/hibernate4` packages, with the minimum version requirement for Hibernate being version 5.
- Most of the deprecated classes in the previous version have been removed.
- Some methods in **JSP Standard Tag Library (JSTL)** have been removed. For example, `FormTag commandName` is no longer available.

Dropped support for frameworks

Spring Framework 5.0 no longer supports the following frameworks:

- Google Guava
- Velocity
- XMLBeans
- JDO
- Portlet
- JasperReports

Using the updated configuration properties

A lot of configuration properties have been renamed/replaced from Spring Boot 1.x to Spring Boot 2.0. So these changes must be incorporated in the `application.yml/application.properties` file to do a successful migration. To ease this process, Spring Boot has released the `spring-boot-properties-migrator` properties migrator, which can be used in the Maven configuration as follows:

```xml
<dependency>
    <groupId>org.springframework.boot</groupId>
    <artifactId>spring-boot-properties-migrator</artifactId>
    <scope>runtime</scope>
</dependency>
```

When this dependency is used, it will analyze the application environment, print out any diagnostics at startup, and even temporarily migrate properties at runtime.

This dependency is only required during migration and could/should be removed when the migration is complete.

Using the changed servlet-specific server properties

With the introduction of Reactive Web Programming out of the box in Spring Boot 2.0, there needs to be a differentiation between properties for a servlet stack and properties for a reactive stack, so that previous properties such as `server.*`, which was related to the server ServletContext path, is not changed to `server.servlet.*`, avoiding verbosity in property naming.

Using the modified template engine extension handling

In Spring Boot 2.0 the file extension for the mustache template engine has been changed from `.html` to `.mustache`. With the `spring.mustache.suffix` configuration property this behavior can be overridden if required.

Using the changed actuator configuration properties

The following changes have been introduced in the Spring Boot Actuator configuration properties in Spring Boot 2.0:

- `endpoints.*` properties have been moved under `management.*`
- `management.*` properties have been moved under `management.server.*`
- `endpoints.<id>.*` properties have been moved under `management.endpoint.<id>.*`
- Shutdown endpoint must be explicitly enabled by setting the `management.endpoint.shutdown.enabled` configuration property to `true`

These changes have the potential to break existing code, and so must be changed accordingly when migrating.

Using the changed actuator base path

Now, the `/actuator` path contains all Spring Boot Actuator-related endpoints. In order to get the previous version's behavior, the `management.endpoints.web.base-path=/` configuration property needs to be set. Another change is the addition of a new purpose for `management.server.servlet.context-path`, which is the counterpart of `server.servlet.context-path` related to Spring Boot Actuator endpoints.

As an example, if `management.server.servlet.context-path=/actuator` is set, along with `management.endpoints.web.base-path=/application`, then the endpoints will be accessible under the `/actuator/application/<endpoint>` path.

Using the renamed actuator endpoints

The following Spring Boot Actuator endpoints have been changed:

- `/autoconfig` has been renamed to `/conditions`
- `/trace` has been renamed to `/httptrace`

Introduction

Applications depending on these endpoints need to be changed to use the renamed endpoints.

Using the changed Embedded Container Configuration

`EmbeddedServletContainer` is changed to `WebServer`. Also, the `org.springframework.boot.context.embedded` package is refactored to `org.springframework.boot.web.embedded`. If `TomcatEmbeddedServletContainerFactory` was used to configure an embedded Tomcat with a custom port in an application as in the following, then it will need to be changed:

```
@Bean
public EmbeddedServletContainerFactory servletContainer() {
  TomcatEmbeddedServletContainerFactory tomcat = new TomcatEmbeddedServletContainerFactory();
  Connector connector = new Connector("org.apache.coyote.http11.Http11NioProtocol");
  connector.setScheme("http");
  connector.setPort(9090);
  tomcat.addAdditionalTomcatConnectors(connector);
  return tomcat;
}
```

It must be changed to use `TomcatServletWebServerFactory` instead, as in the following:

```
@Bean
public TomcatServletWebServerFactory webServer() {
    TomcatServletWebServerFactory tomcat = new TomcatServletWebServerFactory(9090);
    return tomcat;
}
```

Using the changed default behavior for path mapping

The default behavior of map extensions such as `.json` and `.xml` to existing controller request mappings has changed in Spring Boot 2.0. Consider the following URL mapping:

```
@GetMapping("/users")
```

[38]

If it is expected to cater to the /users.json URL in a Spring Boot 1.x application, then it won't be supported in Spring Boot 2.0. This means new mappings need to be added as necessary.

Using the changed default dispatcher types for the servlet filter

The default dispatcher type for the servlet filter in Spring Boot 2.0 is DispatcherType.REQUEST. This is changed to be in line with the default in the servlet specification. If other dispatcher types are required then a FilterRegistrationBean must be used to register the filter.

Using the modified transitive dependency to spring-boot-web-starter

Spring Boot 1.x had the transitive dependency spring-boot-starter-web whenever one of the following template engine starters was used:

- spring-boot-starter-freemarker
- spring-boot-starter-thymeleaf
- spring-boot-starter-mustache

This was done because Spring Web MVC was running on top of the Servlet API, which is the only web application framework that was available at that time.

Now, with the introduction of the Spring Reactive Web starter spring-boot-starter-webflux, which is completely independent of the Servlet API, transitive dependencies from those template engine starters have been removed. This means that, when a template engine starter dependency is added, a developer needs to manually add a dependency to either Spring Web MVC starter or Spring Web Flux starter based on the requirement.

Using the changed default proxying strategy

Spring Boot 2.0 uses CGLIB as the default proxying strategy including for **aspect-oriented programming (AOP)**. If proxy based proxying is required, the following configuration property needs to be set:

    spring.aop.proxy-target-class=false.

Using the modified configuration location strategy

With Spring Boot 2.0, the `spring.config.location` configuration will no longer append to the list of configurations; instead, it will replace it. So, if append logic is required, then `spring.config.additional-location` must be used.

Using the changed Jackson/JSON support

With Spring Boot 2.0, Jackson's configuration was modified to write JSR-310 dates as ISO-8601 strings. For its previous behavior, the property `spring.jackson.serialization.write-dates-as-timestamps=true` needs to be set.

Using the changed Spring Boot Actuator security

The separate security auto-configuration for actuators has been removed in Spring Boot 2.0; thus, `management.security.*` properties are no longer supported. The `endpoints.<id>.sensitive` flag for each endpoint is no longer available, and if an application is dependent on this behavior then it must use a custom configuration for Spring Security to permit or restrict access to those endpoints.

Using the changed HikariCP default connection pool for JPA

With Spring Boot 2.0, the default connection pool for JPA has been changed from Tomcat to HikariCP. Thus it is no longer required to use the configuration property `spring.datasource.type` as an override to use HikariCP. Using the following dependency will by default use HikariCP:

```xml
<dependency>
        <groupId>org.springframework.boot</groupId>
        <artifactId>spring-boot-starter-data-jpa</artifactId>
</dependency>
```

Using the changed default database initialization strategy

With Spring Boot 2.0, the default basic DataSource initialization is only enabled for embedded databases and will be disabled as soon as a production database is used. The configuration property `spring.datasource.initialization-mode` (with values `always` or `never`), which replaces the old `spring.datasource.initialize` configuration property, can be used for more control.

Using the changed database schema creation strategy

The default behavior for embedded databases used with a schema manager such as Liquibase, Flyway, and so on will be dropping existing tables and creating a new one, which is similar to `create-drop` for the configuration property `spring.jpa.hibernate.ddl-auto`. If no schema manager is used then the default behavior is to do nothing, which is similar to setting `none` for the aforementioned configuration property.

Using the changed testing support

The following test annotations are no longer supported for Mockito 1.x:

- `@MockBean`
- `@SpyBean`

If testing needs to be done using the aforementioned annotations then Spring Boot 2.0 `spring-boot-starter-test` must be used or Mockito 2.x must be used explicitly.

Using the revised Spring Security

There are some Spring Security-related changes made for Spring Boot 2.0's release, which need to be incorporated when migrating. Some of the most notable ones are explained in the following sections.

Using the changed default security auto-configuration strategy

Spring Security has changed its auto-configuration strategy to make use of defaults in most cases instead of enabling multiple configuration options. Notable cases are when Spring Security authorization with content negotiation is used.

Spring Security OAuth2 is migrated to Spring Security core

The OAuth2 project is now part of the Spring Security core project and released out of the box. Thus dependencies for OAuth2 will not be maintained separately as of Spring Security 5.0. If a Spring Boot application makes use of a non-migrated feature then dependencies for those need to be added explicitly.

Using the AuthenticationManager bean

Exposing a custom `AuthenticationManager` bean can now be done with an overriding `WebSecurityConfigurerAdapter.authenticationManagerBean` method annotated with a `@Bean` annotation.

Understanding removed features

Some features that were available in Spring Boot 1.x but are no longer supported in Spring Boot 2.0 are as follows:

- Disabled CRaSH support—Spring Boot 1.x had an integrated Java shell that was used to SSH and Telnet in a Spring Boot application. This is no longer available and the `spring-boot-starter-remote-shell` dependency can no longer provide support in monitoring and manage Spring Boot applications.
- Removed auto-configuration support for Spring Mobile.
- Removed auto-configuration support for Spring Social.
- Removed dependency management support for `commons-digester`.

Summary

Congratulations on completing the first chapter. This chapter talked about what Spring Boot is, and explained its unique characteristics in depth by talking about Spring Boot's standalone, production-grade, flexible, and extensible capabilities in detail with examples.

Also, it talked about how to get started with Spring Boot application development by going through the anatomy of a Spring Boot application. It explained what makes a Spring Boot application different from a standard Maven Java application. Also, it talked about the ways a Spring Boot application can be run.

Next, it talked about what has changed from Spring Boot 1.x to Spring Boot 2.0, as it is a major version release, and how to successfully migrate from Spring Boot 1.x to Spring Boot 2.0 by going through each change and explaining how it affects an existing Spring Boot application. It also covered how to mitigate any adverse effects successfully without breaking the application.

Furthermore, it talked about what is in the pipeline for the next minor release of Spring Boot 2.0. These are enhancements that are proposed and discussed by the Spring Boot community, which they deem necessary for the next minor release. These features, along with more features, enhancements, and bug fixes, can be expected in the next minor release, Spring Boot 2.1.0.

Introduction

This chapter has set the pace for coming chapters, which contain more exciting, hands-on Spring Boot 2.0 applications. The contents of this chapter will help greatly in upcoming chapters when it comes to understanding what makes a Spring Boot application work. This chapter also touched on different parts of the Spring Framework ecosystem such as Spring Security, Spring Data JPA, and so on, which will be covered in detail in coming chapters. This chapter has enabled us to write Spring Boot 2.0 applications that just run easily and effectively.

Questions

Please answer the following questions to see whether you have successfully mastered this chapter:

1. What is Spring Boot?
2. What is the bare minimum code to start a Spring Boot application?
3. What is the minimum platform required to run a Spring Boot 2.0 application?
4. What is HTTP/2?
5. What is the default dispatcher type for a Spring Boot 2.0 servlet filter?
6. What is the next minor release version of Spring Boot 2.0?
7. What is the name of the default connection pool framework for a Spring Boot 2.0 application with the JPA starter?

Further reading

In order to improve your knowledge of Java and Spring Boot, the following books are recommended. They will be helpful in the coming chapters:

- *Learning Reactive Programming with Java 8*: `https://www.packtpub.com/application-development/learning-reactive-programming-java-8`
- *Learning Spring Boot 2.0 – Second Edition*: `https://www.packtpub.com/application-development/learning-spring-boot-20-second-edition`

2
Building a Basic Web Application

This chapter will help readers get started developing web applications using Spring Boot 2.0. It will enable experts as well as beginners with Spring Boot web application development to understand the concepts behind a web application. It will explain these concepts by walking the reader through the process of developing a web application that enables the submitting of comments to a scrum retrospective meeting. This web application will use an embedded database for persistence, Spring Data JPA for a model, Spring Thymeleaf for a view, and Spring Web MVC for controllers.

The following topics will be covered in this chapter:

- Using Spring Data JPA for persistence
- Using Thymeleaf for view
- Using Spring Web MVC with servlet 3.x for controller
- Using Spring Security for authentication and authorization
- Demonstrating Retro Board

Technical requirements

In order to implement a web application using Spring Boot, the following build tools need to be downloaded and installed:

- To install **Java Development Kit (JDK)** 8, download it from its official page at http://www.oracle.com/technetwork/java/javase/downloads/jdk8-downloads-2133151.html
- To install Maven 3, download it from its official page at https://maven.apache.org/download.cgi

- To install IntelliJ IDEA, download it from its official page at `https://www.jetbrains.com/idea/download/`
- To install **Spring Tool Suite (STS)**, download it from its official page at `https://spring.io/tools`

The source code for this chapter can be found at `https://github.com/PacktPublishing/Spring-Boot-2.0-Projects-Fundamentals-of-Spring-Boot-2.0`, under the `Chapter02` directory.

Getting started

In this section, readers will get an overview of the web application being developed. The requirements, design, and implementation details will be discussed in brief.

Web application architecture

A web application is exposed to multiple concurrent users over a public or private network as opposed to a standalone application. Let's get started developing a basic web application that uses the well known **Model-view-controller** (**MVC**) pattern to build a three-tier application. The MVC pattern is known for its separation of concerns by decoupling presentation logic (what the user sees in a browser), routing and business logic (what the application needs to accomplish), and persistence (where the data is finally stored). This has made MVC a very developer-friendly pattern as different tiers of an application can be developed and tested by experts in that area independently and without knowledge of the other tiers.

For example, a **user interface** (**UI**) developer can work on the presentation while a database administrator works on database optimization. Also, this layering has made maintenance easier than in conventional web applications, which usually have spaghetti code without any layering.

In this chapter, Spring Web MVC Framework will be used to implement the MVC pattern inside our web application. Let's have a look at the workflow of Spring Web MVC in detail.

Workflow of Spring Web MVC

Spring Web MVC is a web framework that is built using a central front controller in the form of a Java servlet known as `DispatcherServlet`. This servlet is responsible for the orchestration of the underlying components required in order to process a request it receives from clients (in most cases from a browser).

Spring Web MVC makes use of the following programming components of its own to make the web framework flexible and able to support different workflows:

- `HandlerMapping`: This is used to map a request to a handler with a set of configurable pre-request and post-request interceptors. For example, a `controller` class with a `@RequestMapping` annotation will be mapped to a corresponding HTTP request by the `RequestMappingHandlerMapping` implementation of `HandlerMapping`.
- `Controller`: This is used to implement handlers to a particular HTTP request, which will be responsible for coordinating the business logic and response generation. For example, an HTTP GET request to the URL `/index` can be mapped to the `@GetMapping("/index")` handler method in a `controller` class.
- `Model`: This is used to send dynamic data in the form of attributes to `View`. Flash messages, lists of domain-specific objects, and so on can be sent using a `Model`.
- `ViewResolver`: This is used to resolve view names usually returned by a `controller` handler method and get the actual `View` in order to return an HTTP response.
- `View`: This is used to generate the final presentation to the end user. These views will contain the syntax that will use `Model` attributes to render responses dynamically. `View` technologies supported by Spring Web MVC include plain **Java Server Pages (JSP)** with **JavaServer Pages Standard Tag Library (JSTL)**, Spring Thymeleaf, Apache Freemarker, and so on.

As an example, an HTTP `GET` request to path `/index` from a web browser will result in the following orchestration when the request reaches `DispatcherServlet`:

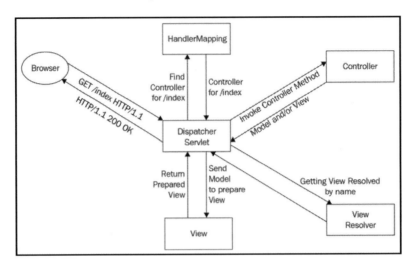

Let's understand the preceding diagram:

- The browser will initiate the HTTP **GET** request for the path **/index** using the **HTTP** protocol
- The HTTP **GET** request in the form of the **HTTP** protocol will be resolved and handed over to **DispatcherServlet** by the Web container (this is a required but transparent step)
- **DispatcherServlet** will use the available **HandlerMapping** implementations to find a **Controller** that contains a handler method matching the path **/index** and HTTP request method **GET**
- **DispatcherServlet** will invoke the handler method from the **Controller** and return the **View** name and **Model** data if there are any
- **DispatcherServlet** will use any configured **View Resolver** to find the view by name and retrieve it
- **DispatcherServlet** will use a model, if any are available, along with the resolved **View** to prepare the final view that will be rendered
- **DispatcherServlet** will hand over the rendered **View** to the web container, which will convert it to an HTTP response and send it to the browser

This complex orchestration will take place for each HTTP request in a Spring Web MVC Framework-based application.

Requirements for our web application

We will be creating a dashboard, which will allow team members to share comments during retrospective meetings. During software development, a team usually carries out scrum retrospective meetings to share their comments on a sprint (a software development period usually a week long). These comments can be positive (plus), improvement (delta), and appreciation (flower).

These comments will be used as feedback to make the team work more efficiently during the following sprints. Usually, this is done using a whiteboard with a table drawn that has columns for pluses, deltas, flowers, and multicolor sticky notes, where each comment from a team member will be placed in a sticky note and posted on the whiteboard under the corresponding column.

Finally, all the comments will be noted and action will be taken in coming sprints accordingly. But this is a tedious process, one that can use technology to simplify the task, making it easier for each member to share their comments on a Sprint easily.

To address this requirement, a web application can be developed that will allow multiple users to log in to the web application and post their respective comments and collaborate in real time.

The use case diagram

The following use case diagram shows the requirement for the dashboard, which is nicknamed Retro Board:

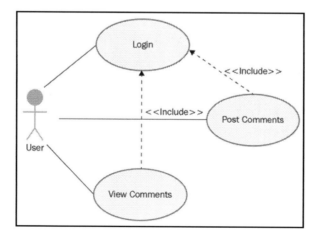

The actor is a **User** of the Retro Board and is a team member who is involved in a sprint. It has the following use cases:

1. **Login**: This is required to authenticate users so that each comment can be uniquely identified
2. **Post Comments**: This is where a logged in user can post their comment under its respective type so that it will be recorded for later, and also collaborate with other users in real time
3. **View Comments**: This is where a logged in user can view comments made by all users

All actions need authentication and authorization to distinguish users and relate the comments they make. All comments need to be saved based on the date when they were made and should be retrievable based on the date also.

Using Spring Data JPA for persistence

In this section, readers will learn what JPA is, as well as how Spring Data JPA helps simplify the development of applications with database persistence.

Understanding the Java Persistence API (JPA)

JPA provides object/relation mapping capabilities to enable mapping between relational database tables and Java objects in order to ease persistence in Java applications. JPA consists of the following features:

- A query language to enable querying from relational database tables in order to retrieve Java objects
- A JPA Criteria API, which can be used to generate queries dynamically
- A set of metadata defined with XML Java annotations in order to successfully map relational database table columns to Java object fields

JPA is not an actual implementation of the preceding features but merely defines the specification. Third-party vendors can perform their own implementation that conforms to the specification. The most popular third-party implementations that support JPA are Hibernate and EclipseLink.

JPA 1.0 was released in 2006 as part of Java Community Process JSR 220. Its latest version is JPA 2.2, which was released in 2017. JPA has made persistence easier and standardized for developers while allowing transactions and data consistency. This has helped a lot, making JPA famous among developers.

Understanding Spring Data JPA

The Spring Data JPA project is an abstraction over JPA which vastly simplifies the process of object/relation mapping, querying, and so on. The following are some of the features of Spring Data JPA:

- Reduces/eliminates unnecessary boilerplate code
- Ease of building repositories with Spring and JPA
- Support for type-and value-safe JPA queries
- Support for database-independent auditing
- Support for database-independent pagination, custom query execution, and so on

Spring Data JPA eases **Create**, **Retrieve**, **Update**, **Delete (CRUD)** operations by allowing the `JpaRespository` interface, which extends from `CrudRepository`. This hides the complexities of plain JPA implementations, which need to be implemented and tested by developers. Using Spring Data JPA could reduce the development time dramatically because of this.

In upcoming chapters, `JpaRepository` with default methods and custom methods will be used extensively to implement business logic and demonstrate how to write Spring Data JPA repositories and test them. The following sections will discuss how to use a domain model designed using a class diagram as a base to implement Spring Data JPA-based entities and repositories.

Class diagram for the domain model

The domain model is the most important part of an application; some applications have run for years on end with multiple frontend technologies but without ever changing the existing domain model. A well-built domain model can easily support multiple business logic and can run an application on limited resources efficiently.

Building a Basic Web Application

The following is the simple class diagram for this web application:

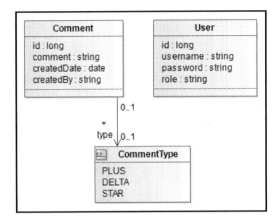

There are two main domain models and one enumeration, as shown in the preceding diagram. Those are as follows:

- **Comment**: This is the main domain model, which will store the actual comment, comment type, comment created date, comment create a user, and so on
- **User**: This is the domain model, which will store the username, password, and role of a registered user
- **CommentType**: This enumeration is to differentiate comments by type

Implementation of the domain model using JPA annotations

This section will explain the details of how to configure and use Spring Data JPA with an embedded database with the domain model designed in the previous section.

Setting up dependencies and configuration

Initially, before implementing the domain model, the dependencies and configuration class need to be specified. The following Maven starter dependency and H2 database dependency need to be included:

```
<dependencies>
    ...
    <dependency>
        <groupId>org.springframework.boot</groupId>
```

```xml
        <artifactId>spring-boot-starter-data-jpa</artifactId>
    </dependency>

    <dependency>
        <groupId>com.h2database</groupId>
        <artifactId>h2</artifactId>
        <version>1.4.196</version>
    </dependency>
</dependencies>
```

The following `RepoConfig` is used, which enables JPA Auditing (here auditing means tracking and logging events related to entities, such as `createdBy` for the `Comment` entity); this will enable auditing of the created date and created a user of an entry in the table:

```java
@Configuration
@EnableJpaAuditing
public class RepoConfig {

}
```

The following configuration properties in the `application.properties` file need to be set to configure `DataSource`:

```
spring.jpa.hibernate.ddl-auto=create
spring.jpa.properties.hibernate.format_sql=true
spring.jpa.properties.hibernate.show_sql=true

spring.datasource.driver-class-name=org.h2.Driver
spring.datasource.url=jdbc:h2:~/retroboard
spring.datasource.username=sa
spring.datasource.password=
```

The preceding configuration does the following:

- Uses `spring.jpa.hibernate.ddl-auto` to set automatically generate **Data Definition Language (DDL)** SQL
- Uses `spring.jpa.properties.hibernate.format_sql` to format SQL generated in a visually pleasing manner
- Uses `spring.jpa.properties.hibernate.show_sql` to show the SQL generated
- Uses `spring.datasource.driver-class-name` to set `org.h2.Driver` as the database driver

Building a Basic Web Application

- Uses `spring.datasource.url` to set the JDBC URL
- Uses `spring.datasource.username` to set the username for the H2 database
- Uses `spring.datasource.password` to set the password for the H2 database

For the complete set of Spring Boot Database configurations, the following documentation URL can be used:

`https://docs.spring.io/spring-boot/docs/current/reference/html/boot-features-sql.html`

Implementing the domain model

In order to successfully populate the `createdUser` property, the `AuditAware` interface needs to be implemented to supply the username and needs to be registered as a Spring Component. More on this in the *Using Spring Security for authentication and authorization* section.

Implementing the domain model `Comment` class using JPA annotations will look like the following:

```
@Entity
@Table(name = "rb_comment")
@EntityListeners(AuditingEntityListener.class)
@Data
public class Comment {

    @Id
    @GeneratedValue
    private Long id;

    private String comment;

    @Enumerated(EnumType.STRING)
    private CommentType type;

    @CreatedDate
    private Timestamp createdDate;

    @CreatedBy
    private String createdBy;

}
```

In the preceding code, the `@Entity` annotation is used to mark the `Comment` class as a JPA entity so that it will be eligible to be used in JPA persistence environment. The `@Table` annotation is used to mention the table name to which the `Comment` class needs to be mapped. The `@EntityListeners` annotation is used with the `AuditingEntityListener` implementation to dynamically populate the `createdDate` and `createdBy` properties annotated with `@CreatedDate` and `@CreatedBy` in the `Comment` domain model when persisting the comment entry into the table. The `@Data` annotation is from the `Lombok` library and used to mark a POJO as a class that will hold data. This means `getters`, `setters`, the `equals` method, the `hashCode` method, and the `toString` method will be generated for that class.

The `@Id` annotation marks the ID property as the identity field of the entity, whereas `@GeneratedValue` marks it as an auto-generated value. The `@Enumerated` annotation with value `EnumType.STRING` on the `type` property is used to notify JPA that the value of the enum `CommentType` needs to be persisted as a `String` type in the database.

Implementing the domain model `User` will look like the following:

```
@Entity
@Table(name = "rb_user")
@Data
@AllArgsConstructor
@NoArgsConstructor
public class User {

    @Id
    @GeneratedValue
    private Long id;

    private String username;

    private String password;

    private String role;

}
```

The preceding class also does the same things as the `Comment` class. The newly added annotations, which are also from the `Lombok` library, are `@AllArgsConstructor`, which will generate a constructor with the `id`, `username`, `password`, and `role` properties, and `@NoArgsConstructor`, which will generate a default constructor.

Implementation of Spring Data JPA repositories

With the domain model implemented successfully, the `JpaRepository` for those can be implemented using Spring Data JPA. The specialty here is that there is no need to implement anything. Just writing an interface that extends from the `JpaRepository` interface will be sufficient to expose methods to find one, find all, save, delete, and so on. The following code shows `CommentRepository`:

```
public interface CommentRepository extends JpaRepository<Comment, Long>
{

    @Query("SELECT c FROM Comment c WHERE year(c.createdDate) = ?1 AND
      month(c.createdDate) = ?2 AND
    day(c.createdDate) = ?3")
    List<Comment> findByCreatedYearAndMonthAndDay(int year, int month,
      int day);

}
```

Since a list of comments for a specific date needs to retrieved to be shown in the frontend, a custom method with a `@Query` annotation is added to the `CommentRepository` interface. This annotation is responsible for using a database-independent SQL query to filter out data from the database.

The following code shows `UserRepository`:

```
public interface UserRepository extends JpaRepository<User, Long> {

    User findByUsername(String username);
}
```

In the preceding code, there is a method named `findByUsername` where `username` is a property of `User` class. In this case, an `@Query` annotation is not required, as the naming of the method will be used to create the filter. There are more things that can be done using Spring Data JPA; see in the official documentation at https://docs.spring.io/spring-data/jpa/docs/current/reference/html/.

Testing Spring Data JPA repositories

Testing is an important part of software engineering and with Spring Boot 2.0 `@DataJpaTest` is introduced to ease the testing of JPA repositories. This annotation will use an embedded database for testing and will auto-configure `TestEntityManager` to verify the JPA Repository operations.

The following is the test for `CommentRepository`:

```java
@RunWith(SpringRunner.class)
@DataJpaTest
public class CommentRepoTest {

    @Autowired
    private TestEntityManager testEntityManager;

    @Autowired
    private CommentRepository commentRepository;

    @Test
    public void
      findByCreatedYearAndMonthAndDay_HappyPath_ShouldReturn1Comment() {
        // Given
        Comment comment = new Comment();
        comment.setComment("Test");
        comment.setType(CommentType.PLUS);
        comment.setCreatedDate(new Timestamp(System.currentTimeMillis()));
        testEntityManager.persist(comment);
        testEntityManager.flush();

        // When
        LocalDate now = LocalDate.now();
        List<Comment> comments =
          commentRepository.findByCreatedYearAndMonthAndDay(now.getYear(),
          now.getMonth().getValue(), now.getDayOfMonth());

        // Then
        assertThat(comments).hasSize(1);
        assertThat(comments.get(0)).hasFieldOrPropertyWithValue("comment",
          "Test");
    }

    @Test
    public void save_HappyPath_ShouldSave1Comment() {
        // Given
        Comment comment = new Comment();
        comment.setComment("Test");
        comment.setType(CommentType.PLUS);
        comment.setCreatedDate(new Timestamp(System.currentTimeMillis()));

        // When
        Comment saved = commentRepository.save(comment);

        // Then
        assertThat(testEntityManager.find(Comment.class,
```

```
            saved.getId())).isEqualTo(saved);
    }
}
```

The preceding test case uses a `TestEntityManager` private member auto-wired (auto-wiring private members should be kept to the minimum as it is not a best practice) to the JUnit test and persists `Comment` by flushing it to the temporary persistence using the `TestEntityManager.flush` method and then, in one test, tests whether it can be successfully retrieved using the `CommentRepository.findByCreatedYearAndMonthAndDay` method. Furthermore, in the next test, it tests whether it could successfully save a `Comment`.

The following is the test for `UserRepository`:

```
@RunWith(SpringRunner.class)
@DataJpaTest
public class UserRepoTest {

    @Autowired
    private TestEntityManager testEntityManager;

    @Autowired
    private UserRepository userRepository;

    @Test
    public void findByUsername_HappyPath_ShouldReturn1User() throws
    Exception {
        // Given
        User user = new User();
        user.setUsername("shazin");
        user.setPassword("shaz980");
        user.setRole("USER");
        testEntityManager.persist(user);
        testEntityManager.flush();

        // When
        User actual = userRepository.findByUsername("shazin");

        // Then
        assertThat(actual).isEqualTo(user);
    }

    @Test
    public void save_HappyPath_ShouldSave1User() throws Exception {
        // Given
        User user = new User();
        user.setUsername("shazin");
```

```
            user.setPassword("shaz980");
            user.setRole("USER");

            // When
            User actual = userRepository.save(user);

            // Then
            assertThat(actual).isNotNull();
            assertThat(actual.getId()).isNotNull();
        }
    }
```

One test, `findByUsername_HappyPath_ShouldReturn1User`, in the preceding test case tests the `UserRepository.findByUsername` method by verifying whether it returns the expected `User` object with a matching username. The other test, `save_HappyPath_ShouldSave1User`, tests for the correct persistence of a `User` object.

Using Spring Boot Devtools for database visualization

In order to ease the testing of database development via Spring Boot Devtools, a dependency can be used that will provide a GUI to visualize the tables created with the data when an embedded database such as H2 is used. This can be seen from the following code:

```
<dependencies>
    <dependency>
        <groupId>org.springframework.boot</groupId>
        <artifactId>spring-boot-devtools</artifactId>
        <optional>true</optional>
    </dependency>
</dependencies>
```

Building a Basic Web Application

With this Spring Boot Devtools enabled after the Spring Boot application's startup, accessing the `http://<host>:<port>/h2-console` (the port will be the same port as the Spring Boot application) URL will display the following H2 database console for ease of development:

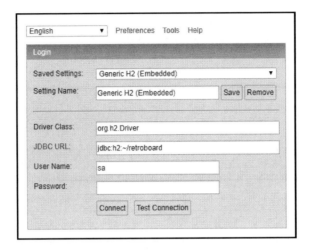

After clicking the **Connect** button with the correct parameters, the following screen with database tables and users will be displayed:

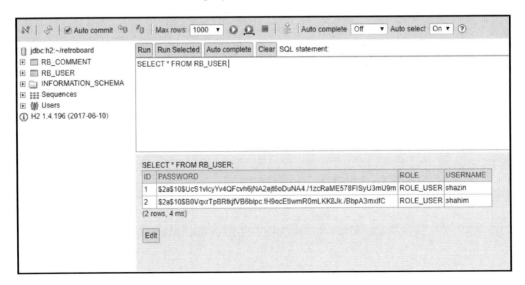

With this tool, entries in the `rb_user` table and the `rb_comment` table can be visualized for ease of development.

Using Services to encapsulate business logic

It is a good practice to encapsulate business logic inside `Service` methods so that controllers and repositories are loosely coupled. The following `Service` is written to encapsulate business logic for `Comment`:

```
@Service
@Transactional(readOnly = true)
public class CommentService {

  private static final Logger LOGGER =
LoggerFactory.getLogger(CommentService.class);

  private final CommentRepository commentRepository;

  public CommentService(CommentRepository commentRepository) {
    this.commentRepository = commentRepository;
  }

  @Transactional(rollbackFor = Exception.class)
  public List<Comment> saveAll(List<Comment> comments) {
    LOGGER.info("Saving {}", comments);
    return commentRepository.saveAll(comments);
  }

  public List<Comment> getAllCommentsForToday() {
    LocalDate localDate = LocalDate.now();
    return
commentRepository.findByCreatedYearAndMonthAndDay(localDate.getYear(),
    localDate.getMonth().getValue(), localDate.getDayOfMonth());
  }
}
```

The `CommentService` method in the preceding code is annotated with the `@Service` stereotype annotation to mark it as a Spring service. Also, it has the `@Transactional` annotation (learn more about Spring Transaction in the `reference documentation`). The `CommentRepository` will be auto-wired using the `CommentService` constructor argument. Another notable thing is that the `CommentService.saveAll` method is annotated with the `@Transactional` annotation with `rollbackFor` set to the `Exception` class. This means that any code inside that method will be enclosed inside a transaction and, if an exception is thrown, `JpaTransactionManager` will roll back the changes it made in the database within that transaction.

Likewise, the following `UserService` is used for `User`:

```
@Service
@Transactional(readOnly = true)
public class UserService implements UserDetailsService {

  private final UserRepository userRepository;

  public UserService(UserRepository userRepository) {
  this.userRepository = userRepository;
  }

  @Override
  public UserDetails loadUserByUsername(String username) throws
  UsernameNotFoundException {
  User user = userRepository.findByUsername(username);

  if(user == null) {
  throw new UsernameNotFoundException(username);
  }

  return new
  org.springframework.security.core.userdetails.User(user.getUsername(),
user.getPassword(),
  Arrays.asList(new SimpleGrantedAuthority(user.getRole())));
  }

  @Transactional(rollbackFor = Exception.class)
  public User create(User user) {
  return userRepository.save(user);
  }
}
```

This is similar to `CommentService` but also implements the Spring Security `UserDetailsService` interface in addition to supporting `User` detail loading. More on this will be discussed in the *Using Spring Security for authentication and authorization* section of this chapter.

Testing Services

`Services` with business logic need to be tested for their correct functionality. In order to do this, `Services` like the following one can be used:

```
@RunWith(SpringRunner.class)
public class CommentServiceTest {
```

```java
    @MockBean
    private CommentRepository commentRepository;

    private CommentService commentService;

    @Before
    public void init() {
        commentService = new CommentService(commentRepository);
    }

    @Test
    public void
       getAllCommentsForToday_HappyPath_ShouldReturn1Comment() {
        // Given
        Comment comment = new Comment();
        comment.setComment("Test");
        comment.setType(CommentType.PLUS);
        comment.setCreatedDate(new
            Timestamp(System.currentTimeMillis()));
        List<Comment> comments = Arrays.asList(comment);
        LocalDate now = LocalDate.now();

when(commentRepository.findByCreatedYearAndMonthAndDay(now.getYear(),
now.getMonth().getValue(),
         now.getDayOfMonth())).thenReturn(comments);

        // When
        List<Comment> actualComments =
          commentService.getAllCommentsForToday();

        // Then
        verify(commentRepository,
           times(1)).findByCreatedYearAndMonthAndDay(now.getYear(),
           now.getMonth().getValue(), now.getDayOfMonth());
        assertThat(comments).isEqualTo(actualComments);
    }

    @Test
    public void saveAll_HappyPath_ShouldSave2Comments() {
        // Given
        Comment comment = new Comment();
        comment.setComment("Test Plus");
        comment.setType(CommentType.PLUS);
        comment.setCreatedBy("Shazin");
        comment.setCreatedDate(new
           Timestamp(System.currentTimeMillis()));

        Comment comment2 = new Comment();
```

Building a Basic Web Application

```java
            comment2.setComment("Test Star");
            comment2.setType(CommentType.STAR);
            comment2.setCreatedBy("Shahim");
            comment2.setCreatedDate(new
              Timestamp(System.currentTimeMillis()));
            List<Comment> comments = Arrays.asList(comment, comment2);
            when(commentRepository.saveAll(comments)).thenReturn(comments);

            // When
            List<Comment> saved = commentService.saveAll(comments);

            // Then
            assertThat(saved).isNotEmpty();
            verify(commentRepository, times(1)).saveAll(comments);

    }
}
```

In the preceding test case for `CommentService`, `CommentRepository` is annotated with `@MockBean`, as testing of its functionality has already been done in the JPA repository testing. During `Service`, test mocking is done using the Mockito library to just mock repository method invocations and verify the correct invocation.

The following is the service test case for `UserService`:

```java
@RunWith(SpringRunner.class)
public class UserServiceTest {

    @MockBean
    private UserRepository userRepository;

    private UserService userService;

    @Before
    public void init() {
        this.userService = new UserService(userRepository);
    }

    @Test
    public void getAllCommentsForToday_HappyPath_ShouldReturn1Comment()
{
        // Given
        User user = new User();
        user.setUsername("shazin");
        user.setPassword("sha908");
        user.setRole("USER");
```

```
            when(userRepository.findByUsername("shazin")).thenReturn(user);

            // When
            UserDetails actual = userService.loadUserByUsername("shazin");

            // Then
            verify(userRepository, times(1)).findByUsername("shazin");
        }

    }
```

In the preceding test case, the `UserRepository.findByUsername` method is mocked to return a given user and finally verify whether that method is invoked exactly once.

Using Spring Thymeleaf for the view

In this section, we will explain in detail what a template engine is, and how to use Spring Thymeleaf to implement the view presentation.

Understanding template engines

Standard **Java Enterprise Edition (Java EE)** applications used JSPs to generate presentation views for the end user. JSP is a mature technology that enables users to use embedded Java code as well as **Java Server Tag Library (JSTL)** elements, which will, in turn, execute Java code to generate a presentation view. All JSPs are eventually compiled as a servlet.

But mixing this Java code with presentation-specific code (HTML, CSS, and many more) is cumbersome and makes separation of concern difficult. Furthermore, presentation views done using plain JSPs are difficult to modify and maintain for UI Engineers. That is where UI template engines are useful.

Template engines provide an easy way of decoupling presentation view code from business logic so that each is layered and can be developed and maintained independently of the others. This helps vastly reduce code duplication and bugs introduced because template engines allow the reuse of previously tested, production-ready code.

Building a Basic Web Application

Spring Thymeleaf

Spring Thymeleaf is a very easy to use and popular template engine used to generate final presentation views. The Spring Thymeleaf Framework offers `ViewResolver` as well as `View` implementations that can be used to generate presentation views. The uniqueness of Spring Thymeleaf comes from the syntax it uses to define presentation view logic.

A snippet of this syntax is as follows:

```html
<!DOCTYPE HTML>
<html xmlns:th="http://www.thymeleaf.org">
  ...
  <body>
    <p th:text="${message}">
  </body>
</html>
```

The uniqueness of this syntax is that it is pure HTML and isn't special code that needs the help of the server side to render. This means that UI engineers can work on styling, animations, and so on without ever knowing anything about Spring Thymeleaf. In order to use Spring Thymeleaf, the following Maven starter dependency needs to be included:

```xml
<dependencies>
    ...
    <dependency>
        <groupId>org.springframework.boot</groupId>
        <artifactId>spring-boot-starter-thymeleaf</artifactId>
    </dependency>
</dependencies>
```

Adding the preceding Maven dependency will import all the required dependencies for Spring Thymeleaf to be used in the web application successfully. The following sections will describe how to sketch-design the Retro Board and then implement it using Spring Thymeleaf.

UI design for the Retro Board

The following is a rough UI design for the Retro Board, which will be designed using Spring Thymeleaf for the web application:

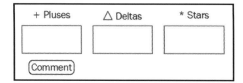

The UI will consist of three columns for each particular comment type and a text area for typing comments. In the end, there will be a button to submit all comments. The UI has an additional requirement where it needs to refresh every 30 seconds to see updated comments from others. This UI will be implemented in a responsive way so that it can be used in desktop devices as well as mobile devices. In order to achieve this, the following UI framework will be used:

- **Bootstrap**: This is a very famous framework for developing responsive UIs for devices with different screen sizes and resolutions
- **Font Awesome**: This is a collection of icons that are usually used in UIs

The preceding frameworks will be used to implement the aforementioned UI design with standard HTML, CSS, and a bit of JavaScript.

UI implementation for the Retro Board using Spring Thymeleaf

The main page for the Retro Board will be a page similar to the design shown in the previous section, implemented using Spring Thymeleaf, Bootstrap, and Font Awesome along with some plain HTML, CSS, and so on.

When you take a closer look at the preceding code, it seems it is mostly very familiar HTML, with some special syntax for Spring Thymeleaf. One of the most notable sections is in the HTML element where the namespace for Spring Thymeleaf is:

```
<html xmlns:th="http://www.thymeleaf.org">
```

The structure of the page is divided into three parts as follows:

- **Header**: This section has the page title and logout button
- **Body**: This section has all the comments and text areas to submit a comment
- **Footer**: This section has author information

Building a Basic Web Application

In order to correctly structure this, Bootstrap-specific styling classes in HTML element attributes are used to define how the UI needs to be rendered responsively:

```
<div class="container">
```

For a full list of such styling classes, the Bootstrap documentation can be referred to, at https://getbootstrap.com/docs/4.0/getting-started/introduction/.

Another notable piece of code is the **Cross-Site Request Forgery (CSRF)** protection token submitted with the POST request when saving comments:

```
<input type="hidden" th:name="${_csrf.parameterName}"
   th:value="${_csrf.token}" />
```

This will be explained in detail in the *Using Spring Security for authentication and authorization* section, but in simple terms it is used to verify that all mutable requests come only from authorized forms. Take note of the Spring Thymeleaf syntax th:name and th:value, which will be rendered into the input name and input value attribute respectively.

From the diagram displayed in the previous section, we can see that there is a main form that has comments for pluses, deltas, and stars along with text areas for submitting comments. Consider the following code:

```
<form action="/comment" method="POST">
    <div class="row form-row">
        <input type="hidden" th:name="${_csrf.parameterName}"
            th:value="${_csrf.token}" />
        <div class="col-md-4"><i class="fa fa-plus"></i> Pluses
            <hr/>
            <div id="pluses" th:each="plus : ${plusComments}">
                <div class="alert alert-info" role="alert">
                    <strong th:text="${plus.createdBy}"></strong>
                    <p th:text="${plus.comment}"></p>
                </div>
            </div>
            <textarea id="plusComment" name="plusComment" class="form-
                control" style="min-width: 100%"></textarea>
        </div>
        ...
    ...
```

In the preceding code snippet, Spring Thymeleaf's th:each tag is used to iterate through the list plusComments sent from the server and render createdBy and comment respectively. Take note that a variable named plus is used to refer to each plus comment individually. The same is true for deltaComments and starComments also.

Eventually, there is a footer section, where copyright and author information will be usually placed, as follows:

```
<footer class="fixed-bottom" style="position: fixed; bottom: 0">
    <div class="container">
        <span class="text-muted">Retro Board by Shazin Sadakath.</span>
    </div>
</footer>
```

The complete source code is available in this chapter's GitHub repository.

Using Spring Web MVC with servlet 3.x for the controller

Controllers are the integration point between the model and view in the MVC paradigm. They act like glue that binds together everything while taking care of business logic execution and routing. The following Maven starter dependency needs to be added to enable Spring Web MVC:

```
<dependencies>
    ...
    <dependency>
        <groupId>org.springframework.boot</groupId>
        <artifactId>spring-boot-starter-web</artifactId>
    </dependency>
</dependencies>
```

The preceding dependency will import servlet, Spring, and Tomcat dependencies to enable successfully writing servlet-based web applications using Spring.

Implementation of Controllers annotations

The following is `CommentController`, which displays and saves comment:

```
@Controller
public class CommentController {

  private final static Logger LOGGER =
LoggerFactory.getLogger(CommentController.class);

  private final CommentService commentService;

  public CommentController(CommentService commentService) {
    this.commentService = commentService;
  }

  @GetMapping("/")
  public String index(Model model) {
    model.addAttribute("time", new SimpleDateFormat("yyyy-MM-dd HH:mm:ss").format(new Date()));
    List<Comment> allComments = commentService.getAllCommentsForToday();
    Map<CommentType, List<Comment>> groupedComments =
    allComments.stream().collect(Collectors.groupingBy(Comment::getType));
    model.addAttribute("starComments", groupedComments.get(CommentType.STAR));
    model.addAttribute("deltaComments", groupedComments.get(CommentType.DELTA));
    model.addAttribute("plusComments", groupedComments.get(CommentType.PLUS));

    return "comment";
  }

  @PostMapping("/comment")
  public String createComment(@RequestParam(name = "plusComment", required = false) String plusComment,
    @RequestParam(name = "deltaComment", required = false) String deltaComment,
    @RequestParam(name = "starComment", required = false) String starComment)
  {
    List<Comment> comments = new ArrayList<>();

    if (StringUtils.isNotEmpty(plusComment)) {
      comments.add(getComment(plusComment, CommentType.PLUS));
    }

    if (StringUtils.isNotEmpty(deltaComment)) {
      comments.add(getComment(deltaComment, CommentType.DELTA));
    }
```

```
    if (StringUtils.isNotEmpty(starComment)) {
    comments.add(getComment(starComment, CommentType.STAR));
    }

    if (!comments.isEmpty()) {
    LOGGER.info("Saved {}", commentService.saveAll(comments));
    }

    return "redirect:/";
    }

    private Comment getComment(String comment, CommentType commentType) {
    Comment commentObject = new Comment();
    commentObject.setType(commentType);
    commentObject.setComment(comment);

    return commentObject;
    }
}
```

The `index` method, which is mapped to the URL /, will load comments made on the day using `CommentService.getAllCommentsForToday()`. After that, it will group all comments by comment type and send those to be displayed on the comment page.

The `createComment` method, which is mapped to the URL /comment, will save comments made on the day using the `CommentService.saveAll()` method.

Testing controllers

Testing controllers for successful routing and view rendering is a must in order to make sure the web application does what is expected. The following is a test case written for `CommentController`, which is annotated with `@WebMvcTest` and has auto-wired `MockMvc`, which will be used to invoke endpoints for testing:

```
@RunWith(SpringRunner.class)
@WebMvcTest(CommentController.class)
public class CommentControllerTest {

  @Autowired
  private MockMvc mockMvc;

  @MockBean
  private CommentService commentService;

  @Test
```

```java
    public void saveComments_HappyPath_ShouldReturnStatus302() throws 
Exception {
    // When
    ResultActions resultActions = 
mockMvc.perform(post("/comment").with(csrf()).with(user("shazin").roles("US
ER")).param("plusComment", "Test Plus"));

    // Then
    resultActions
    .andExpect(status().is3xxRedirection())
    .andExpect(redirectedUrl("/"));

    verify(commentService, times(1)).saveAll(anyList());
    verifyNoMoreInteractions(commentService);
    }

    @Test
    public void getComments_HappyPath_ShouldReturnStatus200() throws Exception 
{
    // Given
    Comment comment = new Comment();
    comment.setComment("Test Plus");
    comment.setType(CommentType.PLUS);
    comment.setCreatedBy("Shazin");
    comment.setCreatedDate(new Timestamp(System.currentTimeMillis()));

    Comment comment2 = new Comment();
    comment2.setComment("Test Star");
    comment2.setType(CommentType.STAR);
    comment2.setCreatedBy("Shahim");
    comment2.setCreatedDate(new Timestamp(System.currentTimeMillis()));
    List<Comment> comments = Arrays.asList(comment, comment2);
    when(commentService.getAllCommentsForToday()).thenReturn(comments);

    // When
    ResultActions resultActions = 
mockMvc.perform(get("/").with(user("shazin").roles("USER")));

    // Then
    resultActions
    .andExpect(status().isOk())
    .andExpect(view().name("comment"))
    .andExpect(model().attribute("plusComments", hasSize(1)))
    .andExpect(model().attribute("plusComments", hasItem(
    allOf(
    hasProperty("createdBy", is("Shazin")),
    hasProperty("comment", is("Test Plus"))
    )
```

```
            )))
            .andExpect(model().attribute("starComments", hasSize(1)))
            .andExpect(model().attribute("starComments", hasItem(
        allOf(
        hasProperty("createdBy", is("Shahim")),
        hasProperty("comment", is("Test Star"))
        )
        )));

        verify(commentService, times(1)).getAllCommentsForToday();
        verifyNoMoreInteractions(commentService);
    }
}
```

One test, `saveComments_HappyPath_ShouldReturnStatus302`, tests the `CommentController.createComment` method by verifying its successful persistence of comments by invoking the `CommentService.saveAll` method exactly once, and verifying it does a redirect to the URL /. Furthermore, it verifies there are no more interactions with `CommentService` after saving all the comments it received.

Another test, `getComments_HappyPath_ShouldReturnStatus200`, tests the `CommentController.index` method by verifying it successfully returns mocked comments to the view `comment` by invoking the `CommentService.getAllCommentsForToday` method exactly once. Furthermore, it verifies there are no more interactions with `CommentService` after returning all the comments for the day.

During both tests, a dummy user authentication and authorization are mocked using the following code snippet:

```
        user("shazin").roles("USER")
```

This code creates a request post processor that will mimic a user with the username `shazin` and role `USER`, which will enable successfully accessing protected endpoints. The following Maven dependencies need to be specified to enable testing:

```
        <dependencies>
            <dependency>
                <groupId>org.springframework.boot</groupId>
                <artifactId>spring-boot-starter-test</artifactId>
                <scope>test</scope>
            </dependency>
            <dependency>
                <groupId>org.mockito</groupId>
                <artifactId>mockito-all</artifactId>
                <version>1.10.19</version>
```

Building a Basic Web Application

```xml
            <scope>test</scope>
        </dependency>
        <dependency>
            <groupId>org.springframework.security</groupId>
            <artifactId>spring-security-test</artifactId>
            <version>4.1.4.RELEASE</version>
          <scope>test</scope>
        </dependency>
</dependencies>
```

Using Spring Security for authentication and authorization

This web application has used Spring Security to authenticate users and to authorize them to submit comments. The Maven Spring Security starter needs to be specified as follows to enable Spring Security in the web application:

```xml
<dependencies>
    <dependency>
        <groupId>org.springframework.boot</groupId>
        <artifactId>spring-boot-starter-security</artifactId>
    </dependency>
</dependencies>
```

The following is the Spring Security configuration:

```java
@Configuration
@EnableWebSecurity
public class SecurityConfig extends WebSecurityConfigurerAdapter {

    @Autowired
    private UserService userDetailService;

    @Override
    public void configure(WebSecurity web) throws Exception {
        web.ignoring().antMatchers("/h2-console/**");
    }

    @Override
    protected void configure(HttpSecurity http) throws Exception {
        http.formLogin()
                .and()
                .logout()
                .permitAll()
                .and()
```

```java
                .authorizeRequests()
                    .antMatchers("/**")
                    .hasRole("USER");
    }

    @Override
    protected void configure(AuthenticationManagerBuilder auth) throws Exception {
        auth.authenticationProvider(authenticationProvider());
    }

    @Bean
    public AuthenticationProvider authenticationProvider() {
        DaoAuthenticationProvider authenticationProvider = new DaoAuthenticationProvider();
        authenticationProvider.setPasswordEncoder(passwordEncoder());
        authenticationProvider.setUserDetailsService(userDetailService);
        return authenticationProvider;
    }

    @Bean
    public PasswordEncoder passwordEncoder() {
        return new BCryptPasswordEncoder();
    }

    @Bean
    public ApplicationRunner applicationRunner() {
        return args -> {
            userDetailService.create(new User(null, "shazin", passwordEncoder().encode("password"),
                "ROLE_USER"));
            userDetailService.create(new User(null, "shahim", passwordEncoder().encode("password"),
                "ROLE_USER"));
        };
    }
}
```

Building a Basic Web Application

The preceding configuration has `@EnableWebSecurity` to configure the filters necessary for Spring Security and override any auto-configuration. The `configure(WebSecurity web)` method ignores Spring Security for the URL `/h2-console/` and all of its sub-URLs. The `configure(HttpSecurity http)` method configures `formLogin`, log out, and access to all URLs (`/**`) that have the user role (`ROLE_USER`) authorization. This, in turn, means the user needs to be authenticated and anonymous users will not be allowed to access anything.

The `configure(AuthenticationManagerBuilder auth)` method is used to configure `AuthenticationProvider` with our implementation for `UserDetailsService` (`UserService`) and `PasswordEncoder`, in our case `BCryptPasswordEncoder`. Finally, `ApplicationRunner` is used to insert some users into the database at startup.

The following code helps to load the currently logged-in user:

```
@Component
public class AuditAwareImpl implements AuditorAware<String> {
    @Override
    public Optional<String> getCurrentAuditor() {
        Authentication authentication =
SecurityContextHolder.getContext().getAuthentication();

        if (authentication == null || !authentication.isAuthenticated()) {
            return Optional.empty();
        }

        return Optional.of(((User)
authentication.getPrincipal()).getUsername());
    }
}
```

Furthermore, to support the `@CreatedUser` annotation used in JPA Auditing, there is `AuditAware` implementation that makes use of `SecurityContextHolder`, which is responsible for holding the `Authentication` object for a logged in user. The principal from the `Authentication` object is retrieved to get the username of the logged in user, which will be persisted with a `Comment` object.

Demonstrating the Retro Board

When everything is put together, build and run the Retro Board, which we will be able to access using the `http://<host>:<port>` URL.

There are several ways to run a Spring Boot application, some of which are:

- Running the Spring Boot application main class using an IDE
- Building a JAR or WAR file using the following Maven command and then running:

    ```
    $ mvn clean install
    $ java -jar target/<package-name>.[jar|war]
    ```

- Running using the Spring Boot Maven plugin:

    ```
    $ mvn clean spring-boot:run
    ```

After running, the Retro Board web application will launch the login screen as follows:

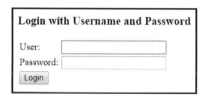

This login screen is the default login screen for form logins in Spring Security. A `username/password` combination created in `SecurityConfig` can be used to log in to the system. After successful login, the user will be routed to the comments page, which is as follows:

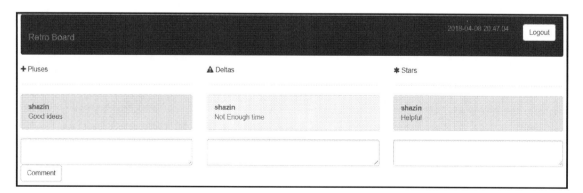

Building a Basic Web Application

In the preceding screenshot, the header is visible with the title of the web application, the current date and time, and the **Logout** button. Additionally, there are three text areas to enter comments and a button to submit comments to be persisted in the relational database. The comments will be shown under their respective type.

As we have used the Bootstrap UI Framework, the comments page is responsive and can be viewed from devices with different screen sizes and resolutions as follows:

The header, body, and footers sections will be re-positioned on the screen so they're displayed properly in the device. Now, with this Retro Board, members of a development team can comment and collaborate successfully using multiple devices simultaneously.

Summary

Congratulations on completing this chapter, where the skills and knowledge required to build a basic web application were discussed in detail. This chapter started off by explaining what a web application is and how a web application can benefit from MVC patterns in terms of both development and maintenance. It talked about the requirements of a web application being developed and used a UML use case diagram to explain the requirement visually.

This chapter also explained how to write the domain model of an application based on the requirements, how to write data repositories for it, how to test those for their correct functioning, and so on. It also discussed how to encapsulate business logic inside services and test them effectively to make sure everything works correctly.

Subsequently, the chapter talked about how to write presentation views to create and display comments using the Spring Thymeleaf Framework. It briefly explained about JSP, JSTL, and how Spring Thymeleaf differs from those. Also, it explained how to use Spring Thymeleaf's syntax to list comments.

Eventually, the chapter discussed how to use Spring Web MVC Controllers to provide routing and coordination for different services. Furthermore, it talked about how to protect controller endpoints using Spring Security to allow proper authentication and authorization for users. Finally, it explained how to test Spring Web MVC Controllers using Web MVC test cases. The chapter also demonstrated the usage of the Retro Board in detail. We'll learn about more complex web application development in upcoming chapters.

Questions

Please answer the following questions to see whether you have successfully mastered this chapter:

1. What is a web application?
2. What is an MVC pattern?
3. What is a relational database?
4. What is JPA?
5. How is the `@Entity` annotation used in JPA?
6. What is a template engine?
7. What is Spring Security used for?

Further reading

In order to improve your knowledge of Spring Web MVC and Spring Security, the following books are recommended and will be helpful in the coming chapters:

- *Spring MVC: Designing Real-World Web Applications*: https://www.packtpub.com/application-development/spring-mvc-designing-real-world-web-applications
- *Spring Security - Third Edition*: https://www.packtpub.com/application-development/spring-security-third-edition

3
Building a Simple Blog Management System

This chapter will introduce the reader to the details of how to build a simple blog management system using Spring Boot 2 as the base application development framework. It will explain how to use Elasticsearch as the persistence layer, which is a widely used data source for storing high-volume, high-velocity data. Subsequently, it will use Apache FreeMarker Template Engine to create presentation views for the blog management system. Furthermore, it will use Spring WebFlux and Spring Security WebFlux to implement controllers and provide authentication and authorization.

The following topics will be covered in this chapter:

- Using Spring Data Elasticsearch for persistence
- Using Apache FreeMarker for the view
- Using Spring WebFlux for the controller
- Using Spring Security for authentication and authorization
- Demonstrating Bloggest

Technical requirements

In order to implement the web application using Spring Boot, the following build tools need to be downloaded and installed:

- To install **Java Development Kit (JDK)** 8, download it from its official page at http://www.oracle.com/technetwork/java/javase/downloads/jdk8-downloads-2133151.html
- To install Maven 3, download it from its official page at https://maven.apache.org/download.cgi

- To install IntelliJ IDEA, download it from its official page at `https://www.jetbrains.com/idea/download/`
- To install **Spring Tool Suite (STS)**, download it from its official page at `https://spring.io/tools`
- To download Elasticsearch server, visit its official page at `https://www.elastic.co/downloads/elasticsearch`

The source code for this chapter can be found under the `https://github.com/PacktPublishing/Spring-Boot-2.0-Projects-Fundamentals-of-Spring-Boot-2.0`, `Chapter03` directory.

Getting started

In this section, the readers will get an overview of the web application that is being developed. The requirements, design, and implementation details will be discussed in brief.

Web application architecture

A web application is exposed to multiple concurrent users over a public or private network, as opposed to a standalone application. Let's get started developing a basic web application that uses the well-known **model-view-controller** (**MVC**) pattern to build a three-tier application. The MVC pattern is known for its separation of concerns by decoupling presentation logic (what the user sees in a browser), routing and business logic (what the application needs to accomplish), and persistence (where the data is finally stored). This has made MVC a very developer-friendly pattern, as different tiers of an application can be developed and tested by experts in that area independently and without knowledge of the other tiers.

For example, a **user interface** (**UI**) developer can work on the beautification of the presentation while a database administrator works on database optimization. Also, this layering has made maintenance easier than with conventional web applications, which usually have spaghetti code without any layering.

In this chapter, Spring WebFlux Framework will be used to implement the MVC pattern inside our web application. Let's have a look at the workflow of Spring WebFlux in detail.

Workflow of Spring WebFlux

The Spring WebFlux workflow is similar to the Spring Web MVC workflow; the main difference is that it doesn't rely on `Servlet` anymore. Instead, it uses a `DispatcherHandler`, which is non-blocking. Furthermore, it makes use of `ServerHttpRequest` and `ServerHttpResponse` instead of `HttpServletRequest` and `HttpServletResponse` from `Servlet` for its request and response representation.

In addition to that, it uses `Flux<DataBuffer>` (this is a non-blocking way to send a 0..N number of messages, data, and so on) instead of `InputStream` and `OutputStream` to read and write data in a non-blocking manner. It uses a `HandlerMapping` and `HandlerAdapter`, which are also non-blocking.

Requirements of the Bloggest system

The problem domain under consideration is a simple blog management system nicknamed **Bloggest**, where users can write articles of interest to them. The Bloggest system must be publicly accessible via the internet and registered users must be able to write, edit, and delete content.

But content available in the Bloggest system must be publicly visible without any need to log in. Each article should have a title, summary, permanent link, and body. The `body` section must be styled using commonly available fonts and font styling, so that articles can be presented in a pleasing manner.

There must be administration capabilities, where an administrator must be able to edit or delete an article written by a user as appropriate.

The Bloggest system should allow the authentication and authorization of users and administrators. Users should be able to create new articles and then edit and delete articles. Administrators should be able to create new articles and edit or delete an article written by anyone to moderate the content.

The use case diagram

The following use case diagram shows the requirement for the dashboard, which is nicknamed Bloggest:

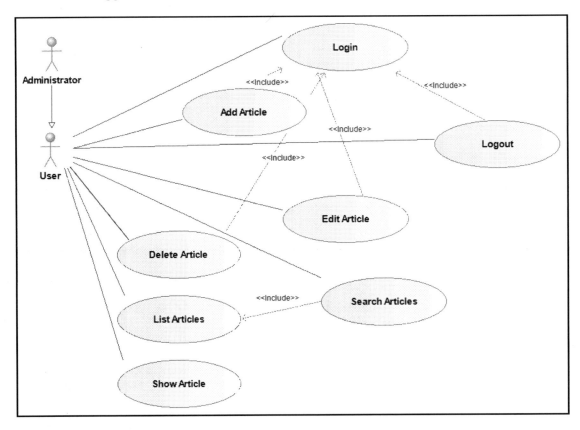

The actors are the **User** and **Administrator** of Bloggest. It has the following use cases:

- **Login**: This use case is required to authenticate users so that each article author can be uniquely identified.
- **Add Article**: This use case is where a user creates a new article in the Bloggest system. It requires the user to be authenticated.
- **Edit Article**: This use case is where a user edits an article he/she created or an administrator edits an article created by any user of the Bloggest system. It requires the user/administrator to be authenticated.

- **Delete Article**: This use case is where a user deletes an article he/she created or an administrator deletes an article created by any user of the Bloggest system. It requires the user/administrator to be authenticated.
- **List Articles**: This use case is where any user of the Bloggest system can list all the articles available in the system. This step doesn't require authentication and is public to everyone.
- **Search Articles**: This use case is where any user of the Bloggest system can search for articles available in the system. This step doesn't require authentication and is public to everyone.
- **Show Article**: This use case is where any user of the Bloggest system can view a particular article of interest. This step doesn't require authentication and is public to everyone.
- **Logout**: This use case is where a logged-in user can log out of the Bloggest system.

Using Spring Data Elasticsearch for persistence

This section will introduce Elasticsearch and how to use Spring Data Elasticsearch repositories to provide **Create, Retrieve, Update, and Delete (CRUD)** operations on Elasticsearch easily.

Understanding Elasticsearch

Elasticsearch is an open source search and analytics engine that can run in a distributed environment. It provides RESTful APIs to ingest and retrieve high-volume, high-velocity data. Elasticsearch is built on top of Apache Lucene and was released in 2010. It has popular use cases such as:

- Log analytics
- Full-text search
- Operational and business intelligence
- Distributed Document Store

Elasticsearch can store new data in the form of documents and it indexes the documents in a cluster by adding searchable references to the document. This enables faster searching for and retrieval of high-volume, velocity documents.

This chapter will use Elasticsearch to store and retrieve blog articles because of the search and indexing capabilities it provides; a blogging system is expected to have a lot of text, which needs to be searched very quickly to provide a good user experience.

Understanding Spring Data Elasticsearch

Spring Data Elasticsearch projects are intended to bring in the concepts of Spring Data repositories, enabling easy development of Elasticsearch repositories. They provide an abstraction layer on top of Elasticsearch to successfully store, retrieve, and modify documents available in the Elasticsearch transparently.

Spring Data Elasticsearch eases CRUD operations by allowing the `ElasticsearchRepository` interface, which extends from `ElasticsearchCrudRepository`. This hides the complexities of plain Elasticsearch implementations, which need to be implemented and tested by developers. Using Spring Data Elasticsearch could reduce the development time dramatically because of this.

In coming chapters, `ElasticsearchRepository`, with default methods and custom methods, will be used extensively to implement business logic and write and test Spring Data Elasticsearch repositories. The following sections will discuss how to use a domain model designed using a class diagram as a base to implement Spring Data Elasticsearch-based documents and repositories.

Class diagram for the domain model

Since the domain model is the most important component of an application, this section will design it first. The following is the simple class diagram for this web application:

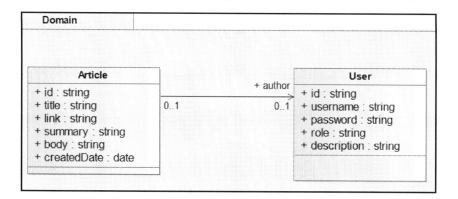

There are two main domain models, as shown in the preceding diagram. They are as follows:

- **Article**: This is the main domain model, which will store the actual article title, body, link, summary, author, created date, and so on
- **User**: This domain model will store the username, password, and role of a registered user

Implementation of the domain model using Spring Data Elasticsearch annotations

This section will explain the details of how to configure and use Spring Data Elasticsearch with an Elasticsearch service with the domain model designed in the previous section.

Setting up dependencies and configuration classes

Initially, before implementing the domain model, the `dependency` and `configuration` class need to be specified. The following Maven starter `dependency` needs to be included:

```
<dependencies>
    <dependency>
        <groupId>org.springframework.boot</groupId>
        <artifactId>spring-boot-starter-data-elasticsearch</artifactId>
    </dependency>
</dependencies>
```

Building a Simple Blog Management System

The following configuration properties in the `application.properties` file need to be set to configure the Elasticsearch cluster nodes:

```
spring.data.elasticsearch.cluster-nodes=localhost:9300
```

The preceding configuration uses `spring.data.elasticsearch.cluster-nodes` to set the Elasticsearch cluster node IP/hostname and port.

Implementing the domain model

The implementation of the domain model `Article` using Elasticsearch annotations will look like the following:

```
@Document(indexName = "springboot2blog_article", type = "article")
@Data
public class Article {

    @Id
    private String id;

    private String title;

    private String link;

    private String summary;

    private String body;

    @Field(type = FieldType.Nested)
    private User author;
    @Field(type = FieldType.Date)
    private Date createdDate = new Date();

}
```

In the preceding code, `@Document` is used to mark the `Article` class as an Elasticsearch document with the index name `"springboot2blog_article"` and the type `"article"`. The `@Id` annotation marks the ID property as the identity field of the document.
The `@Data` annotation is from Lombok library and is used to mark a **plain old Java object (POJO)** as a class that will hold data. This means `getters`, `setters`, the `equals` method, the `hashCode` method, and the `toString` method will be generated for that class. The `author` field and the `createdDate` field are annotated with the `@Field` annotation, which specifies the type of those fields as they are complex, composite fields.

The implementation of the domain model `User` will look like the following:

```
@Document(indexName = "springboot2blog_user", type = "user")
@Data
@NoArgsConstructor
@AllArgsConstructor
public class User {

    @Id
    private String id;

    private String username;

    private String password;

    private String role;
    private String description;
}
```

The preceding class also does the same things as the `User` class. The newly added annotations, which are also from Lombok library and `@AllArgsConstructor`, will generate a constructor with the `id`, `username`, `password`, `role`, and `description` properties and `@NoArgsConstructor`, which will generate a default constructor.

Implementation of Spring Data Elasticsearch repositories

With the domain models implemented successfully, `ElasticsearchRepository` for those can be implemented using Spring Data Elasticsearch. The specialty here is that there is no need to implement anything. Just writing an interface that extends from the `ElasticsearchRepository` interface would be sufficient to expose methods to find one, find all, save, delete, and so on. The following code shows `ArticleRepository`:

```
public interface ArticleRepository extends
ElasticsearchRepository<Article, String> {
    Optional<Article> findByLink(String link);
    Page<Article> findByTitleContainingAndBodyContaining(String title,
      String body, Pageable pageable);
}
```

Since there are use cases in the application to show `Article` with a link to that `Article`, the `findByLink` method is introduced in the preceding repository; this will return `Optional`, which may or may not have a value inside. Furthermore, in order to enable the search use case for all the available articles, the `findByTitleContainingAndBodyContaining` method is introduced, which will return a `Page` object that will have the content, number of total elements, number of total pages, and so on. So, that full-text search can be done on the `title` and `body` properties of `Article`.

The following code shows `UserRepository`:

```
public interface UserRepository extends ElasticsearchRepository<User,
String> {
  User findByUsername(String username);
}
```

In the preceding code, there is a method name `findByUsername`, where `username` is a property of the `User` class.

Using Apache FreeMarker for the view

In this section, it will be explained in detail what a template engine is, and then we will talk about how to use Spring Apache FreeMarker to implement the view presentation.

Understanding template engines

Standard Java **Jakarta Enterprise Edition (Jakarta EE)** applications use **JavaServer Pages (JSPs)** to generate presentation views for the end user. JSP is a mature technology that enables the use of embedded Java code as well as **JavaServer Pages Standard Tag Library (JSTL)** elements, which will, in turn, execute Java code, which can generate presentation views. All JSPs are eventually compiled as a `Servlet`.

But mixing these Java codes and presentation-specific codes (HTML, CSS, and many more) is cumbersome and makes the separation of concerns difficult. Furthermore, presentation views mad using plain JSPs are difficult to modify and be maintained by UI engineers. That is where UI template engines are useful.

Template engines provide an easy way of decoupling presentation view code from business logic so that each is layered and can be developed and maintained independently of the other. This helps vastly reduce code duplication and the number of bugs introduced because template engines allow the reuse of previously tested, production-ready code.

Apache FreeMarker

Apache FreeMarker is a popular template engine that can generate a text output based on the template and variable data. Apache FreeMarker templates use a custom programming language named **FreeMarker Template Language** (FTL), which is used to write programming constructs in presentation views.

A controller is used to prepare the data required, which is then passed on to the template in order to render the presentation views. Apache FreeMarker focuses on how to present the data that is sent to it in an aesthetically pleasing manner.

Apache FreeMarker adheres to the MVC pattern and templates can be developed by UI engineers, while the data required to render the final presentation views can be computed in the backend and sent by developers independently and transparently.

Some features of Apache FreeMarker are as follows:

- FTL has common programming syntaxes for conditional blocks, iterations, assignments, string, arithmetic operations, and so on
- It is lightweight and flexible
- It has internationalization (i18n support)

A snippet of this syntax is as follows:

```
<!DOCTYPE HTML>
<html>
  ...
  <body>
    <#if message??>
        <p>${message}</p>
    </#if>
  </body>
</html>
```

The preceding Apache FreeMarker code basically checks if a variable by the name `message` is present, and if so, displays it inside of a paragraph tag. More details on Apache FreeMarker can be referenced from the following documentation:

https://freemarker.apache.org/docs/dgui_quickstart_basics.html.

In order to use Apache FreeMarker, the following Maven starter `dependency` needs to be included:

```
<dependencies>
    <dependency>
        <groupId>org.springframework.boot</groupId>
        <artifactId>spring-boot-starter-freemarker</artifactId>
    </dependency>
</dependencies>
```

Adding the preceding Maven `dependency` will import all the required dependencies for Apache FreeMarker to be used in the web application successfully. The following sections will describe how to sketch design the Bloggest application and then implement it using Apache FreeMarker.

UI design for Bloggest

The following is a rough UI design for Bloggest, which will be designed using Apache FreeMarker for the web application:

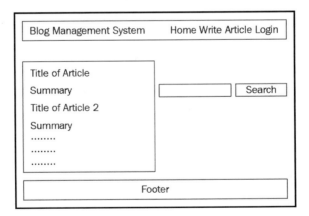

Chapter 3

The preceding UI sketch is for the **List Articles** use case, which will be the main landing page of the Bloggest web application. There are some common UI elements that are common to almost all of the use cases, such as a header, navigation links, search bar, and a footer. Consider this use case diagram:

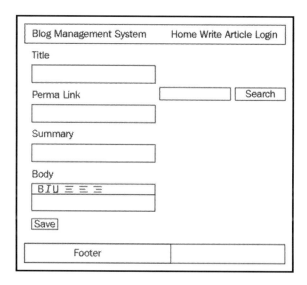

The preceding UI sketch is for **Add Article**, **Edit Article**, and **Delete Article** use cases where the **Title**, **Perma Link**, **Summary**, and **Body** of an `Article` can be specified to be created or edited. Now, consider this diagram:

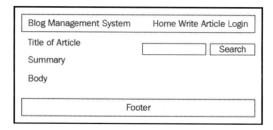

The preceding UI sketch is for the **Show Article** use case, where a user can view an `Article` available on the Bloggest platform.

This UI will be implemented in a responsive way so that it can be used on desktop devices as well as mobile devices. In order to achieve this, the Bootstrap UI Framework will be used. Bootstrap is a very famous framework for developing a responsive UI for devices with different screen sizes and resolutions.

The preceding frameworks will be used to implement the aforementioned UI design with standard HTML, CSS, and a bit of JavaScript.

UI implementation for Bloggest using Apache FreeMarker

The main page for Bloggest will be a page similar to the design shown in the previous section, implemented using Apache FreeMarker and Bootstrap along with some plain HTML, CSS, and so on.

Upon taking a closer look at the preceding code, it seems it is mostly very familiar HTML, with some special syntax for Apache FreeMarker. One of the most notable sections is where Apache FreeMarker specific tags will start as follows:

```
<#element>
```

These tags end as follows:

```
</#element>
```

The structure of the page is divided into three parts as follows:

- **Header**: This section has the page title and the **login**, **logout**, and **Write Article** buttons
- **Body**: This section has all the content
- **Footer**: This section has author information

In order to structure this correctly, Bootstrap-specific styling classes in HTML element attributes are used to define how the UI needs to be rendered responsively. In order to speed up development, this section uses an opensource Bootstrap template specifically designed for blogging systems, which is available at the following URL:

```
https://blackrockdigital.github.io/startbootstrap-blog-post/
```

Implementing a common layout using Apache FreeMarker

There are so many common elements in the aforementioned UI sketches, it makes sense to use a common layout to avoid code duplication and enable centralized code in all the pages. The following `common/standardPage.ftl` template file is used for this purpose:

```
<#macro page title>
<!DOCTYPE html>
<html lang="en">

  <head>

    <meta charset="utf-8">
    <meta name="viewport" content="width=device-width, initial-scale=1,
      shrink-to-fit=no">
    <meta name="description" content="Blog Management System">
    <meta name="author" content="Shazin Sadakath">

    <title>${title}</title>
    <link rel="stylesheet" type="text/css"
      href="/webjars/bootstrap/4.0.0/css/bootstrap.min.css"/>

    <!-- Custom styles for this template -->
    <link href="/css/blog-post.css" rel="stylesheet">

    <script src="/webjars/jquery/3.3.1-1/jquery.min.js"></script>

  </head>
```

The preceding `head` section imports Bootstrap, Blog CSS, and the JQuery JavaScript library. Going ahead, we see the following code:

```
<body>

  <!-- Navigation -->
  <nav class="navbar navbar-expand-lg navbar-dark bg-dark fixed-top">
    <div class="container">
      <a class="navbar-brand" href="/article">Blog Management
        System</a>
      <button class="navbar-toggler" type="button" data-
        toggle="collapse" data-target="#navbarResponsive"
        aria-controls="navbarResponsive" aria-expanded="false" aria-
        label="Toggle navigation">
          <span class="navbar-toggler-icon"></span>
      </button>
      <div class="collapse navbar-collapse" id="navbarResponsive">
```

Building a Simple Blog Management System

```
            <ul class="navbar-nav ml-auto">
              <li class="nav-item active">
                <a class="nav-link" href="/article">Home
                  <span class="sr-only">(current)</span>
                </a>
              </li>
              <li class="nav-item">
                <a class="nav-link" href="/article/new">Write Article
                  <span class="sr-only">(current)</span>
                </a>
              </li>
              <li class="nav-item">
                <#if user??>
                  <a class="nav-link" href="#">Welcome, ${user.username}
                  </a>
                <#else>
                  <a class="nav-link" href="/login">Login</a>
                </#if>
              </li>
              <li class="nav-item">
                <a class="nav-link" href="/logout">Logout</a>
              </li>
            </ul>
          </div>
        </div>
      </nav>
```

Then, inside the body section, the preceding code is responsible for rendering the header and menu at the top of the page:

```
<!-- Page Content -->
<div class="container">

  <div class="row">

    <#nested>

    <!-- Sidebar Widgets Column -->
    <div class="col-md-4">

      <!-- Search Widget -->
      <div class="card my-4">
        <h5 class="card-header">Search</h5>
        <div class="card-body">
        <form action="/article">
          <div class="input-group">
            <input type="text" name="q" class="form-control"
              placeholder="Search for...">
```

```
                    <span class="input-group-btn">
                      <input type="submit" class="btn btn-secondary"
                         value="Go!"/>
                    </span>
                  </div>
                </form>
              </div>
            </div>

          </div>
        </div>
        <!-- /.row -->

      </div>
      <!-- /.container -->
```

Furthermore, for dynamic content, there is a notable Apache FreeMarker tag, which is the following. We wire content here using `@p.page`:

```
<#nested>
```

Dynamic content specific to a web page will be rendered inside this part of the template:

```
      <!-- Footer -->
      <footer class="py-5 bg-dark">
        <div class="container">
          <p class="m-0 text-center text-white">Copyright &copy; Shazin
             Sadakath 2018</p>
        </div>
        <!-- /.container -->
      </footer>

      <!-- Bootstrap core JavaScript -->
      <script src="/webjars/bootstrap/4.0.0/js/bootstrap.bundle.min.js">
      </script>

    </body>

</html>
</#macro>
```

Finally, the template has the `footer` section, which is common to all pages, and also imports any JavaScript libraries that need to be loaded lazily.

Some noticeable things in the preceding template are that it begins and ends with the following `macro` tag:

```
<#macro page title>
```

All of the common JavaScript, CSS, and HTML will go inside this tag.

Implementing a List Articles page

Let's have a look at the `article/index.ftl` page, which implements the **List Articles** page and makes use of the common template shown in the preceding section:

```
<#import "../common/standardPage.ftl" as p>

<@p.page title="Posts">
        <!-- Post Content Column -->
        <div class="col-lg-8">

          <#if message??>
          <div id="success-alert" class="alert alert-success">
            ${message}
          </div>
          <script type="text/javascript">
            $( document ).ready(function() {
                $("#success-alert").fadeTo(2000, 500).slideUp(500,
                  function(){
                    $("#success-alert").slideUp(500);
                });
            });
          </script>
          </#if>
```

The preceding section is responsible for showing any message to the user for up to two seconds. The message can be anything from information, to a warning, or an error. The code actually uses the JQuery slide up animation and fade effect. Now, consider the following code:

```
          <#if articles?? >
            <#list articles.content as article>
            <!-- Title -->
            <h1 class="mt-4"><a
             href="/article/show/${article.link}">${article.title}</a>
            </h1>
```

```
<!-- Author -->
<p class="lead">
  by
  <#if article.author??>
      <a href="#">${article.author.username}</a>
  <#else>
      Anonymous
  </#if>
</p>

<hr>
<!-- Date/Time -->
<p>Posted on ${article.createdDate?string
('dd.MM.yyyy HH:mm:ss')}</p>

<p>${article.summary}</p>
```

If there are articles to be shown, then the preceding code will loop through each of them and show the title of the `Article` that will be linked to that article's link. Also, it will show the name of the author of the `Article`, the `Article` that was created, and also a summary of the `Article`:

```
<#if article.author?? && user??>
  <#if article.author.username == user.username || user.role?
    contains("ADMIN")>
    <form id="form_delete_${article.id}" method="post"
     action="/article/delete/${article.id}"></form>
    <p><a class="btn btn-success"
     href="/article/edit/${article.id}">Edit</a>
    <a href="#" class="btn btn-danger"
     onclick="$('#form_delete_${article.id}').submit();">Delete
    </a></p>
  </#if>
</#if>

<hr>
</#list>
```

These objects, `??`, these objects are the ones that are sent in the `Model` object. If there is a user logged-in, the preceding logic will check whether the logged in user is actually the author of `Article` or an administrator. In both of those cases, only then will it show the **Edit** and **Delete** buttons.

Finally, the previous code generates the pagination for the list of articles available in the **List Articles** page. Consider the following code:

```
<nav aria-label="Page navigation example">
    <ul class="pagination">
      <#if articles.hasPrevious()>
        <li class="page-item"><a class="page-link"
        href="/article?
         page=${articles.previousPageable().pageNumber}&size=20">
          Previous</a></li>
        </#if>
        <#list 1..articles.totalPages as i>
          <li class="page-item"><a class="page-link"
            href="/article?page=${i-1}&size=20">${i}</a></li>
        </#list>
        <#if articles.hasNext()>
          <li class="page-item"><a class="page-link"
            href="/article?
         page=${articles.nextPageable().pageNumber}&size=20">
          Next</a></li>
        </#if>
      </ul>
    </nav>
    </#if>

      </div>
</@p.page>
```

The common template is imported using the following Apache FreeMarker tag:

```
<#import "../common/standardPage.ftl" as p>
```

This tag imports the `common/standardPage.ftl` as the variable p, and dynamic content for the page is specified inside the tags `p.page` as follows:

```
<@p.page title="Posts">
```

The content within the preceding tags will be replaced with the `<#nested>` tag available in the common template, and the value specified in `title` will replace `${title}` in the common template.

Implementing a Create Article page

Let's have a look at the `article/create.ftl` page, which implements the **Create Article** page and makes use of the common template shown in the preceding section's code:

```
<#import "../common/standardPage.ftl" as p>


<@p.page title="${(article.title)!'New Post'}">
<script type="text/javascript"
src="/webjars/ckeditor/4.7.0/standard/ckeditor.js"></script>
```

The preceding code imports the CKEditor JavaScript library to enable rich text writing for the `content` section:

```
<!-- Post Content Column -->
<div class="col-lg-8">
<form action="/article" method="post">
```

The preceding code creates a form that can be submitted to a URL/article as a `POST` request to create or update a blog article:

```
<#if article?? >
  <input type="hidden" id="id" name="id" value="${article.id}"/>
  <div class="form-group">
    <label for="postTitle">Title</label>
    <input type="text" class="form-control" id="title" name="title"
     placeholder="Post Title" value="${article.title}" required="true">
  </div>
  <div class="form-group">
    <label for="postLink">Perma Link</label>
    <input type="text" class="form-control" id="link" name="link"
     placeholder="Post Perma Link" value="${article.link}"
     required="true">
  </div>
  <div class="form-group">
    <label for="postSummary">Summary</label>
    <textarea class="form-control" id="summary" name="summary" rows="3"
     required="true">${article.summary}</textarea>
  </div>
  <div class="form-group">
    <label for="postBody">Body</label>
    <textarea class="form-control" id="body" name="body" rows="10"
     required="true">${article.body}</textarea>
  </div>
```

Building a Simple Blog Management System

If an article is already there (update article scenario) then the preceding code will store the ID of that article in a hidden field to be submitted and will populate the `Title`, `Perma Link`, `Summary`, and `Body` with the existing values so that they can be edited, shown as follows:

```
<#else>
  <div class="form-group">
    <label for="postTitle">Title</label>
    <input type="text" class="form-control" id="title" name="title"
     placeholder="Post Title" required="true">
  </div>
  <div class="form-group">
    <label for="postLink">Permalink</label>
    <input type="text" class="form-control" id="link" name="link"
     placeholder="Post Permalink" required="true">
  </div>
  <div class="form-group">
    <label for="postSummary">Summary</label>
    <textarea class="form-control" id="summary" name="summary" rows="3"
    required="true"></textarea>
  </div>
  <div class="form-group">
    <label for="postBody">Body</label>
    <textarea class="form-control" id="body" name="body" rows="10"
    required="true"></textarea>
  </div>
</#if>
  <div class="form-group">
    <input class="form-control btn btn-primary" type="submit"
    value="Save"/>
  </div>
```

If it is an entirely new article then the preceding code will create empty `Title`, `Perma Link`, `Summary`, and `Body` fields. Eventually, the page will have a **Save** button for both the create and update use cases:

```
<script type="text/javascript">
  CKEDITOR.replace( 'body' );

  $("#title").keyup(function(){
      var str = $(this).val();
      str = str.replace(/[^a-zA-Z0-9\s]/g,"");
      str = str.toLowerCase();
      str = str.replace(/\s/g,'-');
      $("#link").val(str);
  });
</script>
```

```
        </form>
    </div>
</@p.page>
```

For styling, the `body` section with `bold`, `italic`, and so on, on a fully fledged JavaScript editor named `CKEDITOR` is used. The following `dependency` in `pom.xml` is required to enable that:

```
<dependencies>
    ...
    <dependency>
        <groupId>org.webjars</groupId>
        <artifactId>ckeditor</artifactId>
        <version>4.7.0</version>
    </dependency>
</dependencies>
```

The following JavaScript code in the front-end page can be used to enable `CKEDITOR` on an HTML element:

```
        <script type="text/javascript">
          CKEDITOR.replace( 'body' );
          ...
        </script>
```

This page also makes use of the common template. It also has a piece of jQuery JavaScript code that takes the text typed in for the title and converts it into a permanent link URL by replacing spaces with `'-'` and rendering all other characters in a simple case.

Implementing a Show Article page

Let's have a look at the `article/show.ftl` page, which implements the **Show Article** page and makes use of the common template shown in the preceding code:

```
    <#import "../common/standardPage.ftl" as p>

<#if article??>
<@p.page title="${article.title}">
        <!-- Post Content Column -->
        <div class="col-lg-8">

            <!-- Title -->
            <h1 class="mt-4">${article.title}</h1>
```

Building a Simple Blog Management System

The previous code will check if it has an article to show, and if it does it will show the article title as the title of the page itself. It will follow this by showing a big header on the page with the article title:

```
<!-- Author -->
  <p class="lead">
   by
  <#if article.author??>
    <a href="#">${article.author.username}</a>
    <#else>
      Anonymous
    </#if>
  </p>

<hr>
```

The preceding code snippet will show the author of the article if it can find one; if not it will show Anonymous.

The following code will show the date when the article was created:

```
<!-- Date/Time -->
<p>${article.createdDate?string('dd.MM.yyyy HH:mm:ss')}</p>
<hr>
```

Furthermore, it has the following code to convert the Article.createdDate property into a string of the format dd.MM.yyyy HH:mm:ss:

```
${article.createdDate?string('dd.MM.yyyy HH:mm:ss')}
<!-- Post Content -->
      ${article.body}
        <hr>
      </div>
</@p.page>
</#if>
```

Eventually, the actual article is shown in its entirety. This page also makes use of the common template.

Implementing an error page

For all the common error scenarios there is a custom error page implemented at `common/error.ftl`, which is shown as follows:

```html
<!DOCTYPE html>
<html lang="en">

  <head>

    <meta charset="utf-8">
    <meta name="viewport" content="width=device-width, initial-scale=1, shrink-to-fit=no">
    <meta name="description" content="">
    <meta name="author" content="">

    <title>Error : ${status}</title>
    <link rel="stylesheet" type="text/css"
    href="/webjars/bootstrap/4.0.0/css/bootstrap.min.css"/>

    <!-- Custom styles for this template -->
    <link href="/css/blog-post.css" rel="stylesheet">

  </head>
  <body>
    <nav class="navbar navbar-expand-lg navbar-dark bg-dark fixed-top">
      <div class="container">
        <a class="navbar-brand" href="/">Blog Management System</a>
      </div>
    </nav>

    <div class="container">

      <div class="row">
        <div class="col-lg-8">

          <!-- Title -->
          <h1 class="mt-4">${status}</h1>

          <p>${exception.message}
        </div>
      </div>
    </div>
  </body>

</html>
```

The preceding page will show the HTTP `status` and `exception.message` in the page for easy troubleshooting regarding what went wrong.

Using Spring WebFlux for controller

Controllers are the integration point between models and views in the MVC paradigm. They act like the glue that binds together everything while taking care of business logic execution and routing. The following Maven starter `dependency` needs to be added to enable Spring WebFlux:

```
<dependencies>
    ...
    <dependency>
        <groupId>org.springframework.boot</groupId>
        <artifactId>spring-boot-starter-webflux</artifactId>
    </dependency>
</dependencies>
```

The preceding `dependency` will import the Reactive Streams, Spring, and Netty dependencies to enable successful writing of `Servlet`-based web applications using Spring.

Implementation of controllers

The following is the `IndexController` that caters the index URL:

```
@Controller
public class IndexController {

    @GetMapping("/")
    public String index() {
        return "redirect:/article";
    }
}
```

The `index` method is mapped to the URL `/`, which will redirect to the `/article` URL when a `GET` request is received at that endpoint.

The following is the `ArticleController`, which is responsible for the CRUD operations of the `Article` domain model:

```java
@Controller
@RequestMapping("/article")
public class ArticleController {

    private final ArticleService articleService;
    private final UserService userService;

    public ArticleController(ArticleService articleService, UserService
      userService) {
        this.articleService = articleService;
        this.userService = userService;
    }

    @GetMapping
    public String index(Model model,
        @AuthenticationPrincipal UserDetails
         userDetails,
        @RequestParam(required = false, value = "q")
         String q,
        @RequestParam(required = false, value = "page") Integer page,
        @RequestParam(required = false, value = "size") Integer size)
        {
        if (q == null) {
         model.addAttribute("articles",
         articleService.getAll(getPageable(page, size)));
        } else {
            model.addAttribute("articles", articleService.search(q,
             getPageable(page, size)));
        }

        return "article/index";
    }
```

All the methods in the preceding controller will be grouped under the URL `/article`. `ArticleController.index`, which is mapped to the `GET` method of the `/article` URL, expects `@AuthenticationPrincipal UserDetails`, and which returns the logged-in user's details and optional `@QueryParams` `q`, `page`, and `size`. Where `q` is used as a search query, `page` and `size` are used to enable pagination on the **List Articles** page.

It uses the `ArticleSearch.getAll` method if a q query parameter is not specified and the `ArticleService.search` method when a q query parameter is specified using the search bar. It also uses the `UserService.getByUsername` method to get the currently logged-in `User` domain model. Finally, it will send all the data using `Model` to `article/index.ftl`. A `Model` is an auto injected into a method, a model usually allows us to submit any reference data to a page that is going to be loaded:

```
@GetMapping("/show/{link}")
public String getPost(@AuthenticationPrincipal UserDetails
 userDetails,
  @PathVariable String link, Model model) {
    Optional<Article> article = articleService.getByLink(link);
    if (article.isPresent()) {
       model.addAttribute("article", article.get());
    } else {
       throwNotFoundException(link);
    }

    return "article/show";
}
```

The `ArticleController.getPost` method is mapped to the GET method `/article/show/{link}` URL, which uses the `@PathVariable link` variable to get the `Article` using the `ArticleService.getByLink` method, which in turn uses the `link` property to get the correct `Article` to show. Finally, it will send the data using `Model` to `article/show.ftl`:

```
@GetMapping("/new")
public String newPost() {
    return "article/create";
}
```

The `ArticleController.newPost` method is mapped to the GET method `/article/new`, which displays the `article/create.ftl` page:

```
@GetMapping("/edit/{id}")
public String editPost(@AuthenticationPrincipal UserDetails
userDetails, @PathVariable String id, Model model) {
    Optional<Article> article = articleService.getById(id);
    if (article.isPresent()) {
        model.addAttribute("article", article.get());
    } else {
        return throwNotFoundException(id);
    }

    return "article/create";
```

```
                    }
    private String throwNotFoundException(@PathVariable String id) {
        throw new NotFoundException("Article Not Found for "+id);
    }
```

The `ArticleController.editPost` method is mapped to the GET method `/article/edit/{id}` URL, which uses the `@PathVariable id` variable to get the `Article` using `ArticleService.getById`. Finally, it will send all the data using `Model` to `article/create.ftl`:

```
    @PostMapping("/delete/{id}")
    public String deletePost(@AuthenticationPrincipal UserDetails
    userDetails, @PathVariable String id, Model model) {
        articleService.deleteById(id);

        model.addAttribute("message", "Article with id " + id + "
        deleted successfully!");
        model.addAttribute("articles", articleService.getAll(new
        PageRequest(0, 10)));

        return "article/index";
    }
```

The `ArticleController.deletePost` method is mapped to the POST method `/article/delete/{id}` URL, which uses the `@PathVariable id` variable to delete the `Article` using the `ArticleService.deleteById` method. Finally, it will send the user to the `article/index.ftl` page to **List Articles** with a message for successfully deleting an `Article`:

```
    @PostMapping
    public String savePost(@AuthenticationPrincipal UserDetails
    userDetails, Article article, Model model) {
        if (article.getId() == null || article.getId().length() == 0) {
            User user =
            userService.getByUsername(userDetails.getUsername());
            article.setAuthor(user);
        } else {
            Optional<Article> optionalArticle =
            articleService.getById(article.getId());
            if (optionalArticle.isPresent()) {
                article.setAuthor(optionalArticle.get().getAuthor());
            }
        }
        articleService.save(article);

        return "redirect:/article/show/"+article.getLink();
```

The `ArticleController.savePost` method is mapped to the `POST` method `/article` URL, which saves the `Article` using the `ArticleService.save` method. Finally, it will redirect to `/article/show/{link}`, where link is the link property of the newly saved `Article`.

Implementation of ControllerAdvice

Furthermore, there is `BaseControllerAdvice`, which is annotated with `@ControllerAdvice` as follows. `ControllerAdvice` is a specialized component that can handle the `@ExceptionHandler`, `@InitBinder`, and `@ModelAttribute` methods:

```
@ControllerAdvice
public class BaseControllerAdvice {

    private final UserService userService;

    public BaseControllerAdvice(UserService userService) {
        this.userService = userService;
    }

    @ExceptionHandler(NotFoundException.class)
    public String handledNotFoundException(NotFoundException e, Model model) {
        model.addAttribute("status", 400);
        model.addAttribute("exception", e);

        return "common/error";
    }
```

The `BaseControllerAdvice.handleNotFoundException` method that is annotated with `@ExceptionHandler` will catch `NotFoundException`, which is as follows:

```
public class NotFoundException extends RuntimeException {

    public NotFoundException(String message) {
        super(message);
    }

    public NotFoundException(String message, Throwable cause) {
        super(message, cause);
    }
}
```

It will set the model properties `status`, `exception` and will eventually forward to the `common/error.ftl` page:

```
@ExceptionHandler(Exception.class)
public String handleException(Exception e, Model model) {
    model.addAttribute("status", 500);
    model.addAttribute("exception", e);

    return "common/error";
}
```

Also, it has the `handleException` method to catch and handle all other `Exception` types, and to forward to `common/error.ftl`:

```
@ModelAttribute
public void addCommonAttributes(@AuthenticationPrincipal
  UserDetails userDetails, Model model) {
    if (userDetails != null) {
        User user =
  userService.getByUsername(userDetails.getUsername());
        model.addAttribute("user", user);
    }
  }
}
```

Additionally, it has the `addCommonAttributes` method to add any common `Model` attributes, which needs to be sent as part of all controller returns. In this case, we send an `@Model` attribute user so that the logged-in username can be shown in the header. `@ModelAttribute` is invoked whenever there is a `GET` request to a controller.

Using Spring Security for authentication and authorization

This web application has used Spring Security for authentication of users and to authorize them to submit comments. The Maven Spring Security starter needs to be specified, as follows, to enable Spring Security in the web application:

```
<dependencies>
  <dependency>
     <groupId>org.springframework.boot</groupId>
     <artifactId>spring-boot-starter-security</artifactId>
  </dependency>
  <dependency>
```

```xml
            <groupId>org.springframework.security</groupId>
            <artifactId>spring-security-webflux</artifactId>
            <version>5.0.0.M2</version>
        </dependency>
    </dependencies>
```

The following is the Spring Security configuration:

```java
@Configuration
@EnableWebFluxSecurity
@EnableReactiveMethodSecurity
public class SecurityConfig {

    @Autowired
    private UserService userService;

    @Bean
    public SecurityWebFilterChain
    springWebFilterChain(ServerHttpSecurity http) throws Exception {
        return http
                .authorizeExchange().pathMatchers(HttpMethod.GET,
    "/article", "/article/show/**", "/webjars/**", "/css/**",
    "/favicon.ico", "/").permitAll()
                .pathMatchers(HttpMethod.POST,
    "/article").authenticated()
                .pathMatchers("/article/edit/**", "/article/new",
    "/article/delete/**").authenticated()
                .and()
                .csrf().disable()
                .formLogin()
                .and()
                .logout()
                .and()
                .build();
    }
}
```

Since the Bloggest application makes use of Spring WebFlux, it also needs to use Reactive Spring Security. This is a new feature introduced in conjunction with Spring Framework 5.0 and Spring WebFlux, so the code may look unfamiliar. The preceding `SecurityConfig` configuration class does the following.

With the `@EnableWebFluxSecurity` annotation, Spring WebFlux controller security is enabled. This will enable us to protect the URLs of the Bloggest application. Also, it has `@EnableReactiveMethodSecurity`, where the `@Secured` annotation can be used on top of methods to be protected.

The `springWebFilterChain(ServerHttpSecurity http)` method, which uses the parameter `http` passed into configure and build `SpringWebFilterChain`, will be used to protect endpoints in the Bloggest application:

```
@Bean
public UserDetailsRepositoryReactiveAuthenticationManager
authenticationManager(BlogReactiveUserDetailsService
blogReactiveUserDetailsService) {
    UserDetailsRepositoryReactiveAuthenticationManager
    userDetailsRepositoryReactiveAuthenticationManager = new
    UserDetailsRepositoryReactiveAuthenticationManager
    (blogReactiveUserDetailsService);
    userDetailsRepositoryReactiveAuthenticationManager.
    setPasswordEncoder(passwordEncoder());
    return userDetailsRepositoryReactiveAuthenticationManager;
}

@Bean
public PasswordEncoder passwordEncoder() {
    return new BCryptPasswordEncoder();
}
```

Furthermore, the method `authenticationManager` returns `UserDetailsRepositoryReactiveAuthenticationManager`, which is configured to have the following `ReactiveUserDetailsService` implementation to load instances of `User` by username using `UserRepository`:

```
@Service
public class BlogReactiveUserDetailsService implements
ReactiveUserDetailsService {

    private final UserRepository userRepository;

    public BlogReactiveUserDetailsService(UserRepository
    userRepository) {
        this.userRepository = userRepository;
    }

    @Override
    public Mono<UserDetails> findByUsername(String s) {
        User user = userRepository.findByUsername(s);
        if (user == null) {
            return Mono.empty();
        }
        return Mono.just(new
        org.springframework.security.core.userdetails.User
        (user.getUsername(), user.getPassword(), Arrays.asList(new
```

```
            SimpleGrantedAuthority(user.getRole())))));
    }
}
```

The preceding implementation finds a User by username, encapsulates the inside of UserDetails and returns it as Mono (UserDetails encapsulated inside of a Mono object). Also, configure the passwordEncoder to be used as follows:

```
@Bean
public ApplicationRunner applicationRunner() {
    return args -> {
        userService.deleteAll();
        userService.save(new User(UUID.randomUUID().toString(),
        "user", passwordEncoder().encode("password"), "USER",
        "User of Blog"));
        userService.save(new User(UUID.randomUUID().toString(),
        "admin", passwordEncoder().encode("password"), "ADMIN",
          "Admin of Blog"));
    };
}
```

The method `applicationRunner()` is used to create and return an ApplicationRunner instance to clear the existing users from the Elasticsearch data store and create some Users.

Demonstrating Bloggest

In order to run the Bloggest web application, it requires that the Elasticsearch data store be up and running. The following command can be used to start Elasticsearch:

```
$ <Path to Elasticsearch>/bin/elasticsearch
```

When everything is put together, build and run the Bloggest, which you will be able to access using the http://<host>:<port> URL.

There are several ways to run a Spring Boot application, some of them are mentioned here:

- Running the Spring Boot application main class using an IDE.
- Building a JAR or WAR file using the following Maven command and then running:

    ```
    $ mvn clean install
    $ java -jar target/<package-name>.[jar|war]
    ```

- Running using a Spring Boot Maven plugin:

    ```
    $ mvn clean spring-boot:run
    ```

After running, the Bloggest web application will show the **List Articles** page as follows:

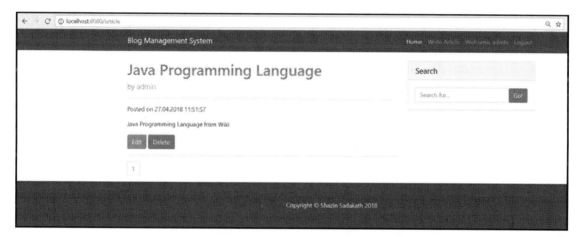

In this page, the header, footer, and right panel with **Search** bar are coming from the `common/standardPage.ftl` common layout. The dynamic content is only available in the middle. Since in this case the **admin** user is already logged in, in the top right the system welcomes the user with the username. If no user is logged in, that section will show the Login link (username `user`, password `password` for **USER** role, username `admin`, password `password` for **ADMIN** role).

When the title link is clicked, the following **Show Article** page is shown:

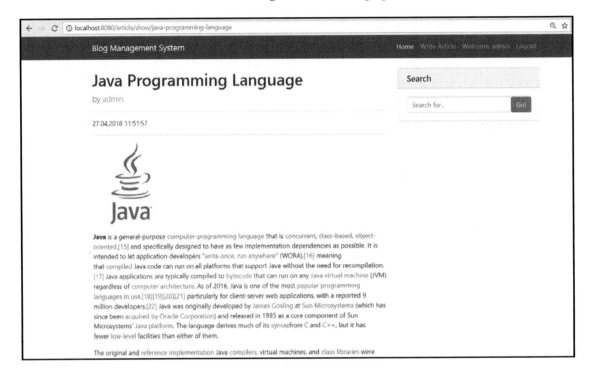

Things to note on this page are that the page is showing the body section of the article in the styled text with even images. Also, the URL is using a permanent link to call the /article/show/ endpoint with. This is important as this URL is now **search engine optimization (SEO)** friendly, meaning it can be indexed easily in search engines such as Google, Bing, and so on to get more leads.

Chapter 3

The following page is for the **Add Article** use case:

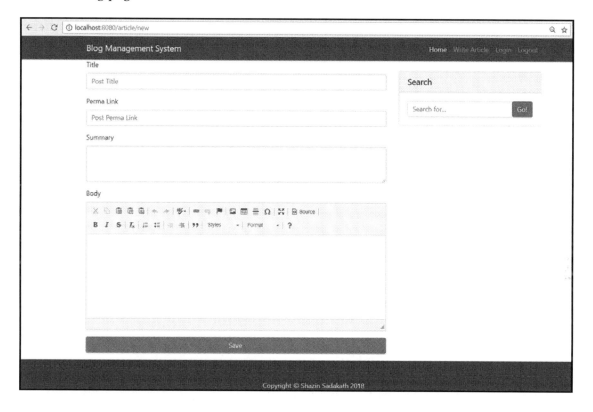

The page has text boxes for **Title**, **Perma Link** (this will be derived dynamically from the title), **Summary**, and **Body**. You can see the CKEDITOR in action for the body section.

The **Edit Article** use case will look like the following:

By clicking on the **Edit** button under the article on the **List Articles** page, this page can be reached. The **Edit** button will be visible only if the logged-in user has the administrator role or is the original author of that particular article.

The following page shows a **Search Article** use case where the keyword Java is searched:

Matching results will be displayed on the **List Articles** page. And finally, the result of the **Delete Article** use case is displayed on the following page:

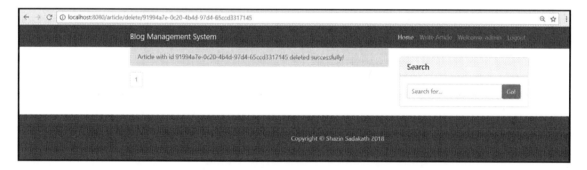

An article can be deleted using the **Delete** button on the **List Articles** page. The **Delete** button will be visible only if the logged-in user has the administrator role or is the original author of that particular article. Eventually, it will redirect to the **List Articles** page.

Since the Bloggest application may be viewed using devices other than a computer, it supports a responsive UI with Bootstrap. All pages are responsive to different screen sizes and resolutions. The following is the **Show Article** page with smaller dimensions:

Chapter 3

The following is the page for the **Login** use case:

This page comes out of the box with Spring Security 5 and it is responsive and more stylish than its predecessor, which was used in `Chapter 2`, *Building a Basic Web Application*.

The following is the page for the **Log out** use case:

Logout can be performed by clicking the **Log Out** link in the header. Unlike the predecessor version of Spring Security, Spring Security 5 asks for confirmation during logout out of the box. When logout is confirmed it will redirect to the **Login** page with a message, as follows:

Summary

Congratulations on completing this chapter, where the skills and knowledge required to build a simple blog management system nicknamed Bloggest were discussed in detail. This chapter started off by explaining what a web application is and how a web application can benefit from the MVC pattern both in terms of development and maintenance. It talked about the requirements of the web application being developed and used a UML use case diagram to explain the requirements visually.

This chapter also talked about how to understand the domain models of an application based on the requirements (Bloggest) and how to use Spring Data Elasticsearch to convert those domain models into documents in the Elasticsearch data store. A UML class diagram was used to explain the domain models in detail.

Furthermore, the chapter explained how to write data repositories for those documents using Spring Data Elasticsearch with minimum effort for commonly used CRUD operations. Moving on, it also explained how to write custom query methods in data repositories, and how to encapsulate business logic inside Spring Service components.

Subsequently, the chapter talked about how to write presentation views to create and display comments using Apache FreeMarker Framework. In addition, it explained how to use Apache FreeMarker syntax to list articles, add an article, edit an article, and show an article.

Eventually, the chapter talked about how to use Spring WebFlux Controllers to provide routing and coordinating of different services. Furthermore, it talked about how to protect controller endpoints using Spring Security to allow proper authentication and authorization for users. The chapter also demonstrated the usage of Bloggest in detail. We'll learn more about some interesting features of Spring Boot 2.0 in coming chapters.

Questions

Please answer the following questions to see whether you have successfully mastered this chapter:

1. What is Elasticsearch?
2. What is Apache FreeMarker?
3. What are the two common constructs in Spring WebFlux?
4. What is a blog management system?
5. What is the use of a `ControllerAdvice`?
6. What is the use of a `PasswordEncoder`?
7. How do you configure Spring Security to use a custom `UserDetailsService`?

Further reading

In order to improve your knowledge of Spring Web MVC, Spring Security, Elasticsearch, and Apache FreeMarker, the following books are recommended to be read, as they will be helpful in the coming chapters:

- *Spring 5.0 By Example*: https://www.packtpub.com/application-development/spring-mvc-designing-real-world-web-applications
- *Spring Security - Third Edition*: https://www.packtpub.com/application-development/spring-security-third-edition
- *Elasticsearch Essentials*: https://www.packtpub.com/big-data-and-business-intelligence/elasticsearch-essentials
- *Instant FreeMarker Starter*: https://www.packtpub.com/web-development/instant-freemarker-starter-instant

Introduction to Kotlin

4

This chapter will introduce the reader to the details of using Kotlin programming with Spring Boot 2 as the base application development framework. It will explain what Kotlin is and how to get started with Kotlin as the main programming language and for testing purposes. Subsequently, it will explain the basic syntax of Kotlin, followed by coding conventions, coding basics, class concepts, and so on. Furthermore, it will delve into the advanced functionalities of Kotlin, such as lambdas, annotations, reflection, and many more, to provide a deep understanding of the programming language.

The following topics will be covered in this chapter:

- Getting started with Kotlin
- Object-oriented programming with Kotlin
- Advanced programming with Kotlin

Technical requirements

In order to implement a web application using Spring Boot, the following build tools need to be downloaded and installed:

- To install **Java Development Kit (JDK)** 8, download it from its official page at `http://www.oracle.com/technetwork/java/javase/downloads/jdk8-downloads-2133151.html`
- To install Maven 3, download it from its official page at `https://maven.apache.org/download.cgi`
- To install IntelliJ IDEA, download it from its official page at `https://www.jetbrains.com/idea/download/`
- To install **Spring Tool Suite (STS)**, download it from its official page at `https://spring.io/tools`

Introduction to Kotlin

The source code for this chapter can be found at `https://github.com/PacktPublishing/Spring-Boot-2.0-Projects-Fundamentals-of-Spring-Boot-2.0`, in the `Chapter04` directory.

Getting started with Kotlin

Kotlin is an up-and-coming programming language that is very versatile and can be used to develop applications in platforms such as server-side, Android, JavaScript, and native. The main features of the Kotlin programming language are as follows:

- **Concise syntax**: Kotlin eliminates a lot of boilerplate code and sticks to the core concepts and functionality
- **Safe coding and runtime**: Kotlin makes sure errors are minimized during coding and while running the application
- **Interoperability**: Kotlin code can make use of existing libraries for JVM (ArrayList), JavaScript (document), and many more
- **Developer friendliness**: Kotlin is supported in a wide array of **integrated development environments** (**IDE**) and command line tools to keep the learning curve gradual

The following sections will cover these features, showcasing each with practical examples to enable easy comprehension.

Default imports

The following packages are imported by default into every Kotlin file:

- `kotlin.*`
- `kotlin.annotation.*`
- `kotlin.collections.*`
- `kotlin.comparisons.*` (since 1.1)
- `kotlin.io.*`
- `kotlin.ranges.*`
- `kotlin.sequences.*`
- `kotlin.text.*`

When running Kotlin applications on the JVM, the following packages are also imported:

```
java.lang.*
kotlin.jvm.*
```

Basic data types

There are a few data types in Kotlin that we need to be aware of, I have listed a few of them in the upcoming sections.

Numeric data types

Kotlin has almost the same data types as Java. The following table lists them:

Data type	No. of bytes	No. of bits
Byte	1	8
Short	2	16
Int	4	32
Long	4	32
Float	8	64
Double	8	64

The only visible difference is that Kotlin has the data type Int as opposed to Integer in Java.

Learning numeric literals

Unlike Java, Kotlin does not support octal literals (which begin with 0 in Java) as a numeric literal. The following numeric literals are supported:

- **Decimals**: We have the following decimals:
    - Int: 123
    - Long: 123L ends with a capital L
- **Hexa-decimals**: Begin with a 0x followed by the value. An example is 0xCAFE for the decimal value 51966.
- **Binary**: Begins with prefix 0b followed by the value. An example is 0b1010 for the decimal value 10.

Introduction to Kotlin

- **Floating point**: Kotlin supports conventional notations for floating points:
    - `Double:123.0, 12.0e10`
    - `Float: 123.0f` or `123.0F` ends with capital `F` or simple `f`

All numeric literals can use _ to separate digits. Some examples are `100_000_000`, `0xA_B_C`, `0b000_000_001`, `100_000F`.

Numeric representation

All numeric values are represented as primitive values in the JVM unless it is a nullable value. For example, if `Long?` or generics are involved. Kotlin has a ternary equals operator (`===`) that can be used to check identity. Consider the following code example:

```
var a : Long = 10L;
println(a === a)
```

The following code will print `true`:

```
var a : Long = 10L;
var b : Long? = a;
var c : Long? = a;
println(b === c)
```

However, it will print `false` if the b and c variables are nullable, will not use primitive data types, and thus will have different identities for each of those respectively. Yet `println(b == c)` will print `true` as it will be checking equality, not the identity.

Numeric operations

Kotlin has bitwise operations available for `Int` and `Long` only, which are very different from those in Java. The following table shows these operations:

Bitwise operation	Purpose	Example
`shl(bits)`	Signed shift left (Java's <<)	`123 shl 1`
`shr(bits)`	Signed shift right (Java's >>)	`123 shr 1`
`ushr(bits)`	Unsigned shift right (Java's >>>)	`123 ushr 1`
`and(bits)`	Bitwise and	`123 and 456`
`or(bits)`	Bitwise or	`123 or 456`
`xor(bits)`	Bitwise xor	`0x101 xor 0x010`
`inv()`	Bitwise inversion	`123.inv()`

String literals

Kotlin has string literal support in the following code:

```
var message = "Hello, World\n";
print(message);
```

Also, unlike Java, Kotlin has multiline string support, as seen in the following code:

```
var csv = """
        Name,Telephone,Email
        Shazin,07743299201,shazin.sadakath@gmail.com
    """.trimIndent();
println(csv);
```

A multiline string literal begins and ends with three double quotes ("""). Inside this, special double quotes can be used without escaping, which is very handy. The `trimIndent()` method trims the indentations inside the string in the preceding code. Without it the string literal will contain tabs and spacing exactly as shown in the previous code; this is shown in the following code:

```
Name,Telephone,Email
Shazin,07743299201,shazin.sadakath@gmail.com
```

The syntax for Kotlin code

Because Kotlin code will be compiled as bytecode to run on top of the **Java virtual machine (JVM)**, it enables us to use the utility classes available in a JVM out of the box. This means Kotlin code can be very familiar to Java developers. But still, as Kotlin is a concise programming language, it has reduced a lot of unnecessary keywords and has simplified many keywords. The following sections will explain this.

The Kotlin packages

Similar to the Java programming language, Kotlin also supports the grouping and categorization of code using packages. The following package declaration can be used to do that:

```
package com.packtpub.springboot2kotlin.gettingstarted

import java.sql.*;
```

Also, whole packages or specific classes inside a package can be imported just as in Java.

String interpolation

Unlike Java, Kotlin supports string interpolation where an actual variable, an expression value, can be used to substitute placeholders ($ sign followed by the variable name or $ sign followed by curly braces) inside string objects. This eliminates the need for memory-expensive string concatenation using the + operator in Java. This is explained using the following code:

```
var sum: Double = calculator.add(1.0, 2.0);
println("Double Sum of 1.0 + 2.0 = $sum");

...
println("No of times methods invoked in StringFormatter = 
${stringFormatter.noOfTimesMethodsInvoked}");
```

In the preceding code snippet `println`, which is passed with string objects containing the placeholders `$sum` and `${stringFormatter.noOfTimesMethodsInvoked}` respectively. Kotlin will replace the actual values with the placeholders before they're sent to be printed on the console.

Functions in Kotlin

As in any programming language, Kotlin does support functions to be written and it enables users to write very concise functions such as the following, without any curly braces, start, and end keywords:

```
// This is an inline function which adds two Int values
fun add(n1: Int, n2: Int): Int = n1 + n2;
```

More descriptive functions with well-defined content are as follows:

```
/*
This is a descriptive function which adds two Double values
 */
fun add(n1: Double, n2: Double): Double {
    return n1 + n2;
}
```

A function that doesn't return anything (effectively a procedure) can be written as follows:

```
fun addAndPrint(n1: Int, n2: Int): Unit {
    println("$n1 + $n2 = ${n1 + n2}");
}

fun substractAndPrint(n1: Int, n2: Int) {
    println("$n1 - $n2 = ${n1 - n2}");
}
```

This is done either by returning `Unit` or by completely omitting it.

Variables in Kotlin

Defining variables in Kotlin can be done in several ways, such as the following:

```
// Immutable
val separatorChar: String = ",";

// Mutable
var noOfTimesMethodsInvoked = 0;
```

The `val` keyword can be used to define `Immutable` variables, and the `var` keyword can be used to define `Mutable` variables. The type of the variable can be specified, but when it isn't, it will be inferred based on what value is being set. In the case of the `noOfTimesMethodsInvoked` variable, the type will be inferred as `Int` by default.

Conditional statements

When writing programming logic, conditional statements are crucial. Similar to Java, Kotlin supports the following statements.

The if statement

An `if` statement can be written as follows:

```
if (i % 2 == 0) {
    println("$i is an even number");
} else {
    println("$i is an odd number");
}
```

This code is very similar to the Java `if` statement.

Introduction to Kotlin

The when statement

The `when` statement here is the same as Java's `switch` statement, but with concise code as follows:

```
var word : String = when(letter) {
    "A" -> "Apple";
    "B" -> "Ball";
    "C" -> "Cat";
    "D" -> "Dog";
    else -> "Don't Know";
}
```

The `else` keyword is used to specify default values in case no match is found.

Type checking and automatic casting

In the Java programming language, if a function accepts a parameter of type `Object`, and if the actual type of that parameter needs to be checked, then the `instanceof` keyword is used. But this alone wasn't sufficient; even if the type of the parameter is found it still needs to be explicitly cast to access any properties or functions within it. This is solved in Kotlin as follows:

```
if (csv is String) {
    return csv.length;
}
```

In the preceding code, the `if` keyword is used to check whether the `csv` parameter is of type `String` or not. If the condition returns true, Kotlin does the implicit casting of `csv` to `String` to enable access to properties or functions and to reduce the chances of errors while keeping the code concise.

Nullable values and compile-time null safety

In contrast to Java, Kotlin enables users to specify whether a variable or function can hold or return `null` as a value. This can be done as follows:

```
fun getStringLength(csv: Any) : Int? {
    noOfTimesMethodsInvoked++;
    if (csv is String) {
        return csv.length;
    }
```

```
        return null;
    }
```

The `getStringLength` function returns an `Int` ending with `?`, which specifies that this method should return `null`. So, the caller of this method must write code to check for null safety. This will be enforced during compile time to reduce the chances of `NullPointerException`.

The for loop

The `for` loop is a very useful and familiar programming syntax that can be used to iterate through an array, collection, or range of values.

The for loop with an array

Using the `for` loop to iterate through an array of values can be done as follows:

```
var animals = arrayOf("Cat", "Lion");
...
for (index in animals.indices) {
    println("This is a great animal : ${animals[index]}")
}
```

Here, the `animals` array has an `indices` property that itself is an array of `Int`, which can be used to loop through each index and print the value of that index.

The for loop with a collection

The `for` loop can also be used to loop through `List` and `Set` as well, as follows:

```
var letters = stringFormatter.csvToList("A,B,C,D,E,F,G,H,I");

if (letters != null) {
    for (letter in letters) {
        var word : String = when(letter) {
            "A" -> "Apple";
            "B" -> "Ball";
            "C" -> "Cat";
            "D" -> "Dog";
            else -> "Don't Know";
        }
```

Introduction to Kotlin

```
        println("$letter for $word");
    }
}
```

Here, the `letters` variable is a `List` of strings objects.

The for loop with a value range

Kotlin, unlike Java, supports looping through a range of values such as 1 to 10 using a `for` loop, as in the following:

```
for (i in 1..10) {
    if (i % 2 == 0) {
        println("$i is an even number");
    } else {
        println("$i is an odd number");
    }
}
```

Here the number range is specified by the `1..10` syntax.

Furthermore, Kotlin supports looping through ranges in reverse as well as with custom specified stepping values, seen as follows:

```
for (i in 10 downTo 0 step 2) {
    println("$i");
}
```

The while loop

The `while` loops are a way to iterate while a condition is being satisfied and are crucial in situations where a `for` loop will not fit. The syntax for a `while` loop is similar to Java and is shown as follows:

```
var animals = arrayOf("Cat", "Lion");

var index = 0;
while (index < animals.size) {
    var animal = animals[index++];
    println("This animal is a $animal");
}
```

Object-oriented programming with Kotlin

Object-oriented programming (OOP) is a very famous and widely used programming methodology. The Java programming language enables OOP with programming concepts such as classes, interfaces, abstraction, inheritance, polymorphism, encapsulation, and many more. The following sections will explain these concepts in Kotlin.

Learning about visibility modifiers

Visibility modifiers can be specified to classes, interfaces, constructors, functions, and properties. In Kotlin, the following visibility modifiers are available:

Visibility modifiers	Classes	Interfaces	Constructors	Functions	Properties
`private`	Visible only inside the file	Visible only inside the file	Visible only inside the file	Visible only inside the file	Visible only inside the file
`protected`	Visible inside file and in subclasses	Visible inside file and in subclasses	Visible inside file and in subclasses	Visible inside file and in subclasses	Visible inside file and in subclasses
`internal`	Visible everywhere inside the same module	Visible everywhere inside the same module	Visible everywhere inside the same module	Visible everywhere inside the same module	Visible everywhere inside the same module
`public`	Visible to all (default)	Visible to all (default)	Visible to all (default)	Visible to all (default)	Visible to all (default)

The `protected` keyword cannot be used to control the visibility of the preceding modifier if it is declared directly under a package. This is because the `protected` keyword expects to subclass. A module in Kotlin can be a Maven project, a Gradle project, an IDE project, and so on; in simple terms, a set of Kotlin files compiled and grouped together.

Classes in Kotlin

The concept of class is used to group the properties and behavior of a particular type of domain model to enable high cohesion. A class is a blueprint that can later be used to create object instances to represent different states. A class in Kotlin will look like the following:

```
class Car(var color : String = "RED") {

    fun accelerate() {
        println("$color car is accelerating...");
    }

    fun brake() {
        println("$color car is decelerating...");
    }

    fun turn(direction: String) {
        println("$color car is turning $direction");
    }

}
```

The preceding class represents a `Car` domain model that has the `color` property and the `accelerate`, `decelerate`, and `turn` behaviors.

Abstract classes

Abstract classes are used to define behavior but not implement it. Implementation of a certain behavior is kept open so that it can be overridden by any implementation later. Let's look at the `Animal` class in the following code:

```
public abstract class Animal() {

    open fun makeNoise(): String? {
        return null;
    }

    open fun name(): String? {
        return null;
    }
}
```

The preceding class is marked as abstract so no instance can be created out of it. Instead, it is meant to be extended and its behavior will override by some other class. Functions of that class, such as makeNoise and name, are kept open with the corresponding keyword so that any subclass implementation can override it later on.

Concrete classes

Concrete classes are used to implement the properties and behaviors of a domain and create instances out of it. The following Lion concrete class will inherit from the Animal abstract class:

```
class Lion : Animal {
    var noise: String

    constructor(noise: String) {
        this.noise = noise;
    }

    override fun name(): String? {
        return "Lion";
    }

    override fun makeNoise(): String? {
        return noise;
    }

}
```

The : symbol is used to specify in the class declaration that one class extends from another.

The concept of interfaces in Kotlin

The concept of an interface is used to define behavior in classes selectively. For example, Cat and Lion can be considered as Animal. But in common practice, Cat can be a more of Pet than Lion. So adding the pet behavior to Animal will cause problems, as all Animal instances will by default have the Pet behavior, which could be dangerous. This is where interfaces come in handy, as they enable us to define behavior selectively as follows:

```
interface Pettable {
    fun play() {
        println("Playing");
```

        };
    }

With the preceding interface named `Pettable`, the `play` behavior can be introduced selectively to classes. For example, `Cat` can be given the `play` behavior while `Lion` can be excluded as follows:

```
class Cat : Animal, Pettable {
    var noise: String

    constructor(noise: String) {
        this.noise = noise;
    }

    override fun name(): String? {
        return "Cat";
    }

    override fun makeNoise(): String? {
        return noise;
    }

    override fun play() {
        println("Fur Ball");
    }
}
```

Kotlin has simplified how a class or an interface is being used in a subclass, and the syntax remains the same.

Learning about extensions

Kotlin has introduced ways to have custom functionality in existing code without subclassing or writing design patterns over it such as decorator patterns. The following method in `String` to count the number of the simple letter A can be written without ever subclassing:

```
fun String.countAs() : Int {
    var count = 0;
    for(i in 0..(this.length - 1)) {
        if (this.get(i) == 'a') {
            count++;
        }
    }
```

```
        return count;
    }
```

It can also be used as follows:

```
println("aaaaabcdefghijkl".countAs());
```

Generic types in Kotlin

Just as in Java 1.5 onwards, Kotlin also has support for generic types to ensure type and value safety at compile time and run-time to reduce boilerplate code and errors. Generics can be used in the following way:

```
class Range<F, T>(var from: F, var to: T) {

    override fun toString() : String {
        return "From $from to $to";
    }
}
```

Generics can also be used with different data types, such as in the following code:

```
var intRange : Range<Int, Int> = Range<Int, Int>(1, 10);
var doubleRange : Range<Double, Double> = Range<Double, Double>(1.0, 10.0);

println(intRange);
println(doubleRange);
```

Enums in Kotlin

Enums are a great way to enforce `type` and `value` safety. Just like in Java, Kotlin also has enums and the following way in which an enum can be defined:

```
enum class Transaction(var code : Char) {
    DEPOSIT('d'),
    WITHDRAW('w')
}
```

Objects in Kotlin

Unlike Java, Kotlin has flexible ways to modify existing functionalities attached to classes without subclassing (anonymous inner classes) them. There are two ways to do that, as follows.

Object expressions

An object expression can be used to create objects without the need to have a class declaration for them. For example, the `Lion` class from previous sections does not implement the `Pettable` interface. This doesn't mean that there can't be extreme cases where exotic tamed animals can be used as pets. So, a one time tamed `Lion` instance can be created on the fly as follows:

```
var tamedLionPet = object : Lion("roar"), Pettable {
    override fun name() : String {
        return "Tamed Pet Lion";
    }
}
```

Using the `object` keyword, a class of `Lion` that implements the `Pettable` interface can be created and an instance can be created out of it for a single use. Also with this, a class is not even required to create an object. This can be explained by the following code:

```
var personObjectWithoutAClass = object {
    var name : String = "Shazin"
    var age : Int = 32
}
```

The preceding code creates a `person` object with `name` and `age` without the need for a class declaration. These expressions can be passed as arguments to methods also. Object expressions are eagerly initialized and executed at the place where they are expressed.

Object declarations

Unlike object expressions, object declarations have a name and cannot be passed into a variable, method argument, and so on, or declared locally. They can be referred by their name and used anywhere within the scope for which they are declared. This is shown with the following code example:

```
object BeanRegister {
    fun registerBean(bean: Any) {
        println("$bean is registered");
```

            }
        }

The declared BeanRegister object at the top level will become a singleton class and its initialization is thread-safe. It can be used as follows:

```
BeanRegister.registerBean("String bean");
```

As with the preceding code, the object's declared name must be used to invoke the methods inside the object declaration. Object declarations are lazily initialized and executed the first time they are called. Object declarations can also have an associated type, like in the following code:

```
object PettableSingleton : Pettable {
    override fun play() {
        super.play()
    }
}
```

Companion objects

An object declaration inside a class can be specified as a companion object of it, just like in the following code:

```
class Bean {
    companion object Factory {
        fun create() : Bean = Bean();
    }
}
```

This means that methods of object declaration inside can be invoked by just specifying the name of the outer class, as follows:

```
var bean = Bean.create();
```

A companion object is initialized when the outer class enclosing it is loaded similarly to a static initializer in Java.

Advanced programming with Kotlin

Kotlin has a lot of features that can be used for advanced programming. This section will explain some of those.

Functions

Unlike in Java, where classes are first-class citizens, functions are first class citizens in Kotlin. This means that a function can exist without being inside a class. This is quite powerful and there are a lot of advanced ways functions can be used to achieve different functionalities.

Infix notation in functions

Infix notations can be used to define functions that can be used, such as 1 + 2, 2 - 3, true && false, a == b statements where there is an operator and two operands. The following function with the infix notation can be used to ZIP (interweave) words together in a way that the letters of each String are joined together to create a new String that has overlapping letters:

```
infix fun String.zip(s1 : String) : String {
    var result : String = "";
    var zipLength : Int = Math.min(s1.length, this.length);
    for(i in 0..zipLength-1) {
        result += this[i];
        result += s1[i];
    }
    return result;
}
```

The preceding function can be called as follows:

```
println("acegikmoqsuwy" zip "bdfhjlnprtvxz");
```

This will produce the following string as a result:

```
abcdefghijklmnopqrstuvwxyz
```

Local functions in Kotlin

In Kotlin, unlike Java, functions can include functions. These nested inner functions will have a local scope where they are defined as follows:

```
fun outerFunction(o : String) {
    var outerFunctionVariable = 0;
    fun innerFunction(i : String) {
        outerFunctionVariable += 1;
        println("Inner Function $i");
        println("Outer Function Variable inside Inner Function
```

```
            $outerFunctionVariable");
    }

    innerFunction(o);

    println("Outer Function $o");
    println("Outer Function Variable $outerFunctionVariable");
}
```

The outer function can be invoked as follows:

```
outerFunction("Hello World!");
```

An inner function can never be invoked from outside its scope but can be accessed from inside it. Also, outer function local variables can be used by inner functions but not vice versa.

Default arguments in functions

Unlike Java function arguments, Kotlin supports default arguments in functions. This enables flexible function writing, as in the following code:

```
fun withDefaultValues(name : String = "Shazin", age : Int = 32) {
    println("Name $name and Age $age");
}
```

The preceding function can be called as follows:

```
withDefaultValues();
withDefaultValues("Shahim", 32);
```

Named arguments in functions

Kotlin functions can be invoked with the name of the arguments. As an example, consider the following function:

```
fun withNamedArguments(firstName : String, lastName : String) {
    println("Hello Mr. $firstName, $lastName");
}
```

This function can be invoked as in the following code:

```
withNamedArguments(firstName = "Shazin", lastName = "Sadakath");
```

This is a really nice feature to enable good readability and reduce the number of errors.

Generics in functions

Kotlin supports generics in functions to avoid code duplication. This is shown with the following code:

```
fun <T> genericFunction(t : T) {
    println(t);
}
```

This function can be invoked as follows:

```
genericFunction("Shazin");
genericFunction(123);
```

Variable number of arguments (vararg) in functions

Kotlin supports a variable number of arguments in functions as in the following code:

```
fun sum(vararg nos: Int): Int {
    var result = 0;
    for(no in nos) {
        result+= no;
    }
    return result;
}
```

These can be invoked with a varying number of arguments, such as the following code:

```
println("Sum of 1, 2, 3 is ${sum(1, 2, 3)}");
println("Sum of 0, 9, 8, 7, 6, 5, 4, 3, 2, 1 is ${sum(0, 9, 8, 7, 6, 5, 4, 3, 2, 1)}");
```

Summary

Congratulations on completing this chapter, where the skills and knowledge required to write applications in the Kotlin language and its features were discussed in detail. This chapter started off by explaining what the Kotlin programming language is and how it differs both in terms of development and maintenance. It talked about the syntax, safety, interoperability, and developer-friendliness of the Kotlin programming language.

This chapter also discussed how to get started using the Kotlin programming language by explaining its basic data types, literals, string interpolation, conditional statements, and so on in detail.

Subsequently, the chapter talked about how to do OOP using Kotlin. It explained the concepts of class, interface, inheritance, extensions, and enums in detail. It also talked about some features unique to Kotlin such as object expressions, object declarations, and companion objects in simple terms.

Eventually, the chapter talked about some of the advanced features of Kotlin such as infix functions, local functions, default arguments in functions, and named arguments in a function. This chapter has provided enough knowledge to help developers learn the Kotlin programming language easily and quickly. This knowledge can be used to build Spring Boot 2.0 applications using the Kotlin programming language. We will learn about more complex Kotlin application development in up coming chapters.

Questions

Please answer the following questions to see whether you have successfully mastered this chapter:

1. Does Kotlin allow string interpolation?
2. What is a nullable variable/argument in Kotlin and how do you define one?
3. What is explicit casting?
4. What are object expressions and object declarations?
5. What is a companion object?
6. What is an infix function?
7. Can a variable define inside a local function accessed by an enclosing function?

Further reading

In order to improve your knowledge of Kotlin, the following books are recommended to be read, as they will be helpful in the coming chapters:

- *Kotlin Programming By Example*: https://www.packtpub.com/application-development/kotlin-programming-example
- *Functional Kotlin*: https://www.packtpub.com/application-development/functional-kotlin
- *Kotlin Programming Cookbook*: https://www.packtpub.com/application-development/kotlin-programming-cookbook

5
Building a Reactive Movie Rating API Using Kotlin

This chapter will help the reader get started in developing RESTful APIs using Spring Boot 2.0 with the Kotlin programming language. It will enable experts, as well as beginners, to Spring Boot web application development, to understand the concepts behind a RESTful API written entirely in Kotlin. It will explain these concepts by walking the reader through the process of developing a RESTful API that enables users to list movies, get movie details, rate movies, and so on. This RESTful API will use an embedded MongoDB platform for persistence, Spring Data MongoDB Reactive for the model, a repository, and Spring WebFlux for controllers.

The following topics will be covered in this chapter:

- Using Spring Data MongoDB for persistence
- Using Spring WebFlux for the controller
- Using Spring Security for basic authorization
- Demonstrating Moviee

Technical requirements

In order to implement the web application using Spring Boot, the following build tools need to be downloaded and installed:

- To install **Java Development Kit (JDK)** 8, it can be downloaded from its official page at http://www.oracle.com/technetwork/java/javase/downloads/jdk8-downloads-2133151.html
- To install Maven 3, download it from its official page at https://maven.apache.org/download.cgi

- To install IntelliJ IDEA, download it from its official page at `https://www.jetbrains.com/idea/download/`
- To install **Spring Tool Suite (STS)**, download it from its official page at `https://spring.io/tools`

The source code for this chapter can be found at `https://github.com/PacktPublishing/Spring-Boot-2.0-Projects-Fundamentals-of-Spring-Boot-2.0`, in the `Chapter05` directory.

Getting started

In this section, readers will get an overview of a RESTful API being developed. The requirements, design, and implementation details will be discussed in brief.

REST architecture

Representational State Transfer (REST) is an architectural style that defines a set of good practices, standards, and properties that can be implemented on top of the **HyperText Transfer Protocol (HTTP)**. A web service that conforms to REST standards enables easy interoperability between devices on the internet.

RESTful web services enable client devices to produce and consume web resources, which are represented by using text with a uniform and predefined set of stateless operations. Web resources were defined by Tim Berners-Lee to be part of the **World Wide Web (WWW)** as resources/documents identified by a **Uniform Resource Locator (URL)**. The flow of a RESTful web service can be defined as follows:

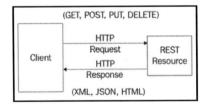

The preceding diagram shows a **Client** accessing a **REST Resource** over the internet. The **Client** initiates the communication by accessing the **REST Resource** identified by a **Uniform Resource Identifier** (URI). The **HTTP Request** can have different request methods based on what operation needs to be performed on the **REST Resource**. If it is just a `read` operation, then most of the time, the **HTTP Request** method **GET** is used. If any manipulation needs to be done on the **REST Resource**, then the appropriate **HTTP Request** method of either **POST**, **PUT**, or **DELETE** is used. Roy Fielding is considered the father of REST, as he was the first person to define the term in his PhD dissertation in 2000.

The following architectural constraints are a part of REST:

- Client-server model
- Statelessness
- Cacheability
- Layerability
- Uniform interface

In this chapter, Spring WebFlux will be used to implement REST controllers.

Requirements of REST architecture

The problem domain under consideration is a movie rating API using RESTful web services nicknamed **Moviee**, where users can list movies, get movie details, and rate movies. The Moviee API must be publicly accessible via the internet and only registered users should be able to perform actions on the API, as a means of security and control.

The Moviee API should allow the authentication and authorization of users without a form using headers. This is important as the API will be accessed by clients using platforms other than the standard browsers.

The use case diagram

The following use case diagram shows the requirements for the Moviee API:

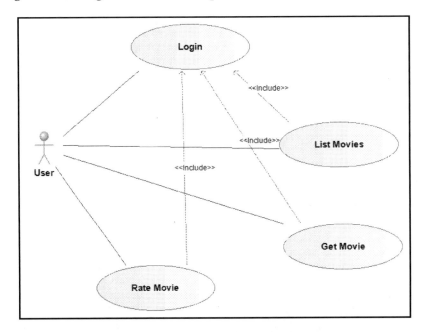

The actor is the **User** of Moviee. It has the following use cases:

- **Login**: This use case is required to authenticate users so that each user can be uniquely identified, and to allow only authenticated users to perform actions.
- **List Movies**: This use case is where a user listed all the movies available inside Moviee. It requires the user to be authenticated.
- **Get Movie**: This use case is where a user sees the details of a movie that is available inside Moviee. It requires the user to be authenticated.
- **Rate Movie**: This use case is where a user rates a movie that is available inside Moviee. It requires the user to be authenticated.

Using Spring Data MongoDB for persistence

This section will introduce MongoDB, and how to use Spring Data MongoDB repositories to provide **Create, Retrieve, Update, and Delete (CRUD)** operations on MongoDB easily.

Understanding MongoDB

MongoDB is a free and open source document store that stores data in a schemaless JSON format that is highly flexible. Each individual document can have different fields. It allows ad-hoc querying, indexing, and aggregation out of the box.

MongoDB can provide high availability, horizontal scalability (scale out), and geographical distribution. MongoDB simplifies development by providing drivers in multiple programming languages, such as C++, C#, JavaScript, Java, and so on.

The following are some of the features of MongoDB:

- High availability with built-in replication
- Horizontal scalability with sharding
- End-to-end security
- Document validation and schema exploration

Understanding Spring Data MongoDB

The Spring Data MongoDB project was intended to introduce the concepts of Spring Data repositories to enable the easy development of MongoDB repositories. It provides an abstraction layer on top of MongoDB to successfully store, retrieve, and modify documents available in MongoDB transparently.

Spring Data MongoDB simplifies **Create, Retrieve, Update, and Delete (CRUD)** operations by providing the `ReactiveMongoRepository` interface, which extends from `ReactiveCrudRepository`. This hides the complexities of plain MongoDB implementations, which need to be implemented and tested by developers. Using Spring Data MongoDB could reduce development time dramatically because of this interface.

In the coming chapters, `ReactiveMongoRepository` along with the default methods will be used extensively to implement business logic and to write Spring Data MongoDB repositories and test them. The following sections will show you how to use a domain model that is designed using a class diagram as a base to implement Spring Data MongoDB-based documents and repositories.

Class diagram for the domain model

Since the domain model is the most important component of an application, in this section we will design it first. The following is the simple class diagram for this web service:

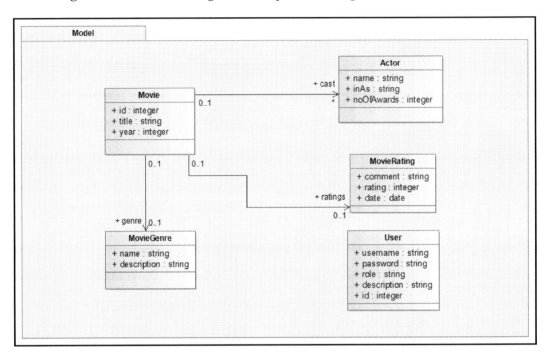

There are five main domain models, as shown in the preceding diagram. These are as follows:

- `Movie`: This is the main domain model, which will store the actual movie title, year, genre, ratings, and cast
- `MovieGenre`: This is the domain model that will store the name and description of the movie genre
- `MovieRating`: This is the domain model that will store the comments, rating, and date of the movie rating
- `Actor`: This is the domain model that will store the name, character name, and number of awards for each actor in the cast
- `User`: This is the domain model that will store the username, password, role, and description for each user in the system

Implementation of the domain model using Spring Data MongoDB annotations

This section will explain the details of how to configure and use Spring Data MongoDB with a MongoDB service and the domain model designed in the previous section. All source code in this chapter is written using Kotlin.

Setting up dependencies and configuration

Initially, before implementing the domain model, the `dependency` and `configuration` classes need to specified. The following Maven starter `dependency` needs to be included:

```xml
<dependencies>
    <dependency>
        <groupId>org.springframework.boot</groupId>
        <artifactId>spring-boot-starter-data-mongodb-reactive</artifactId>
    </dependency>
    ...
    <dependency>
        <groupId>de.flapdoodle.embed</groupId>
        <artifactId>de.flapdoodle.embed.mongo</artifactId>
    </dependency>
</dependencies>
```

The preceding entries import all the dependencies of the MongoDB Reactive stack and an embedded MongoDB, which can be used to store documents.

Implementing the domain model

Implementing the `Movie` domain model using MongoDB annotations will look like the following:

```kotlin
@Document(collection = "movies")
data class Movie(@Id val id : Int,
                 val title : String,
                 val year : Int,
                 val genre : MovieGenre,
                 val ratings : MutableList<MovieRating>,
                 val cast : List<Actor>)
```

The preceding model is written in Kotlin. There are some interesting things about the preceding code:

- **The `data` keyword**: The `data` keyword in Kotlin can be used to mark classes whose sole purpose is to hold and transfer data. Classes with this keyword will get the `equals()`, `hashCode()`, `toString()`, and `copy()` functions auto-generated by the compiler.
- **The `val` keyword**: The `val` keyword is used to define immutable properties right after the class name, which will generate the proper accessors and modifiers accordingly.

Furthermore, the `@Document` annotation is used to mark the `Movie` class as a document in MongoDB and the `@Id` annotation is used to mark the `id` property as the identifier of the `Movie` class.

Implementing the `MovieGenre` domain model will look like the following:

```
data class MovieGenre(val name : String,
                     val description : String)
```

Implementing the `MovieRating` domain model will look like the following:

```
data class MovieRating(val comment : String,
                      val rating : Int,
                      val date : Date)
```

Implementing the `Actor` domain model will look like the following:

```
data class Actor(val name : String,
                val inAs : String,
                val noOfAwards : Int)
```

Implementing the `User` domain model will look like the following:

```
@Document(collection = "users")
data class User(@Id val id : Int,
               val username : String,
               val password : String,
               val role : String,
               val description: String)
```

All the models will have all argument constructors, which can be used to create instances out of them.

Implementing of Spring Data MongoDB repositories

With the domain model implemented successfully, its `MovieRepository` can be implemented using Spring Data MongoDB. The specialty of this is that there is no need to implement anything. Just writing an interface that extends from the `ReactiveMongoRepository` interface would be sufficient to expose the methods to find one, find all, save, delete, and so on. The following code shows `MovieRepository`:

```
interface MovieRepository : ReactiveMongoRepository<Movie, Int>
```

The following code shows, `UserRepository`:

```
interface UserRepository : ReactiveMongoRepository<User, Int> {
    fun findByUsername(username : String) : Flux<User>;
}
```

The preceding `UserRepository` has a custom method written to query the MongoDB user's collection and find users by `username`.

Using a service to encapsulate business logic

It is a good practice to encapsulate business logic inside `Service` methods so that controllers and repositories are loosely coupled. The following is a `Service` written to encapsulate the business logic for `Movie`:

```
@Service
class MovieService constructor(val movieRepository: MovieRepository) {

    fun findAll() = this.movieRepository.findAll();

    fun save(movie : Movie) : Mono<Movie> =
this.movieRepository.save(movie);

    fun findOne(id : Int) : Mono<Movie> = this.movieRepository.findById(id)
            .switchIfEmpty(Mono.error(MovieNotFoundException.create(id)));

    fun rate(id : Int, comment : String, rating : Int) : Mono<Movie> {
        var movieMono: Mono<Movie> = this.findOne(id);
        return
      movieMono.switchIfEmpty(Mono.error
(MovieNotFoundException.create(id))).map({ movie ->
            movie.ratings.add(MovieRating(comment, rating, Date()));
            movie;
```

```
        }).map({ movie ->
            this.save(movie).subscribe();
            movie;
        });
    }

}
```

in the preceding code, `MovieService` is annotated with the `@Service` stereotype annotation to mark it as a Spring Service. When a movie specified by an ID does not exist, `MovieNotFoundException` is thrown. The following is the implementation of this:

```
class MovieNotFoundException : Exception {

    constructor(message : String) : super(message);

    companion object {
        fun create(id : Int) : MovieNotFoundException {
            return MovieNotFoundException("Movie by id $id, not
            found");
        }
    }

}
```

The `MovieNotFoundException` phrase extends the `Exception` class and has a companion object to create instances with an appropriate message.

Likewise, the following `UserService` is used for `User`:

```
@Service
class UserService(val userRepository: UserRepository) {

    fun getByUsername(username : String) : Flux<User> {
        return userRepository.findByUsername(username);
    }

    fun save(user : User) : Mono<User> {
        return userRepository.save(user);
    }
}
```

This `Service` class has functions to save and get the user using their username. Also, there is a Spring Security Reactive-specific service that is implemented to load users by username using `UserService` and return as a Spring Security user to successfully authenticate users. The following `MovieeReactiveUserDetailsService` implements the `ReactiveUserDetailsService.findByUsername()` function:

```
@Service
class MovieeReactiveUserDetailsService(val userService : UserService) :
ReactiveUserDetailsService {

    override fun findByUsername(username: String?): Mono<UserDetails> {
        if (username != null) {
            return userService.getByUsername(username).toMono().map({
                user -> User.withUsername(user.username).password
                  (user.password).roles(user.role).build();
            });
        }

        return Mono.empty();
    }
}
```

The preceding service makes use of `UserService` to get the user using their username and convert them into a Spring Security user, before returning `Mono<UserDetails>`.

Testing Services

A `Service` with business logic needs to be tested to ensure it functions correctly. In order to do this, a `Service` like the following can be used:

```
@RunWith(MockitoJUnitRunner::class)
@ActiveProfiles("dev")
class MovieServiceTest {

    @Mock
    lateinit var movieRepository: MovieRepository;

    lateinit var movieService: MovieService;
```

In the preceding test case for `MovieService`, `MovieRepository` is annotated with `@Mock`. During `Service`, test mocking is done using the Mockito library just to mock repository method invocations and verify the correct invocation. Consider the following code:

```
@Before
fun setup() {
    movieService = MovieService(movieRepository);
}
```

The preceding code is used to create an instance of `MovieService` with a mocked `MovieRepository`. Consider the following code:

```
@Test
fun `Saving a Movie - Happy Path`() {
    // Given
    var expected = getMovie();
    `when`(movieRepository.save(expected)).
     thenReturn(Mono.just(expected));

    // When
    val actual = movieService.save(expected);

    // Then
    actual.subscribe({movie ->
     assertThat(movie).isEqualTo(expected)});
    verify(movieRepository, times(1)).save(expected);
}
```

The preceding code snippet tests the `Saving a Movie` scenario's happy path:

```
@Test
fun `Find a Movie by Id - Happy Path`() {
    // Given
    var expected = getMovie();
    `when`(movieRepository.findById(1)).
     thenReturn(Mono.just(expected));

    // When
    val actual = movieService.findOne(1);

    // Then
    actual.subscribe({movie ->
     assertThat(movie).isEqualTo(expected)});
    verify(movieRepository, times(1)).findById(1);
}
```

The preceding code snippet tests the `Find a Movie by Id` scenario's happy path:

```
@Test
fun `Find a Movie by Id - Failure Path`() {
    // Given
    var expected = getMovie();
    `when`(movieRepository.findById(1)).thenReturn(Mono.empty());

    // When
    val actual = movieService.findOne(1);

    // Then
    actual.doOnError({t ->
    assertThat(t).isInstanceOf(MovieNotFoundException::
     class.java)}).
     subscribe();
    verify(movieRepository, times(1)).findById(1);
}
```

The preceding code snippet tests the `Find a Movie by Id` scenario's failure path:

```
@Test
fun `Rate a Movie - Happy Path`() {
    // Given
    var expected = getMovie();
    `when`(movieRepository.findById(1)).
     thenReturn(Mono.just(expected));
    `when`(movieRepository.save(expected)).
     thenReturn(Mono.just(expected));

    // When
    var actual = movieService.rate(1, "Great", 5);

    // Then
    actual.subscribe({movie ->
     assertThat(movie.ratings).hasSize(1)});
    verify(movieRepository, times(1)).findById(1);
    verify(movieRepository, times(1)).save(expected);
}
```

The preceding code snippet tests the `Rate a Movie` scenario's happy path:

```
@Test
fun `Rate a Movie - Failure Path`() {
    // Given
    `when`(movieRepository.findById(1)).thenReturn(Mono.empty());

    // When
```

```
        var actual = movieService.rate(1, "Great", 5);

        // Then
        actual.doOnError({t ->
        assertThat(t).isInstanceOf(MovieNotFoundException::
        class.java)}).subscribe();
    }
```

The preceding code snippet tests the `Rate a Movie` scenario's failure path:

```
fun getMovie() : Movie {
    return Movie(1, "Avengers", 2018, MovieGenre("Action",
      "Action"), ArrayList<MovieRating>(), ArrayList<Actor>())
}


}
```

The preceding code snippet creates mock `Movie` data for testing.

The following is the service test case for `UserService`:

```
@RunWith(MockitoJUnitRunner::class)
@ActiveProfiles("dev")
class UserServiceTest {

    @Mock
    lateinit var userRepository: UserRepository;

    lateinit var userService: UserService;

    @Before
    fun setup() {
        this.userService = UserService(userRepository);
    }

    @Test
    fun `Saving a User - Happy Path`() {
        // Given
        var user : User = getUser();
        `when`(userRepository.save(user)).thenReturn(Mono.just(user));

        // When
        var actual = userService.save(user);

        // Then
        actual.subscribe({u -> assertThat(user).isEqualTo(u)});
        verify(userRepository, times(1)).save(user);
```

```
    }

    @Test
    fun `Find by Username - Happy Path`() {
        // Given
        var user : User = getUser();
        `when`(userRepository.findByUsername("shazin")).
         thenReturn(Flux.just(user));

        // When
        var actual = userService.getByUsername("shazin");

        // Then
        actual.subscribe({u -> assertThat(user).isEqualTo(u)});
        verify(userRepository, times(1)).findByUsername("shazin");
    }

    fun getUser() : User {
        return User(1, "shazin", "password", "USER", "User of Moviee");
    }

}
```

The preceding tests use lazy initialization with the lateinit keyword for variables that are mocked, autowired, or initialized inside the @Before function. This is done because any variable that is not nullable must be initialized either during declaration or in the constructor.

Also, Kotlin allows descriptive function names for methods, which describe the scenario being tested, enclosed inside two "`".

Using Spring WebFlux for controllers

Controllers are the integration point between the model and resources in a RESTful web service. They act like the glue that binds everything together while taking care of business logic execution and responses. The following Maven starter dependency needs to be added to enable Spring WebFlux:

```
<dependencies>
    ...
    <dependency>
        <groupId>org.springframework.boot</groupId>
        <artifactId>spring-boot-starter-webflux</artifactId>
    </dependency>
</dependencies>
```

The preceding `dependency` will import the Reactive Stream, Spring, and Netty dependencies to enable the successful writing of Reactive web applications using Spring.

Implementation of controllers

The following is `MovieController`, which caters for listing and rating movies:

```
@RequestMapping("/movies")
@RestController
class MovieController constructor(val movieService : MovieService) {

    @GetMapping
    fun getMovies() : Flux<Movie> {
        return this.movieService.findAll();
    }

    @GetMapping("/{id}")
    fun getMovie(@PathVariable id : Int) : Mono<Movie> {
        return this.movieService.findOne(id);
    }

    @PutMapping("/{id}/rate")
    fun rateMovie(@PathVariable id : Int, @RequestParam rating : Int,
     @RequestParam comment : String) : Mono<Movie> {
        return this.movieService.rate(id, comment, rating);
    }
}
```

The `getMovies` function is mapped to the `/movies` URL and will load movies from MongoDB by using the `MovieService.findAll()` function as `Flux<Movie>` and sending it as a JSON response to the caller.

The `getMovie` function is mapped to the `/movies/{id}` URL and will load the movie identified by the `id` path variable from MongoDB by using the `MovieService.findOne()` function as `Mono<Movie>` and sending it as a JSON response to the caller.

The `rateMovie` function is mapped to the `/movies/{id}/rate` URL and will load the movie identified by the `id` path variable from MongoDB and rate it with the `comment` and `rating` query strings passed in by using the `MovieService.rate()` function as `Mono<Movie>` and sending it as a JSON response to the caller.

Furthermore, to show meaningful information when `MovieNotFoundException` is thrown instead of a white label page, `ErrorDTO` is introduced as follows:

```
data class ErrorDTO(val code : Int, val message : String?) : Serializable
```

This has the `code` phrase, which is the HTTP status code, and a `message` property. A `@ControllerAdvice` is used to catch `MovieNotFoundException` and convert it to a `ReponseEntity` containing `ErrorDTO`, as follows:

```
@ControllerAdvice
class BaseController {

    @ExceptionHandler(value = MovieNotFoundException::class)
    fun handleMovieNotFoundException (e : MovieNotFoundException) :
     ResponseEntity<ErrorDTO> {
        return ResponseEntity<ErrorDTO>(ErrorDTO(400, e.message),
        HttpStatus.BAD_REQUEST);
    }
}
```

The `handleMovieNotFoundException` function accepts an argument of `MovieNotFoundException` and is annotated with `@ExceptionHandler` to catch that exception. Inside the function, the correct message and HTTP status code are returned as part of `ErrorDTO`.

Testing controllers

You should test the controller for successful business logic execution and response generation. The following test case is written for `MovieController`, which is annotated with `@WebFluxTest` and has an autowired `WebTestClient`, which will be used to invoke the endpoints:

```
@RunWith(SpringRunner::class)
@WebFluxTest(MovieController::class)
@ActiveProfiles("dev")
class MovieControllerTest {

    @MockBean
    lateinit var movieService: MovieService;

    @MockBean
    lateinit var movieRepository: MovieRepository;

    @Autowired
    lateinit var webTestClient: WebTestClient;
```

Building a Reactive Movie Rating API Using Kotlin

The preceding code snippet performs creates mocking beans and the testing utility:

```
@Test
fun `List Movies - Happy Path`() {
    // Given
    var movieFlux: Flux<Movie> = Flux.fromIterable(listOf(getMovie()));
    `when`(movieService.findAll()).thenReturn(movieFlux);

    // When
    webTestClient.get().uri("/movies")
            .header(HttpHeaders.CONTENT_TYPE, "application/json")
            .exchange()
            .expectStatus().isOk()
            .expectBody()
            .json("""
      [{"id":1,"title":"Avengers","year":2018,"genre":
    {"name":"Action","description":"Action"},"ratings":[],
    "cast":[]}]""");

    // Then
    verify(movieService, times(1)).findAll();
}
```

The preceding code snippet performs the controller testing for the `List Movies` scenario's happy path:

```
@Test
fun `Rate Movie - Happy Path`() {
    // Given
    var movie = getMovie();
    movie.ratings.add(MovieRating("Great", 5, Date()))
    `when`(movieService.rate(1, "Great",
     5)).thenReturn(Mono.just(movie));

    // When
    webTestClient.put().uri("/movies/1/rate?comment=Great&rating=5")
            .exchange()
            .expectStatus().isOk()
            .expectBody()
            .json("""
     {"id":1,"title":"Avengers","year":2018,"genre":
     {"name":"Action","description":"Action"},"ratings":
      [{"comment":"Great","rating":5}],"cast":[]}""")

    // Then
    verify(movieService, times(1)).rate(1, "Great", 5)
}
```

The preceding code snippet performs the controller testing for the `Rate Movie` scenario's happy path:

```
@Test
fun `Rate Movie - Failure Path`() {
    // Given
    `when`(movieService.rate(2, "Great",
     5)).thenReturn(Mono.error(MovieNotFoundException.create(2)));

    // When
    webTestClient.put().uri("/movies/2/rate?comment=Great&rating=5")
            .exchange()
            .expectStatus().isBadRequest()
            .expectBody()
            .json("""{"code":400,"message":"Movie by id 2, not
             found"}""")

    // Then
    verify(movieService, times(1)).rate(2, "Great", 5)
}
```

The preceding code snippet performs the controller testing of the `Rate Movie` scenario's failure path:

```
@Test
fun `Get Movie by Id - Happy Path`() {
    // Given
    `when`(movieService.findOne(1))
    .thenReturn(Mono.just(getMovie()));

    // When
    webTestClient.get().uri("/movies/1")
            .exchange()
            .expectStatus().isOk()
            .expectBody()
            .json("""
            {"id":1,"title":"Avengers","year":2018,"genre":
            {"name":"Action","description":"Action"},
            "ratings":[],"cast":[]}""")

    // Then
    verify(movieService, times(1)).findOne(1);
}
```

The preceding code snippet does the controller testing of the `Get Movie by Id` scenario's happy path:

```
fun getMovie() : Movie {
    return Movie(1, "Avengers", 2018, MovieGenre("Action",
    "Action"), ArrayList<MovieRating>(), ArrayList<Actor>())
    }
}
```

The preceding code snippet creates mock `Movie` data for testing.

In the preceding controller test case, `WebTestClient` is used to hit particular endpoints of the controller and verify whether it returns the correct status codes, bodies, and so on.

Using Spring Security for basic authorization

The Moviee web service uses Spring Security to authenticate users and authorize them to list, get, and rate movies. The Maven Spring Security starter needs to be specified as follows to enable Spring Security in the web service:

```
<dependencies>
    <dependency>
        <groupId>org.springframework.boot</groupId>
        <artifactId>spring-boot-starter-security</artifactId>
    </dependency>
</dependencies>
```

The Moviee web service uses basic authentication, an authentication mechanism that uses a header named `Authorization` with the `"Basic "+base64encode(username:password)` value. The following is the Spring Security configuration:

```
@Configuration
@EnableWebFluxSecurity
class SecurityConfig {

    @Bean
    fun securityWebFilterChain(http : ServerHttpSecurity) :
SecurityWebFilterChain {
        http.authorizeExchange()
                .pathMatchers("/movies/**")
                .authenticated()
                .and()
```

```
                .httpBasic()
                .and()
                .csrf()
                .disable();

        return http.build();
    }
```

The preceding configuration uses @EnableWebFluxSecurity to configure the web filters necessary for Spring Security Reactive and override any auto-configurations. The securityWebFilterChain function uses its ServerHttpSecurity argument to protect all the endpoint sets under /movies/** and ensure they're accessible only after authentication. This in turns means the user needs to be authenticated; anonymous users will not be allowed to access anything:

```
    @Bean
    fun authenticationManager(movieeReactiveUserDetailsService:
    MovieeReactiveUserDetailsService):
      UserDetailsRepositoryReactiveAuthenticationManager {
        val userDetailsRepositoryReactiveAuthenticationManager =
          UserDetailsRepositoryReactiveAuthenticationManager
          (movieeReactiveUserDetailsService)
        userDetailsRepositoryReactiveAuthenticationManager.
        setPasswordEncoder(passwordEncoder())

        return userDetailsRepositoryReactiveAuthenticationManager
    }

    @Bean
    fun passwordEncoder(): PasswordEncoder {
        return BCryptPasswordEncoder()
    }
```

The authenticationManager function is used to configure an instance of ReactiveAuthenticationManager with MovieeReactiveUserDetailsService, implemented earlier, along with BCryptPasswordEncoder:

```
    @Bean
    @Profile("default")
    fun applicationRunner(userService : UserService): ApplicationRunner
    {
        return ApplicationRunner {
    userService.save(com.packtpub.springboot2movierating.model.User
    (1, "user", passwordEncoder().encode("password"), "USER", "User of
    Moviee")).subscribe();
    userService.save(com.packtpub.springboot2movierating.model.User(2,
```

```
        "admin", passwordEncoder().encode("password"), "ADMIN", "Admin of
        Moviee")).subscribe()
            }
        }
    }
```

Finally, `ApplicationRunner` is used to insert some users into the database at startup.

Demonstrating Moviee

When everything is put together, built, and run, the Retro board can be accessed using the `http://<host>:<port>` URL.

There are several ways to run a Spring Boot application; some of them are mentioned in the following list:

- Running the Spring Boot application main class using an IDE.
- Building a JAR or WAR file using the following Maven command and then running it:

    ```
    $ mvn clean install
    $ java -jar target/<package-name>.[jar|war]
    ```

- Running the Spring Boot application using the Spring Boot Maven plugin:

    ```
    $ mvn clean spring-boot:run
    ```

Integration testing

To verify the everything works as expected in a real world scenario, an integration test can be written that, which puts everything together and tests each endpoint. The following is an integration test for the Moviee web service:

```
@RunWith(SpringRunner::class)
@SpringBootTest(webEnvironment = SpringBootTest.WebEnvironment.RANDOM_PORT)
class SpringBoot2MovieRatingApplicationTests {

    @Autowired
    lateinit var webTestClient : WebTestClient;

    @Test
    fun `Get Movies - Happy Path`() {
```

```
webTestClient
    .get()
    .uri("/movies")
    .header("Authorization", getBasicAuthorization())
    .exchange()
    .expectStatus()
    .isOk()
    .expectBody()
    .json("""[{"id":1,"title":"Titanic","year":1999,"genre":
{"name":"Romantic","description":"Romantic"},"cast":
[{"name":"Lionardo Dicaprio","inAs":"Jack","noOfAwards":1},
{"name":"Kate Winslet","inAs":"Rose","noOfAwards":2}]}]""");
}
```

The preceding code snippet performs the integration testing for the Get Movies scenario's happy path:

```
@Test
fun `Get Movies - Failure Path (No Authorization)`() {
    webTestClient
        .get()
        .uri("/movies")
        .exchange()
        .expectStatus()
        .isUnauthorized()
}
```

The preceding code snippet performs the integration testing for the Get Movies scenario's failure path:

```
@Test
fun `Get Movie - Happy Path`() {
    webTestClient
        .get()
        .uri("/movies/1")
        .header("Authorization", getBasicAuthorization())
        .exchange()
        .expectStatus()
        .isOk()
        .expectBody()
        .json("""{"id":1,"title":"Titanic","year":1999,"genre":
{"name":"Romantic","description":"Romantic"},"cast":
[{"name":"Lionardo Dicaprio","inAs":"Jack","noOfAwards":1},
{"name":"Kate Winslet","inAs":"Rose","noOfAwards":2}]}""")

}
```

The preceding code snippet performs the integration testing for the `Get Movie` scenario's happy path:

```
@Test
fun `Rate Movie - Happy Path`() {
    webTestClient
        .put()
        .uri("/movies/1/rate?comment=Ok Movie&rating=3")
        .header("Authorization", getBasicAuthorization())
        .exchange()
        .expectStatus()
        .isOk()
        .expectBody()
        .json("""{"id":1,"title":"Titanic","year":1999,"genre":
    {"name":"Romantic","description":"Romantic"},"ratings":
    [{"comment":"Good Movie","rating":5},{"comment":"Ok
    Movie","rating":3}],"cast":[{"name":"Lionardo
    Dicaprio","inAs":"Jack","noOfAwards":1},{"name":"Kate
    Winslet","inAs":"Rose","noOfAwards":2}]}""")
}
```

The preceding code snippet performs the integration testing for the `Rate Movie` scenario's happy path:

```
    fun getBasicAuthorization() : String {
        val plainCreds = "user:password"
        val plainCredsBytes = plainCreds.toByteArray()
        val base64CredsBytes =
        Base64.getEncoder().encode(plainCredsBytes);
        val base64Creds = String(base64CredsBytes)

        return "Basic $base64Creds";
    }

}
```

The preceding code snippet returns the `Base64` encoded username and password to be sent as part of the authorization header.

The preceding integration test class is annotated with `@SpringBootTest`, which configures a `webEnvironment` that will start on a random port. By using `WebTestClient`, each particular endpoint can be invoked with a proper basic authentication header and verified responses. Integration tests are used to test from end to end before deploying to production.

Demonstrating the use of Postman

Postman is a famous GUI tool widely used to invoke RESTful web services. It offers a free tier for small, individual projects, such as Moviee.

Accessing the List Movies endpoint

In the following Postman `GET` request, the `Basic Auth` authorization type is used, along with a **username** of `user` and a **password** of `password`, to authenticate. When the **Send** button is clicked, a JSON array of movies will be returned, as shown in the following screenshot:

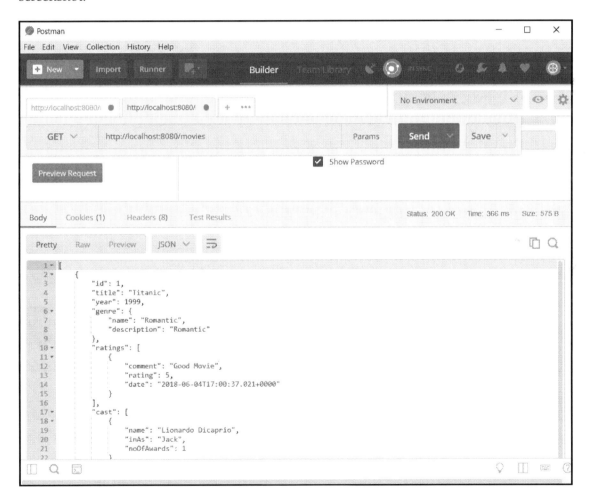

Accessing the Get Movie endpoint

In the following Postman GET request, the Basic Auth authorization type is used, along with a **username** of user and a **password** of password, to authenticate. When the **Send** button is clicked, the JSON of a single movie will be returned, along with the HTTP status code 200, as shown in the following screenshot:

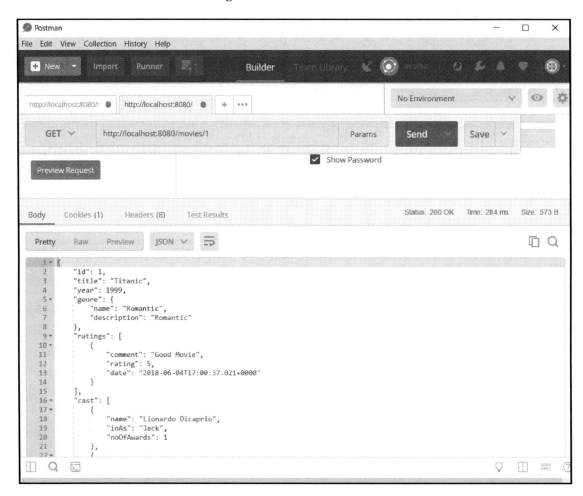

Accessing the Get Movie endpoint with an invalid Movie ID

In the following Postman GET request, the Basic Auth authorization type is used, along with a **username** of user and a **password** of password, to authenticate. When the **Send** button is clicked, the JSON of a single error will be returned, along with the HTTP status code 400, as shown in the following screenshot:

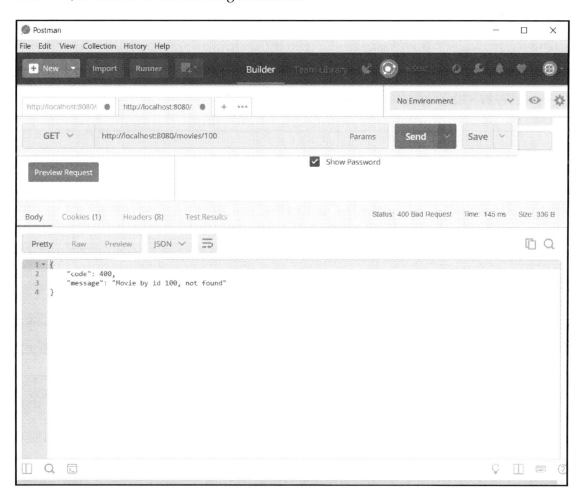

Accessing the Rate Movie endpoint

In the following Postman PUT request, the Basic Auth authorization type is used, along with a **username** of user and a **password** of password, to authenticate comment, rating query strings. When the **Send** button is clicked, the JSON of a single movie with a newly added rating will be returned, along with the HTTP status code 200, as shown in the following screenshot:

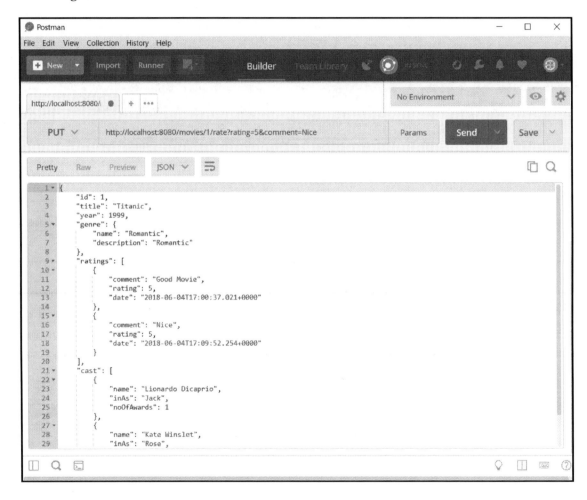

Summary

Congratulations on completing this chapter, where the skills and knowledge required to build a RESTful web service were discussed in detail. This chapter started off by explaining what REST is and how a web service can benefit by being RESTful, in terms of both development and maintenance. It talked about the requirements of the RESTful web service being developed, and used a UML use case diagram to explain the requirement visually.

This chapter also talked about how to understand the domain model of an application based on the requirements (the Moviee app), and used Spring Data MongoDB to convert domain model entities into MongoDB documents. A UML class diagram was used to explain the domain model in detail. Furthermore, the chapter explained how to write data repositories for those entities, using Spring Data MongoDB with minimum effort, in commonly used CRUD operations. It also explained how to write custom query methods in data repositories and how to encapsulate business logic inside Spring service components. Finally, it explained how to test these service components.

Toward the end, the chapter talked about how to use Spring WebFlux REST controllers to provide coordination between different services. Furthermore, it talked about how to protect controller endpoints using Spring Security to allow the basic authentication and authorization of users. Finally, it explained how to test Spring WebFlux controllers using WebFlux test cases. The chapter also demonstrated the use of Moviee in detail. Let's learn more about application development in the next chapter.

Questions

Please answer the following questions to see whether you have successfully mastered this chapter:

1. What is REST?
2. What is MongoDB?
3. What is Kotlin?
4. What is the use of the data keyword in Kotlin?
5. What is basic authentication?
6. What is integration testing?
7. What is Postman?

Further reading

In order to improve your knowledge of Spring Web MVC and Spring Security, the following books are recommended, which will be helpful in the coming chapters:

- *Building RESTful Web Services with Spring 5, Second Edition*: `https://www.packtpub.com/application-development/building-restful-web-services-spring-5-second-edition`
- *Mastering MongoDB 3.x*: `https://www.packtpub.com/big-data-and-business-intelligence/mastering-mongodb-3x`

6
Building an API with Reactive Microservices

This chapter will help readers get started on developing reactive microservices using Spring Boot 2.0. It will enable experts as well as beginners in Spring Boot web application development to understand the concepts behind a microservice and how easy it is to use Spring Boot 2.0 to develop a microservice application. It will explain these concepts by walking the reader through the process of developing two microservices related to a Taxi Hailing System, where one will be for the Taxi Service, including functions such as getting available taxis, finding the status of a taxi, updating taxi location, and registering taxis, and the other one will be for the Taxi Booking Service, which will allow users to book a taxi, cancel a taxi, and so on. These two microservices will be running inside a container platform named Docker and will use a Redis instance for persistence, Spring Data Redis Reactive for the model and repository, and Spring WebFlux for controllers.

The following topics will be covered in this chapter:

- Using Spring Data Redis for persistence
- Using Spring WebFlux for controllers
- Using asynchronous data transfer for cross-microservice communication
- Using Docker to support microservices
- Demonstrating Saber

Technical requirements

In order to implement the web application using Spring Boot, the following build tools need to be downloaded and installed:

- To install **Java Development Kit (JDK)** 8, download it from its official page at http://www.oracle.com/technetwork/java/javase/downloads/jdk8-downloads-2133151.html
- To install Maven 3, download it from its official page at https://maven.apache.org/download.cgi
- To install IntelliJ IDEA, download it from its official page at https://www.jetbrains.com/idea/download/
- To install **Spring Tool Suite (STS)**, download it from its official page at https://spring.io/tools
- To install Docker, download it from its official page at https://www.docker.com/get-docker

The source code for this chapter can be found at https://github.com/PacktPublishing/Spring-Boot-2.0-Projects-Fundamentals-of-Spring-Boot-2.0, **under** the Chapter06 **directory.**

Getting started

In this section, the reader will get an overview of the reactive microservices being developed. The requirements, design, and implementation details will be discussed in brief.

Microservices architecture

Microservices architecture has become a buzzword within the last five years with the emergence of cloud-based hosting services. There is no fixed definition of this architecture, but in general terms, microservices architecture is a way of designing and implementing software as a collection of independently deployable services that are highly coherent and loosely coupled. Each of these services will be designed, implemented, deployed, and maintained by a team of usually 5 to 10 members with complete ownership and accountability. Each microservice will address a particular domain of a system (user, sales, and others), can be developed using different programming languages, and can have its own persistence and an API to enable synchronous communication and/or a publisher/subscriber model for asynchronous communication.

Microservices architecture was preceded by monolithic architecture, where all the functionality was grouped into a single application that loaded and ran inside a single process. This monolithic software was really heavy and took a lot of time to load, and scaling required the entire application to be scaled by replicating it in multiple servers. There was no way to scale a particular functionality alone. This is depicted in the following diagram:

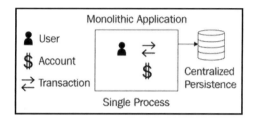

Microservices architecture addressed these pain points by enabling us to run small, highly cohesive applications that do one functionality really well. This could load fast and require fewer resources to function. Scaling of a microservice can be done by distributing it across servers and by replicating it as and when needed. Consider the following diagram:

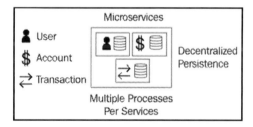

There are some characteristics that can be found in any **Microservices** architecture-based software application, which are as follows:

- **Service components**: The components in a microservice architecture are services that can communicate via a web request, RPC call, and so on. Unlike library components in a monolithic application where communication happens between library components via in-memory, in-process calls internally without an external API.
- **Organized by business domain**: In a monolithic application, layering of the application was done using techniques such as user interface, business logic, and database. But in a microservices architecture, layering is not like that; instead, it is based on a business domain such as user, or transaction.

- **Building products, not projects**: A monolithic application is considered to be a project, where it will be developed by a groups of engineers, deployed by another group of engineers, and maintained by another group, whereas microservices architecture-based software applications are built as products, which are owned by the group of engineers that developed them. They are accountable for the deployment, smooth running, and maintenance of that microservice product.
- **Smart Microservices, dumb queues**: Instead of using an **Enterprise Service Bus (ESB)**, which is capable of doing complex tasks such as transforming, filtering, routing, and aggregating of the messages being communicated, microservices rely on using dumb queues, which are just to communicate between two microservices asynchronously. All heavy lifting should be done in microservices.
- **Decentralized persistence**: Polyglot persistence, as it is commonly known, lets each microservice use its own persistence (Database, Key/Value store—whichever suits it well), instead of relying on a single persistence store.
- **Fail tolerance**: Microservices should be able to work under predictable and unpredictable failures.
- **Automation**: Microservices should be able to be deployed using continuous integration and continuous deployment tools.
- Future-proof with the ability to evolve.

The requirements of microservices architecture

The application being developed is a Taxi Hailing API nicknamed **Saber**, which uses microservices architecture to break down its two most core features into independently running microservices. We will be learning about the following:

1. **Taxi Service**: This service is responsible for registering, updating taxi location, updating taxi status, getting taxi status, and searching for taxis in a geographical area
2. **Taxi Booking Service**: This service is responsible for registering, accepting, canceling, and searching for bookings in a geographical area

The microservices will be placed behind a secure API Gateway that will be responsible for handling the authentication and authorization of users, which is out of scope for this implementation. The API Gateway will be calling the microservices that are internally accessible to it in order to perform taxi and taxi booking actions.

Each microservice has a REST API to expose operations of its own to the outside world, and also uses asynchronous communication to communicate among them using a publisher/subscriber model.

The use case diagram

The following use case diagram shows the requirements for the microservice, which is nicknamed Saber:

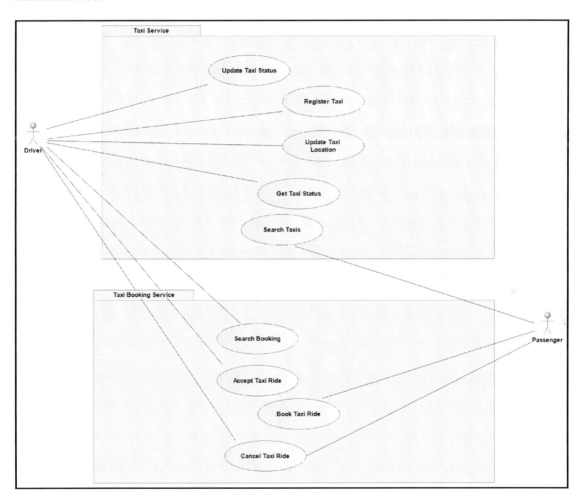

There are two main actors, named the **Driver** and the **Passenger** of the Saber. The use cases are grouped into two different microservices.

The Taxi Microservice has the following use cases:

- **Register Taxi**: This use case is required to register a Taxi by a driver, a physical vehicle with a vehicle type to provide a transportation service to passengers
- **Update Taxi Location**: This use case is required to update the location of a registered Taxi while it moves around
- **Update Taxi Status**: This use case is required to update the status of a registered Taxi such as available, occupied, and so on
- **Get Taxi Status**: This use case is required to get the status of a registered Taxi
- **Search Taxi**: This use case is required to search for registered Taxis close to a passenger, given a geographical coordinate (latitude, longitude) and a radius in kilometers

The Taxi Booking microservice has the following use cases:

- **Book Taxi Ride**: This use case is required to book a Taxi ride by a passenger, given a start location, end location, taxi type, and so on
- **Accept Taxi Ride**: This use case is required to accept a Taxi booking made by a passenger by a driver
- **Cancel Taxi Ride**: This use case is required to cancel a Taxi booking made by a passenger, either by the driver or by the passenger
- **Search Booking**: This use case is required to search Taxi Bookings close to a driver, given a geographical coordinate (latitude, longitude) and a radius in kilometers

The project structure to develop microservices

In order to develop microservices in this chapter, there may be a lot of code that could be reused between the two microservices. To accommodate this, the following project structure is used in this chapter:

`spring-boot-2-taxi/`: This is the parent Maven project of all the following projects:

- ├── `spring-boot-2-taxi-config/`: This is a Maven project that will have all the common configurations
- ├── `spring-boot-2-taxi-model/`: This is a Maven project that will have all the common data transfer objects

- ├── `spring-boot-2-taxi-service/`: This is a Maven project that will be responsible for the Taxi Microservice
- ├── `spring-boot-2-taxi-book-service/`: This is a Maven project that will be responsible for the Taxi Booking microservice

This project structure follows a Maven module approach, which enables code reuse and faster building of the projects.

Using Spring Data Redis for persistence

This section will introduce Redis and how to use Spring Data Redis repositories to provide **Create, Retrieve, Update, Delete (CRUD)** operations on Redis easily, and also how to use the reactive capabilities of Spring Data with Redis. The decision to use Redis was made because the data in a Taxi domain is highly volatile and tends to change very often (such as the location of a moving Taxi), and also because of its out-of-the-box Geo data support. This is because Redis holds in memory most of the time; it suits well for this.

Understanding Redis

Redis is a distributed, in-memory, key-value store that provides high scalability, reliability, and performance. Redis is much more than a distributed cache; it stores not only key-value pairs but also collections such as lists, sets, sorted sets, maps, and many more. Redis also provides a set of algorithms that can be performed on those collections.

Redis supports scalability by enabling client-side sharing and server-side master/slave replication. Redis stores encoded data in memory, so a large amount of data can be stored with a minimal memory footprint. Redis can also be configured to write data to a file for fault tolerance based on the timing and frequency of data writing.

Understanding Spring Data Redis

Spring Data Redis is intended to bring the concepts of Spring Data repositories to enable easy development of Redis repositories. It provides an abstraction layer on top of Redis to successfully store, retrieve, and modify documents available in Redis transparently.

Spring Data Redis eases CRUD operations by allowing the `CrudRepository` interface, which extends from the repository. This hides the complexities of plain Redis implementations, which need to be implemented and tested by developers. Using Spring Data Redis could reduce the development time dramatically because of this.

Furthermore, Spring Data Redis provides a set of templates to enable reactive programming in the form of `ReactiveRedisTemplate` and `ReactiveRedisOperations`.

In coming chapters, `CrudRepository` with default methods and `ReactiveRedisTemplate` will be used extensively to implement business logic and to write Spring Data Redis repositories and test them. The following sections will discuss how to use a domain model designed using a class diagram as a base to implement Spring Data Redis-based documents and repositories.

Class diagram for the domain model

Since the domain model is the most important component of an application, this section will design it first. The following is a simple class diagram for these microservices:

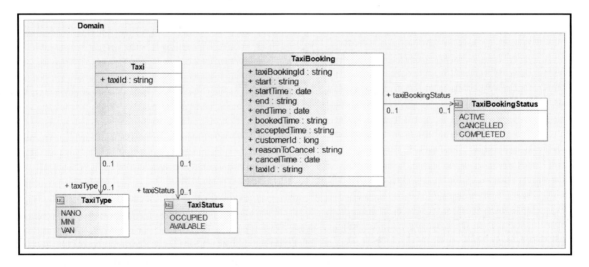

There are two main domain models shown in the preceding diagram. They are as follows:

- **Taxi**: This is the main domain model, which will store the `taxiid`, `TaxiType`, and `TaxiStatus` of an actual physical taxi
- **TaxiBooking**: This is the domain model, which will store the `taxiBookingId`, `TaxiBookingStatus`, start location, end location, start time, end time, and so on.

Also, the model uses `TaxiType`, `TaxiStatus`, and `TaxiBookingStatus` enumerations to specify some type-and value-safe properties.

Implementation of domain model using Spring Data Redis annotations

This section will explain the details of how to configure and use Spring Data Redis with a Redis service with the domain model designed in the previous section.

Setting up dependencies and configuration

Initially, before implementing the domain model, the dependency and configuration classes need to be specified. The following Maven starter dependency needs to be included and available in the `spring-boot-2-taxi-config` project:

```
<dependencies>
    <dependency>
        <groupId>org.springframework.boot</groupId>
        <artifactId>spring-boot-starter-data-redis-reactive</artifactId>
    </dependency>
</dependencies>
```

Implementing the domain model

Implementing the domain model `Taxi` using Spring Data Redis annotations will look like the following, which is available in `spring-boot-2-taxi-service`:

```
@RedisHash("Taxi")
@Data
@AllArgsConstructor
@NoArgsConstructor
public class Taxi implements Serializable {
    @Id
    private String taxiId;

    private TaxiType taxiType;

    private TaxiStatus taxiStatus;
}
```

Implementing the domain model `TaxiBooking` using Spring Data Redis annotations will look like the following which is available in `spring-boot-2-taxi-book-service`:

```
@RedisHash("TaxiBooking")
@Data
@AllArgsConstructor
@NoArgsConstructor
public class TaxiBooking {
    @Id
    private String taxiBookingId;

    private Point start;

    private Date startTime;

    private Point end;

    private Date endTime;

    private Date bookedTime;

    private Date acceptedTime;

    private Long customerId;

    private TaxiBookingStatus bookingStatus;

    private String reasonToCancel;

    private Date cancelTime;

    private String taxiId;
}
```

The `@RedisHash` annotation is used to store the contents of this domain model as a Redis Map with `@Id` used to mark the `id` field for this model. The annotations `@Data` is from Lombok library to generate `toString`, `equals`, `hashCode`, and getters/setters for this model. The start and end attributes are of type `org.springframework.data.geo.Point`, which is used to store coordinates. The `@AllArgsConstructor` annotation is used to generate the all arguments constructor and `@NoArgsConstructor` is used to generate a default constructor without any arguments.

Implementation of Spring Data Redis repositories

With the domain model implemented successfully, `CrudRepository` for those can be implemented using Spring Data Redis. The specialty here is that there is no need to implement anything. Just writing an interface that extends from the `CrudRepository` interface would be sufficient to expose methods to find one, find all, save, delete, and so on. The following code shows the `TaxiRepository`, which is available in the `spring-boot-2-taxi-service`:

```
@Repository
public interface TaxiRepository extends CrudRepository<Taxi, String> {

}
```

The `@Repository` annotation is used to mark this interface as a data repository component of Spring. The following code shows `TaxiBookingRepository`, which is available in `spring-boot-2-taxi-book-service`:

```
@Repository
public interface TaxiBookingRepository extends CrudRepository<TaxiBooking, String> {

}
```

Using a Service to encapsulate business logic

It is a good practice to encapsulate business logic inside `Service` methods so that controllers and repositories are loosely coupled. The following is a `Service` written for encapsulating business logic for `Taxi`, and is available in `spring-boot-2-taxi-service`:

```
@Service
public class TaxiService {

  private final ReactiveRedisTemplate<String, String> reactiveRedisTemplate;
  private final TaxiRepository taxiRepository;
  private final LocationToPointConverter locationToPointConverter = new LocationToPointConverter();

  public TaxiService(ReactiveRedisTemplate<String, String> reactiveRedisTemplate, TaxiRepository taxiRepository) {
    this.reactiveRedisTemplate = reactiveRedisTemplate;
    this.taxiRepository = taxiRepository;
  }
```

```
public Mono<Taxi> register(TaxiRegisterEventDTO taxiRegisterEventDTO) {
    Taxi taxi = new Taxi(taxiRegisterEventDTO.getTaxiId(),
    taxiRegisterEventDTO.getTaxiType(), TaxiStatus.AVAILABLE);
    return Mono.just(taxiRepository.save(taxi));
}
```

The preceding `register` method saves `Taxi` in the system so that it can fulfill rides. This will return a result that is a reactive single object:

```
public Mono<Taxi> updateLocation(String taxiId, LocationDTO locationDTO) {
    Optional<Taxi> taxiOptional = taxiRepository.findById(taxiId);
    if (taxiOptional.isPresent()) {
    Taxi taxi = taxiOptional.get();
    return
reactiveRedisTemplate.opsForGeo().add(taxi.getTaxiType().toString(),
locationToPointConverter.convert(locationDTO), taxiId.toString()).flatMap(l
-> Mono.just(taxi));
    } else {
    throw getTaxiIdNotFoundException(taxiId);
    }
}
```

The preceding `updateLocation` method will use the `ReactiveRedisTemplate.opsForGeo().add` method to update the location and `taxiId` of a `Taxi` grouped into taxi type. This will return a result that is a reactive single object:

```
    public Flux<GeoResult<RedisGeoCommands.GeoLocation<String>>>
      getAvailableTaxis(TaxiType taxiType, Double latitude, Double
longitude,
     Double radius) {
        return
reactiveRedisTemplate.opsForGeo().radius(taxiType.toString(), new
        Circle(new Point(longitude, latitude), new Distance(radius,
        Metrics.KILOMETERS)));
    }
```

The preceding `getAvailableTaxis` method will return all the `Taxi` IDs falling inside of a circle which has a center geo coordinate depicted by latitude, longitude, and radius in kilometers. This will return a result that is a reactive collection of objects:

```
    public Mono<TaxiStatus> getTaxiStatus(String taxiId) {
        Optional<Taxi> taxiOptional = taxiRepository.findById(taxiId);
        if (taxiOptional.isPresent()) {
            Taxi taxi = taxiOptional.get();
            return Mono.just(taxi.getTaxiStatus());
        } else {
```

```
            throw getTaxiIdNotFoundException(taxiId);
        }

    }
```

The preceding `getTaxiStatus` method will return `TaxiStatus` of a taxi identified by `taxiId`. This will return a result that is a reactive single object:

```
    public Mono<Taxi> updateTaxiStatus(String taxiId, TaxiStatus taxiStatus) {
        Optional<Taxi> taxiOptional = taxiRepository.findById(taxiId);
        if (taxiOptional.isPresent()) {
            Taxi taxi = taxiOptional.get();
            taxi.setTaxiStatus(taxiStatus);
            return Mono.just(taxiRepository.save(taxi));
        } else {
            throw getTaxiIdNotFoundException(taxiId);
        }
    }

    private TaxiIdNotFoundException getTaxiIdNotFoundException(String taxiId) {
        return new TaxiIdNotFoundException("Taxi Id "+taxiId+" Not Found");
    }
}
```

The preceding `updateTaxiStatus` method will update the `TaxiStatus` of a taxi identified by the `taxiId`. This will return a result that is a reactive single object.

The `TaxiService` class in the preceding code is annotated with the `@Service` stereotype annotation to mark it as a Spring Service. All methods of this service return either a `Mono` or `Flux`, enabling those to be used Reactively. When a Taxi specified by an ID does not exist, `TaxiIdNotFoundException` is thrown. The following is the implementation for it:

```
public class TaxiIdNotFoundException extends RuntimeException {
    public TaxiIdNotFoundException(String message) {
        super(message);
    }

    public TaxiIdNotFoundException(String message, Throwable cause) {
        super(message, cause);
    }
}
```

Building an API with Reactive Microservices

`TaxiIdNotFoundException` **extends from the** `Exception` **class. Likewise, the following** `TaxiBookingService` **class is used for** `TaxiBooking,` **which is available in** `spring-boot-2-taxi-book-service`:

```
@Service
public class TaxiBookingService {

    private final static Logger LOGGER =
    LoggerFactory.getLogger(TaxiBookingService.class);

    private final RedisTemplate<String, String> redisTemplate;
    private final ReactiveRedisTemplate<String, String> reactiveRedisTemplate;
    private final TaxiBookingRepository taxiBookingRepository;
    private final ObjectMapper objectMapper = new ObjectMapper();
    private final LocationToPointConverter locationToPointConverter = new LocationToPointConverter();

    public TaxiBookingService(RedisTemplate<String, String> redisTemplate,
    ReactiveRedisTemplate<String, String> reactiveRedisTemplate,
    TaxiBookingRepository taxiBookingRepository) {
        this.redisTemplate = redisTemplate;
        this.reactiveRedisTemplate = reactiveRedisTemplate;
        this.taxiBookingRepository = taxiBookingRepository;
    }

    public Mono<TaxiBooking> book(TaxiBookedEventDTO taxiBookedEventDTO) {
        TaxiBooking taxiBooking = new TaxiBooking();
taxiBooking.setEnd(locationToPointConverter.convert(taxiBookedEventDTO.getEnd()));
taxiBooking.setStart(locationToPointConverter.convert(taxiBookedEventDTO.getStart()));
        taxiBooking.setBookedTime(taxiBookedEventDTO.getBookedTime());
        taxiBooking.setCustomerId(taxiBookedEventDTO.getCustomerId());
        taxiBooking.setBookingStatus(TaxiBookingStatus.ACTIVE);
        TaxiBooking savedTaxiBooking =
taxiBookingRepository.save(taxiBooking);
        return
reactiveRedisTemplate.opsForGeo().add(getTaxiTypeBookings(taxiBookedEventDTO.getTaxiType()), taxiBooking.getStart(),
taxiBooking.getTaxiBookingId()).flatMap(l -> Mono.just(savedTaxiBooking));
    }
```

The preceding `book` method will enable a passenger to save a `TaxiBooking` in Redis based on the supplied `TaxiBookedEventDTO`, and will use the `reactiveRedisTemplate.opsForGeo().add()` method to add the taxi booking by its type, to be listed by its starting location and `taxiBookingId` so that it can be queried using geo-location search queries:

```
public Mono<TaxiBooking> cancel(String taxiBookingId,
TaxiBookingCanceledEventDTO canceledEventDTO) {
        Optional<TaxiBooking> taxiBookingOptional =
        taxiBookingRepository.findById(taxiBookingId);
        if (taxiBookingOptional.isPresent()) {
            TaxiBooking taxiBooking = taxiBookingOptional.get();
            taxiBooking.setBookingStatus(TaxiBookingStatus.CANCELLED);
            taxiBooking.setReasonToCancel(canceledEventDTO.getReason());
            taxiBooking.setCancelTime(canceledEventDTO.getCancelTime());
            return Mono.just(taxiBookingRepository.save(taxiBooking));
        } else {
            throw getTaxiBookingIdNotFoundException(taxiBookingId);
        }
}
```

The preceding `cancel` method retrieves a Taxi Booking by its `taxiBookingId` and updates the booking status to canceled along with the reason and canceled time:

```
public Mono<TaxiBooking> accept(String taxiBookingId,
TaxiBookingAcceptedEventDTO acceptedEventDTO) {
        Optional<TaxiBooking> taxiBookingOptional =
        taxiBookingRepository.findById(taxiBookingId);
        if (taxiBookingOptional.isPresent()) {
            TaxiBooking taxiBooking = taxiBookingOptional.get();
            taxiBooking.setTaxiId(acceptedEventDTO.getTaxiId());
taxiBooking.setAcceptedTime(acceptedEventDTO.getAcceptedTime());
            return
Mono.just(taxiBookingRepository.save(taxiBooking)).doOnSuccess(t ->
            {
                try {
redisTemplate.convertAndSend(RedisConfig.ACCEPTED_EVENT_CHANNEL,
objectMapper.writeValueAsString(acceptedEventDTO));
                } catch (JsonProcessingException e) {
                    LOGGER.error("Error while sending message to Channel
{}",
                    RedisConfig.ACCEPTED_EVENT_CHANNEL, e);
                }
            });
```

```
        } else {
            throw getTaxiBookingIdNotFoundException(taxiBookingId);
        }
    }
```

The preceding accept method will enable a driver to accept a TaxiBooking to fulfill the ride. After updating the taxiId and acceptedTime the taxiBooking will be saved and a Booking Accepted Event will be triggered to notify any listeners:

```
        public Flux<GeoResult<RedisGeoCommands.GeoLocation<String>>>
          getBookings(TaxiType taxiType, Double latitude, Double longitude,
    Double
            radius) {
            return
    reactiveRedisTemplate.opsForGeo().radius(getTaxiTypeBookings(taxiType),
                new Circle(new Point(longitude, latitude), new Distance(radius,
                Metrics.KILOMETERS)));
        }
```

The preceding getBookings method will return TaxiBooking by taxiType, geo-location, and radius. So any taxiBookings that match the type and fall inside the circle whose center is marked by the geo-coordinates and has the same radius:

```
        public Mono<TaxiBooking> updateBookingStatus(String taxiBookingId,
    TaxiBookingStatus taxiBookingStatus) {
            Optional<TaxiBooking> taxiBookingOptional =
              taxiBookingRepository.findById(taxiBookingId);
            if (taxiBookingOptional.isPresent()) {
                TaxiBooking taxiBooking = taxiBookingOptional.get();
                taxiBooking.setBookingStatus(taxiBookingStatus);
                return Mono.just(taxiBookingRepository.save(taxiBooking));
            } else {
                throw getTaxiBookingIdNotFoundException(taxiBookingId);
            }
        }
```

The preceding updateBookingStatus will update the bookingStatus of a TaxiBooking identified by the taxiBookingId passed in:

```
        private TaxiBookingIdNotFoundException
          getTaxiBookingIdNotFoundException(String taxiBookingId) {
            return new TaxiBookingIdNotFoundException("Taxi Booking Id
            "+taxiBookingId+" Not Found");
        }
```

```
        private String getTaxiTypeBookings(TaxiType taxiType) {
            return taxiType.toString()+"-Bookings";
        }

}
```

The `TaxiBookingService` in the preceding code is also annotated with `@Service` stereotype annotation to mark it as a Spring Service. All methods of this service return either a `Mono` or `Flux`, enabling those to be used Reactively. When a Taxi booking specified by an ID does not exist, `TaxiBookingIdNotFoundException` is thrown. Following is the implementation:

```
public class TaxiBookingIdNotFoundException extends RuntimeException {

    public TaxiBookingIdNotFoundException(String message) {
        super(message);
    }

    public TaxiBookingIdNotFoundException(String message, Throwable cause) {
        super(message, cause);
    }

}
```

`TaxiBookingIdNotFoundException` extends from `Exception`.

Using Spring WebFlux for a controller

Controllers are the integration point between Model and Resources in an AI. They act like the glue that binds together everything while taking care of business logic execution and response. The following Maven starter `dependency` needs to be added to enable Spring WebFlux:

```xml
<dependencies>
    ...
    <dependency>
        <groupId>org.springframework.boot</groupId>
        <artifactId>spring-boot-starter-webflux</artifactId>
    </dependency>
</dependencies>
```

The preceding dependency will import Reactive Stream, Spring, and Netty dependencies to enable successful writing of Reactive-based web applications using Spring.

Implementation of controllers

The following code is the `TaxiController`, which caters to the registering, searching, status updating, and so on, of Taxis; it is available in `spring-boot-2-taxi-service`:

```
@RequestMapping("/taxis")
@RestController
public class TaxiController {

    private final TaxiService taxiService;

    public TaxiController(TaxiService taxiService) {
        this.taxiService = taxiService;
    }

    @GetMapping
    public Flux<TaxiAvailableResponseDTO>
      getAvailableTaxis(@RequestParam("type") TaxiType taxiType,
      @RequestParam("latitude") Double latitude, @RequestParam("longitude")
      Double longitude, @RequestParam(value = "radius", defaultValue = "1")
       Double radius) {
        Flux<GeoResult<RedisGeoCommands.GeoLocation<String>>> availableTaxisFlux
           = taxiService.getAvailableTaxis(taxiType, latitude, longitude, radius);
        return availableTaxisFlux.map(r -> new
        TaxiAvailableResponseDTO(r.getContent().getName()));
    }

    @GetMapping("/{taxiId}/status")
    public Mono<TaxiStatusDTO> getTaxiStatus(@PathVariable("taxiId") String taxiId) {
        return taxiService.getTaxiStatus(taxiId).map(s -> new
        TaxiStatusDTO(taxiId, s));
    }

    @PutMapping("/{taxiId}/status")
    public Mono<TaxiStatusDTO> updateTaxiStatus(@PathVariable("taxiId") String
        taxiId, @RequestParam("status") TaxiStatus taxiStatus) {
        return taxiService.updateTaxiStatus(taxiId, taxiStatus).map(t -> new
        TaxiStatusDTO(t.getTaxiId(), t.getTaxiStatus()));
    }

    @PutMapping("/{taxiId}/location")
    public Mono<TaxiLocationUpdatedEventResponseDTO>
```

```
    updateLocation(@PathVariable("taxiId") String taxiId, @RequestBody
     LocationDTO locationDTO) {
        return taxiService.updateLocation(taxiId, locationDTO).map(t -> new
        TaxiLocationUpdatedEventResponseDTO(taxiId));
    }

    @PostMapping
    public Mono<TaxiRegisterEventResponseDTO> register(@RequestBody
    TaxiRegisterEventDTO taxiRegisterEventDTO) {
        return taxiService.register(taxiRegisterEventDTO).map(t -> new
        TaxiRegisterEventResponseDTO(t.getTaxiId()));
    }

}
```

We can understand the following from the previous code:

- The `getAvailableTaxis` function is mapped to the URL `/taxis` and accepts taxi type, latitude, longitude, and radius in kilometers, and returns Taxis available in that geographical area
- The `getTaxiStatus` function is mapped to the URL `/taxis/{taxiId}/status` and returns the status of the Taxi identified by the `taxiId` path variable
- The `updateTaxiStatus` function is mapped to the URL `/taxis/{taxiId}/status` with the request method `PUT` and updates the status of the Taxi identified by the `taxiId` path variable
- The `updateLocation` function is mapped to the URL `/taxis/{taxiId}/location` with the request method `PUT` and updates the location of the Taxi identified by the `taxiId` path variable
- The `register` function is mapped to the URL `/taxis` with request method `POST` and registers a new Taxi into the system

The following code is `TaxiBookingController`, which caters to the registering, searching, status updating, and so on, of Taxis; it is available in `spring-boot-2-taxi-book-service`:

```
@RequestMapping("/taxibookings")
@RestController
public class TaxiBookingController {

    private final TaxiBookingService taxiBookingService;

    public TaxiBookingController(TaxiBookingService taxiBookingService) {
        this.taxiBookingService = taxiBookingService;
```

```java
    }

    @PostMapping
    public Mono<TaxiBookedEventResponseDTO> book(@RequestBody TaxiBookedEventDTO
    taxiBookedEventDTO) {
        return taxiBookingService.book(taxiBookedEventDTO).map(t -> new
        TaxiBookedEventResponseDTO(t.getTaxiBookingId()));
    }

    @PutMapping("/{taxiBookingId}/cancel")
    public Mono<TaxiBookingCanceledEventResponseDTO>
     cancel(@PathVariable("taxiBookingId") String taxiBookingId,
@RequestBody
      TaxiBookingCanceledEventDTO taxiBookingCanceledEventDTO) {
        return taxiBookingService.cancel(taxiBookingId,
       taxiBookingCanceledEventDTO).map(t -> new
       TaxiBookingCanceledEventResponseDTO(t.getTaxiBookingId()));
    }

    @PutMapping("/{taxiBookingId}/accept")
    public Mono<TaxiBookingAcceptedEventResponseDTO>
      accept(@PathVariable("taxiBookingId") String taxiBookingId,
@RequestBody
       TaxiBookingAcceptedEventDTO taxiBookingAcceptedEventDTO) {
        return taxiBookingService.accept(taxiBookingId,
        taxiBookingAcceptedEventDTO).map(t -> new
        TaxiBookingAcceptedEventResponseDTO(t.getTaxiBookingId(),
t.getTaxiId(),
        t.getAcceptedTime()));
    }

    @GetMapping
    public Flux<TaxiBookingResponseDTO> getBookings(@RequestParam("type")
     TaxiType taxiType, @RequestParam("latitude") Double latitude,
     @RequestParam("longitude") Double longitude, @RequestParam(value =
"radius",
     defaultValue = "1") Double radius) {
        return taxiBookingService.getBookings(taxiType, latitude,
longitude,
         radius).map(r -> new
TaxiBookingResponseDTO(r.getContent().getName()));
    }


}
```

We infer the following from the previous code:

- The `book` function is mapped to the URL `/taxibookings` with request method `POST` and creates a Taxi booking for a particular Taxi type with start and end location
- The `cancel` function is mapped to the URL `/taxibookings/{taxiBookingId}/cancel` and cancels a Taxi booking identified by the `taxiBookingId` path variable
- The `accept` function is mapped to the URL `/taxibookings/{taxiBookingId}/accept` and enables a driver to accept a Taxi booking identified by the `taxiBookingId` path variable
- The `getBookings` function is mapped to the URL `/taxibookings` and accepts taxi type, latitude, longitude, radius in a kilometers, and returns Taxi bookings available in that geographical area

Using asynchronous data transfer for cross-microservice communication

Microservices need to communicate with each other from time to time. The HTTP APIs that microservices expose are usually reserved for the external systems invoking them, but when they need to talk internally, it is best to use an asynchronous way to communicate so that they can still communicate even when one microservice is down or not functioning properly.

Asynchronous data transfer using Redis

Redis offers asynchronous data transfer between an application using a publisher/subscriber model, which enables one application to publish to a channel and another application to subscribe to that channel and perform actions when an event is received. The publishers need not know about the subscribers, and vice versa in this model, which enables loose coupling and high scalability.

In the case of these two microservices, the Taxi Microservice needs to know when a Taxi Booking is accepted in the Taxi Booking Microservice so that it can update the status of a Taxi. For this reason, the Taxi Booking microservice will publish a Taxi Booking Accepted Event, and the Taxi Microservice will subscribe to it.

Building an API with Reactive Microservices

The following code snippet in the `TaxiBookingService.accept` function is responsible for publishing that event to the Redis Pub/Sub Channel:

```
try {
    redisTemplate.convertAndSend(RedisConfig.ACCEPTED_EVENT_CHANNEL,
objectMapper.writeValueAsString(acceptedEventDTO));
} catch (JsonProcessingException e) {
    LOGGER.error("Error while sending message to Channel {}",
RedisConfig.ACCEPTED_EVENT_CHANNEL, e);
}
```

The following bean configuration snippet in the Taxi Microservice in `SpringBoot2TaxiServiceApplication` is required to set up the Subscriber as a listener:

```
@Bean
public RedisMessageListenerContainer container(RedisConnectionFactory
connectionFactory, TaxiBookingAcceptedEventMessageListener
taxiBookingAcceptedEventMessageListener) {
   RedisMessageListenerContainer container = new
    RedisMessageListenerContainer();
   container.setConnectionFactory(connectionFactory);
   container.addMessageListener(taxiBookingAcceptedEventMessageListener,
new
   PatternTopic(RedisConfig.ACCEPTED_EVENT_CHANNEL));
   return container;
}
```

The following `Listener` implementation is required to take action when a Taxi Booking Accepted Event is sent from the Taxi Booking Microservice to the Taxi Microservice:

```
@Component
public class TaxiBookingAcceptedEventMessageListener implements
MessageListener {

    private static final Logger LOGGER =
    LoggerFactory.getLogger(TaxiBookingAcceptedEventMessageListener.class);

    private final TaxiService taxiService;
    private final ObjectMapper objectMapper = new ObjectMapper();

    public TaxiBookingAcceptedEventMessageListener(TaxiService taxiService)
{
        this.taxiService = taxiService;
    }

    @Override
    public void onMessage(Message message, @Nullable byte[] bytes) {
        try {
```

```
                TaxiBookingAcceptedEventDTO taxiBookingAcceptedEventDTO =
                objectMapper.readValue(new String(message.getBody()),
                TaxiBookingAcceptedEventDTO.class);
                LOGGER.info("Accepted Event {}", taxiBookingAcceptedEventDTO);
            taxiService.updateTaxiStatus(taxiBookingAcceptedEventDTO.getTaxiId(),
            TaxiStatus.OCCUPIED);
            } catch (IOException e) {
                LOGGER.error("Error while updating taxi status", e);
            }
        }
    }
```

The preceding listener's `onMessage` method will be activated whenever an event is received and will update the status of the Taxi.

Using Docker to support microservices

Microservice architectures need to be able to scale up and scale down as and when required based on demand. It is best to use a container platform such as Docker to achieve this.

Understanding Docker

Docker is a very popular container platform. Containerization, as opposed to virtualization, is the process of deploying applications in a portable and predictable manner by packaging components along with their dependencies into isolated, standard process environments called **containers**. Docker is used by many developers and IT operations staff to provide independence from the underlying infrastructure and applications they run. Docker can be run on on-premise hardware, in the cloud, or in a hybrid setup. Docker containers are lightweight and ideal for microservices development. Docker provides the following features for microservices:

- Accelerated development of microservices
- Ease of deployment
- Ease of rollback
- Lightweight
- Portability
- Predictability

Docker uses a Dockerfile with the steps to initialize a container that can be deployed. Also, Docker provides Docker Compose in order to compose multiple Docker images to work together to create a system.

Using Maven to build Docker images

Since the projects already use Maven as the dependency management and build tool, it makes sense to use a Maven plugin that can be used to build Docker images. For this purpose, Spotify's open source `dockerfile-maven` plugin is used in both the `spring-boot-2-taxi-service` and `spring-boot-2-taxi-booking-service` projects as follows:

```xml
<plugins>
    ...
    <plugin>
        <groupId>com.spotify</groupId>
        <artifactId>dockerfile-maven-plugin</artifactId>
        <version>${dockerfile-maven.version}</version>
        <executions>
            <execution>
                <id>default</id>
                <goals>
                    <goal>build</goal>
                    <goal>push</goal>
                </goals>
            </execution>
        </executions>
        <configuration>
            <contextDirectory>${project.build.directory}</contextDirectory>
            <repository>packtpub-spring-boot-2/${project.artifactId}
        </repository>
            <tag>${project.version}</tag>
        </configuration>
    </plugin>
</plugins>
```

This is with the Dockerfile, which is placed inside `/src/resources/docker/Dockefile`:

```
FROM frolvlad/alpine-oraclejdk8:slim
VOLUME /tmp
ADD PROJECT_JAR app.jar
RUN sh -c 'touch /app.jar'
ENV JAVA_OPTS=""
ENTRYPOINT [ "sh", "-c", "java $JAVA_OPTS -jar /app.jar" ]
```

A Docker image can be built by issuing the following usual Maven build command while being inside the `spring-boot-2-taxi` project:

$ mvn clean install

The preceding Dockerfile does the following code:

- Downloads `alpine-oraclejdk8` and uses it to run the Spring Boot app
- Goes into the `/tmp` volume
- Adds the file mentioned by the placeholder `PROJECT_JAR` (will be explained later) as `app.jar`
- Creates an empty file by the name `app.jar` in the root
- Sets the environment variable `JAVA_OPTS`
- Creates the entry point into the Docker image with the Spring Boot 2.0 application, which is instructed to start `app.jar` using the `java` command

This Dockerfile is available for both `spring-boot-2-taxi-service` and `spring-boot-2-taxi-booking-service`. There are two more plugins used to help with this Dockerfile, which are listed as follows:

```
<plugins>
    ...
    <plugin>
        <artifactId>maven-resources-plugin</artifactId>
        <executions>
            <execution>
                <id>copy-resources</id>
                <phase>process-resources</phase>
                <goals>
                    <goal>copy-resources</goal>
                </goals>
                <configuration>
                    <outputDirectory>${basedir}/target</outputDirectory>
                    <resources>
                        <resource>
                            <directory>src/main/resources/docker</directory>
                            <includes>
                                <include>Dockerfile</include>
                            </includes>
                        </resource>
                    </resources>
                </configuration>
            </execution>
        </executions>
    </plugin>
```

```xml
<plugin>
    <groupId>com.google.code.maven-replacer-plugin</groupId>
    <artifactId>replacer</artifactId>
    <version>1.5.3</version>
    <executions>
        <execution>
            <phase>prepare-package</phase>
            <goals>
                <goal>replace</goal>
            </goals>
        </execution>
    </executions>
    <configuration>
        <file>${basedir}/target/Dockerfile</file>
        <replacements>
            <replacement>
                <token>PROJECT_JAR</token>
                <value>${project.build.finalName}.jar</value>
            </replacement>
        </replacements>
    </configuration>
</plugin>
...
</plugins>
```

The `maven-resource-plugin` will copy the Dockerfile from the `/src/resources/docker` directory to the `/target` directory in order to create a Docker image successfully, while the `replacer` plugin will replace the `PROJECT_JAR` placeholder in the file `/target/Dockerfile` to have the Maven project build the final JAR name (an example is `spring-boot-2-taxi-service-0.0.1-SNAPSHOT.jar`).

Building a system of microservices with Docker

The final system is expected to be built in the following shape:

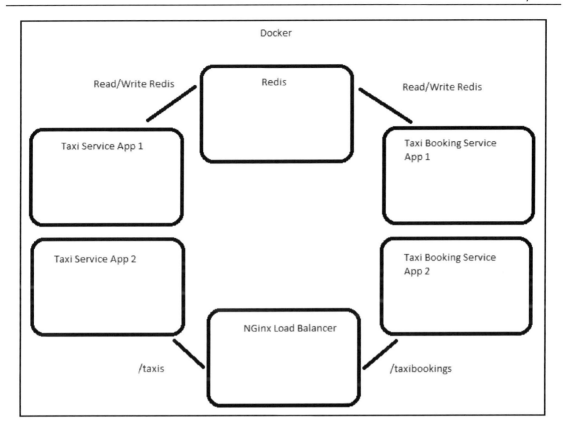

In the preceding diagram, everything resides inside of **Docker** as containers. Each small rectangle is a Docker container with a process of its own. There is one **Redis** container that acts as the in-memory data store for replication to have multiple instances of the Taxi Service Apps and Taxi Booking Service Apps.

All the apps are running behind an **NGinx Load Balancer** so that it can handle the load by distributing traffic among different apps.

The following `docker-compose.yml` file is used to define the preceding layout in Docker's understandable configuration:

```
version: '2'
services:
  taxi-service-app:
    build: ./spring-boot-2-taxi-service/target
    networks:
      - backend
    depends_on:
```

```yaml
      - db

  taxi-booking-service-app:
    build: ./spring-boot-2-taxi-booking-service/target
    networks:
      - backend
    depends_on:
      - db

  db:
    hostname: redis
    image: "redis:alpine"
    ports:
      - "6379:6379"
    networks:
      - backend

  nginx-lb:
    container_name: nginx-lb
    image: nginx:1.13
    restart: always
    ports:
      - 80:80
      - 443:443
    volumes:
      - ./nginx/conf.d:/etc/nginx/conf.d
    networks:
      - backend
    depends_on:
      - taxi-service-app
      - taxi-booking-service-app

networks:
  backend:
    driver: bridge
```

The `services` section lists all the services required to be defined, while the `networks` section lists the networks connecting those services together. The `db` service, in this case, the Redis data store, is the first service to be initialized, as both the `taxi-service-app` and `taxi-booking-service-app` services depend on it. The `db` service will be listening on port `6379` both inside and outside of the network `backend`. This service is created using an already existing Docker image from the Docker repository named `redis:alpine`.

After that, either the `taxi-service-app` or `taxi-booking-service-app` service can be initialized. It will be created from the Docker image that was created in the previous step and placed inside the respective `/target` directory. Both of these services depend on `db` as mentioned earlier and connect to the network `backend`.

Finally, the `nginx-lb` service will be initialized when both the `taxi-service-app` and `taxi-booking-service-app` services are up and running. This service will expose port `80` for non-secure connections and `443` for secure connections. This service will also use the `app.conf` configuration file available in the `/nginx/conf.d` directory, which is inside the `/spring-boot-2-taxi` project.

The `app.conf` file does the following:

```
server {
    listen 80;
    charset utf-8;
    access_log off;

    location /taxibookings {
        proxy_pass http://taxi-booking-service-app:9090;
        proxy_set_header Host $host:$server_port;
        proxy_set_header X-Forwarded-Host $server_name;
        proxy_set_header X-Real-IP $remote_addr;
        proxy_set_header X-Forwarded-For $proxy_add_x_forwarded_for;
    }

    location /taxis {
        proxy_pass http://taxi-service-app:8080;
        proxy_set_header Host $host:$server_port;
        proxy_set_header X-Forwarded-Host $server_name;
        proxy_set_header X-Real-IP $remote_addr;
        proxy_set_header X-Forwarded-For $proxy_add_x_forwarded_for;
    }
}
```

It will listen on port `80`, as mentioned in the preceding code explanation, and will route any requests that come into `http://<host>/taxibookings` to `http://taxi-booking-service-app:9090` (`9090` is the port for the Taxi Bookings service and is configured with `server.port` in `application.properties` file for that project).

Building an API with Reactive Microservices

It will route any requests that come into `http://<host>/taxis` to `http://taxi-service-app:8080`. Also, it will send some headers along with the forwarded requests.

This is all there for the composing of the final system.

Deploying microservices with Docker

Now, with Docker images being built and the Docker composing layout defined, it is possible to build the composing layout and start it so that it can cater requests. The following command, issued from inside the `spring-boot-2-taxi` project, composes everything:

```
$ docker-compose build
```

The preceding command will generate a somewhat familiar output:

```
db uses an image, skipping
Building taxi-booking-service-app
...
Successfully built 8e77b030d54c
Successfully tagged spring-boot-2-taxi_taxi-booking-service-app:latest
Building taxi-service-app
...
Successfully built a2f9c5cf28af
Successfully tagged spring-boot-2-taxi_taxi-service-app:latest
nginx-lb uses an image, skipping
```

The preceding output shows that `db` and `nginx-lb` use an existing image, so they are not built from scratch, whereas `taxi-booking-service-app` and `taxi-service-app` are built from scratch using the Dockerfile and initialize everything.

Next, the following command can be used to start all the Docker containers of the system:

```
$ docker-compose up -d
```

The preceding command will create all the containers in daemon mode (will run in the background) and will generate the following familiar-looking output:

```
Creating network "spring-boot-2-taxi_backend" with driver "bridge"
Creating spring-boot-2-taxi_db_1 ... done
Creating spring-boot-2-taxi_taxi-service-app_1 ... done
Creating spring-boot-2-taxi_taxi-booking-service-app_1 ... done
Creating nginx-lb ... done
```

As explained earlier, the output shows that the network is being created first, followed by `db`, followed by the apps, and finally `nginx load balancer`.

Individual apps can be scaled up or down using the following command:

```
docker-compose up --scale <APP_NAME>=2 -d
```

`APP_NAME` can be either `taxi-service-app` or `taxi-booking-service-app` based on the requirement. The number after the equals sign depicts the number of containers required to be running for that app.

Consider the following example:

```
docker-compose up --scale taxi-service-app=2 -d
```

Also, in order to stop and bring down all the services started, the following command can be used:

```
docker-compose down
```

Demonstrating Saber

Demonstrating this system is done using Postman, as explained in the following sections.

Submitting to the Register Taxi endpoint

In the following Postman, a `POST` request is sent to the URL `http://localhost/taxis` with this body:

```
{
    "taxiType":"NANO"
}
```

Building an API with Reactive Microservices

When the **Send** button is pressed, a JSON of a map with `taxiId` will be returned back, along with the HTTP status code `200`:

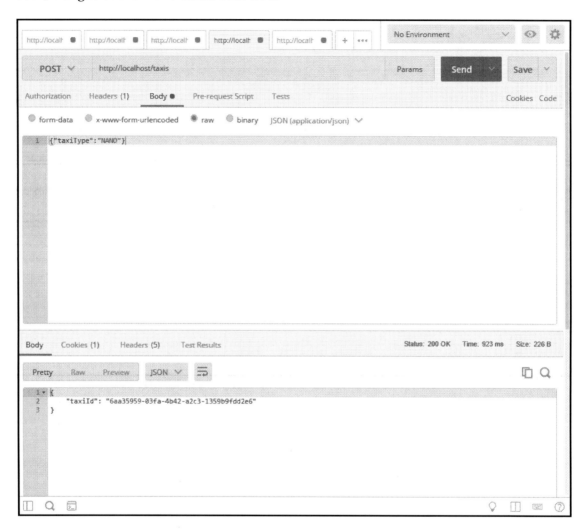

Submitting location to update Taxi Location endpoint

In the following Postman, a `PUT` request is sent to the URL `http://localhost:8080/taxis/<TaxiId>` with the following JSON body:

```
{"latitude":6.938020, "longitude":79.963855}
```

When the **Send** button is pressed, a JSON of a map with `taxiId` will be returned along with the HTTP status code `200`:

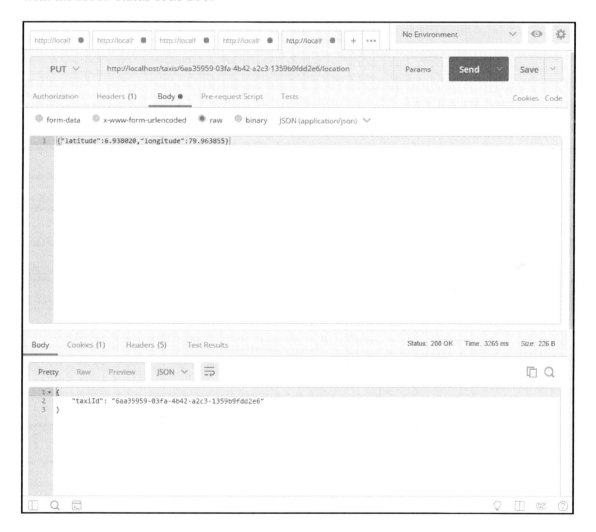

Submitting to Update Taxi Status endpoint

In the following Postman `PUT` request, a `PUT` request is sent to the URL `http://localhost:8080/taxis/<TaxiId>/status?status=OCCUPIED`, and when the **Send** button is pressed a JSON of a map with `taxiId`, after updating the status of the taxi identified by the TaxiID and status will be returned along with the HTTP status code `200`:

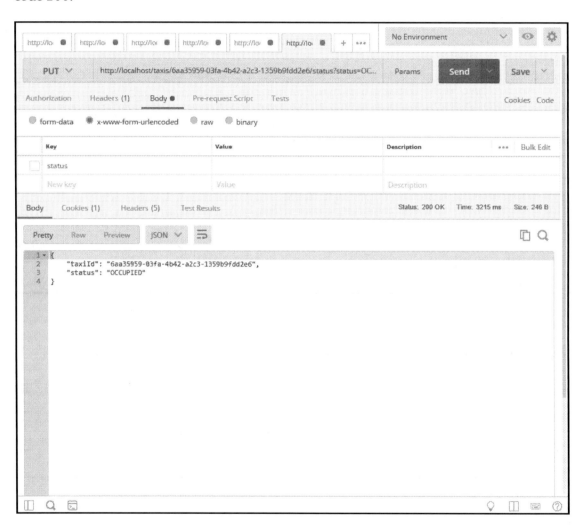

Accessing the Get Taxi Status endpoint

In the following Postman GET request, when the **Send** button is pressed, a JSON of a map with taxiId and status will be returned along with the HTTP status code 200:

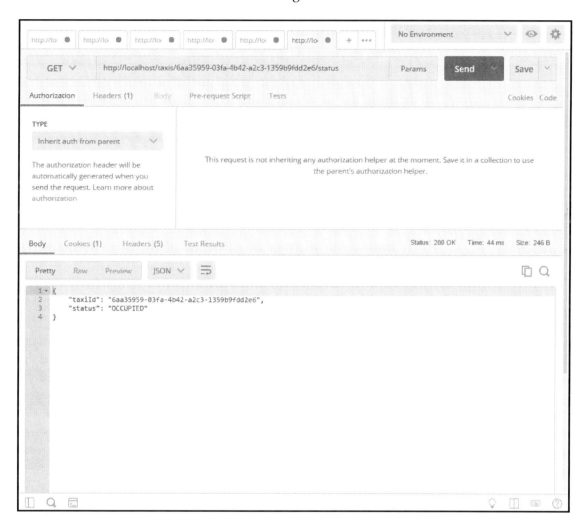

Accessing the GET available Taxis endpoint

In the following Postman GET request with taxi type, latitude, longitude, and radius parameters, when the **Send** button is pressed, a JSON of a list of maps with taxiId will be returned, along with the HTTP status code 200:

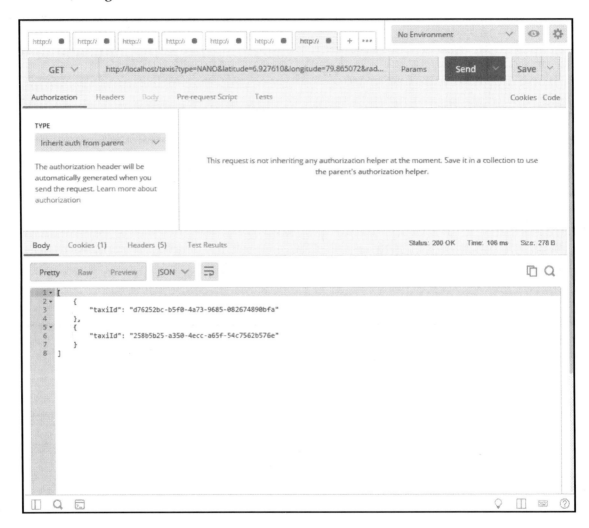

Submitting to Book Taxi endpoint

In the following Postman POST request, the JSON body is filled:

```
{
    "start": {"latitude":6.938020, "longitude":79.963855},
    "end": {"latitude":6.938021, "longitude":79.963857},
    "customerId": 101,
    "taxiType": "NANO"
}
```

When the **Send** button is pressed, a JSON of a map with taxiBookingId will be returned, along with the HTTP status code 200:

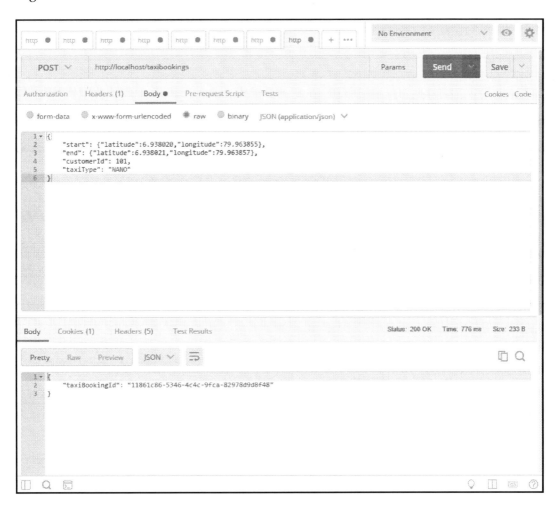

Submitting to Accept Taxi Booking endpoint

In the following Postman PUT request, when the **Send** button is pressed, a JSON of a map with taxiBookingId, taxiId, and acceptedTime will be returned along with the HTTP status code 200:

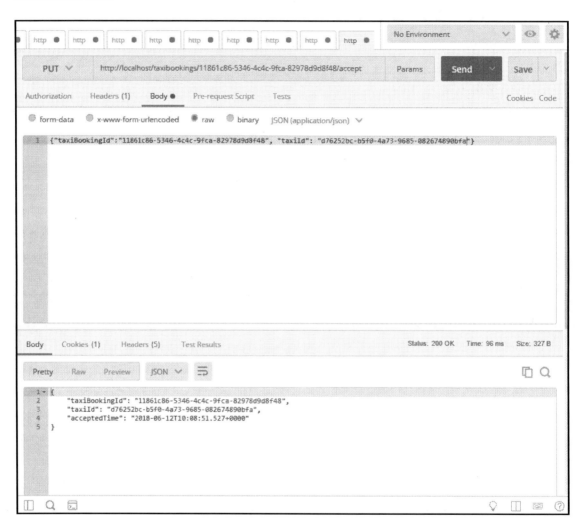

Submitting to cancel Taxi Booking endpoint

In the following Postman `PUT` request, when the **Send** button is pressed, a JSON of a map with `taxiBookingId` will be returned, along with the HTTP status code `200`:

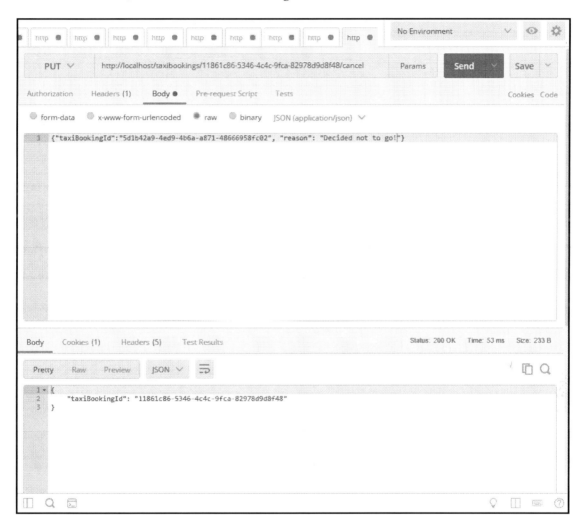

Accessing Taxi Bookings endpoint

In the following Postman `GET` request with taxi type, latitude, longitude, and radius parameters, when the **Send** button is pressed, a JSON of a list of maps with `taxiBookingId` will be returned, along with the HTTP status code `200`:

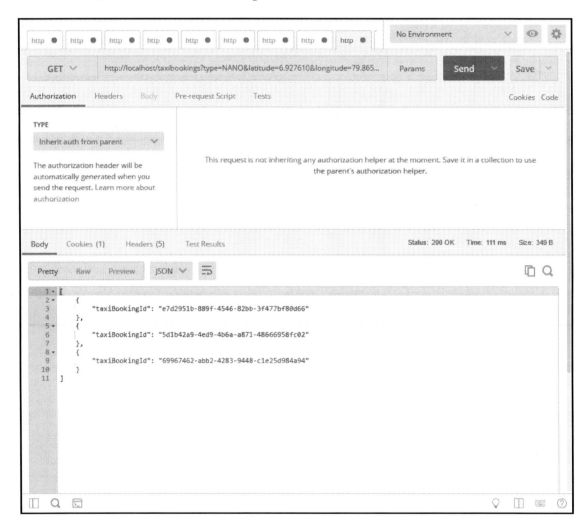

Summary

Congratulations on completing this chapter, where the skills and knowledge required to build microservices were discussed in detail. This chapter started off by explaining what a microservices architecture is and how it is beneficial both in terms of development and maintenance. It talked about the requirements of the microservice architecture being developed and used a UML use case diagram to explain the requirement visually.

This chapter also talked about how to understand the domain model of an application based on the requirements (Saber) and use Spring Data Redis to convert those domain model entities into Redis maps. A UML class diagram was used to explain the domain model in detail. Next, it explained how to write data repositories for those entities using Spring Data Redis with minimum effort for commonly used CRUD operations. It also explained how to write custom query methods in data repositories. Also, it explained how to encapsulate business logic inside Spring Service components. It also talked about how to use Spring WebFlux REST controllers to provide coordination of different services.

Furthermore, it talked about the Docker container platform, explaining what a container is before diving into creating and deploying Spring Boot 2.0 applications as Docker images. Finally, this chapter showed how to use Docker Compose to create complex systems using Docker containers. The chapter also demonstrated the usage of Saber in detail. We'll learn more about application development in coming chapters.

Questions

Please answer the following questions to see whether you have successfully mastered this chapter:

1. What is a Maven module?
2. What is Redis?
3. What is a microservices architecture?
4. What are the benefits of a microservices architecture?
5. What is containerization?
6. What is Docker?
7. What is nginx?

Further reading

In order to improve your knowledge of microservices and Docker, the following books are recommended to be read, as they will be helpful in the coming chapters:

- *Spring: Microservices with Spring Boot*: `https://www.packtpub.com/application-development/spring-microservices-spring-boot`
- *Docker and Kubernetes for Java Developers*: `https://www.packtpub.com/virtualization-and-cloud/docker-and-kubernetes-java-developers`

7
Building a Twitter Clone with Spring Boot

This chapter will introduce the reader to the details of how to build a Twitter clone, nicknamed **Tweety**, using Spring Boot 2 as the backend development framework and Angular 5 as the frontend framework. We will explain how to use JPA as the persistence layer, which is a widely used data source. Subsequently, it will use Angular Material to create the presentation views for the blog management system. Furthermore, it will also use Spring WebFlux and Spring Security OAuth2 to implement controllers and provide authentication and authorization.

The following topics will be covered in this chapter:

- Using Spring Data JPA for persistence
- Using Angular 5 for the frontend
- Using Spring Web Flux for the REST controller
- Using Spring Security for authentication and authorization
- Demonstrating Tweety

Technical requirements

In order to implement the web application using Spring Boot, the following build tools need to be downloaded and installed:

- To install **Java Development Kit (JDK)** 8, you can download it from its official page at http://www.oracle.com/technetwork/java/javase/downloads/jdk8-downloads-2133151.html

- To install Maven 3, download it from its official page at `https://maven.apache.org/download.cgi`
- To install IntelliJ IDEA, it can be downloaded from its official page at `https://www.jetbrains.com/idea/download/`
- To install **Spring Tool Suite (STS)**, you can download it from its official page at `https://spring.io/tools`
- To install Node.js, you can download it from its official page at `https://nodejs.org/en/download/`

The source code for this chapter can be found at `https://github.com/PacktPublishing/Spring-Boot-2.0-Projects-Fundamentals-of-Spring-Boot-2.0`, in the `Chapter07` directory.

Getting started

In this section, readers will get an overview of the Twitter clone being developed. The requirements, design, and implementation details will be discussed in brief.

Beginning with the Tweety architecture

The application architecture for Tweety will have a RESTful API backend and a **model-view-viewmodel (MVVM)** frontend. MVVM is a design pattern used to enable two-way data binding between the view and the model so that one changes when the other does. Angular is a very famous framework that conforms to the MVVM design pattern, which allows highly responsive frontend applications that efficiently update when data from the server changes or a user interacts with the application. Apart from this, Angular provides routing, dependency injection, components, templates, and so on to enable flexible, modular development.

The Tweety application will have the **user interface (UI)** implemented using Angular Material, which is a module provided out of the box to simplify UI development using custom tags and themes.

Tweety requirements

Tweety, being a Twitter clone, is supposed to act like a social media application that allows multiple users to communicate and interact with each other. (This application, however, is being made purely to demonstrate the features of Angular, Spring Boot 2, and their ability to integrate together. This application is in no way a competitor or replacement for Twitter and doesn't include all the features of such a social media application.) The Tweety application must be publicly accessible via the internet, and registered users must be able to send out tweets and mention another user in a tweet.

The main feed must be visible without any authentication and the user feed must only be visible after authentication.

The use case diagram

The following use case diagram shows the requirement for Tweety:

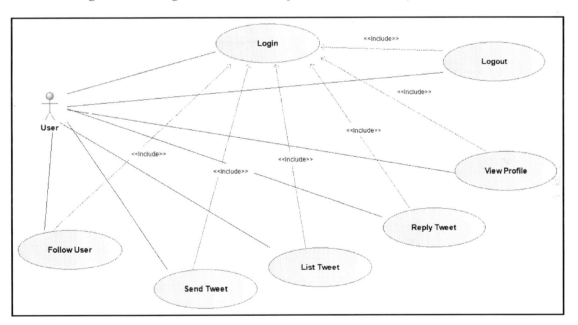

The actor is the **User** of the Tweety application. It has the following use cases:

- **Login**: This use case is required to authenticate users so that each user can be uniquely identified, to allow only authenticated users to perform actions.
- **List Tweet**: This use case is where a user can list all the tweets available for that user. It requires the user to be authenticated.
- **Reply Tweet**: This use case is where a user can reply to a Tweet. It requires the user to be authenticated.
- **Send Tweet**: This use case is where a user can send a Tweet. It requires the user to be authenticated.
- **Follow User**: This use case is where a user can follow another user. It requires the user to be authenticated.
- **View Profile**: This use case is where a user's profile can be viewed by another. It requires the user to be authenticated.
- **Logout**: This use case is where a logged in user can log out.

Using Spring Data JPA for persistence

This section will introduce JPA and how to use Spring Data JPA repositories to provide **Create, Retrieve, Update, and Delete (CRUD)** operations in JPA easily.

Class diagram for the domain model

Since the domain model is the most important component of an application, in this section, we will design it first. The following is the simple class diagram for this web service:

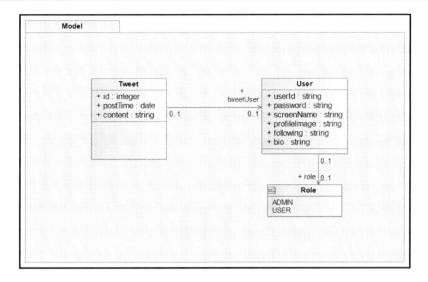

There are three main domain models shown in the preceding diagram. Those are as follows:

- **Tweet**: This is the main domain model, which will store the actual tweet content, posted time, and posted user
- **User**: This is the domain model that will store the username, password, role, and bio of each user on the system
- **Role**: This is the enumeration to describe the role of the user

Implementation of the domain model using Spring Data JPA annotations

This section will explain the details of how to configure and use Spring Data JPA and an H2 embedded database with the domain model designed in the previous section.

Setting up dependencies and configuration

Initially, before implementing the domain model's dependencies and configuration, the class needs to be specified. The following Maven starter dependency needs to be included:

```
<dependencies>
    <dependency>
        <groupId>org.springframework.boot</groupId>
```

```
        <artifactId>spring-boot-starter-data-jpa</artifactId>
    </dependency>
    ...
    <dependency>
        <groupId>com.h2database</groupId>
        <artifactId>h2</artifactId>
        <version>1.4.197</version>
    </dependency>
</dependencies>
```

The preceding entries will import all the `dependencies` of the JPA stack, and an embedded H2 database that can be used to store entities.

Implementing the domain model

Implementing the `Tweet` domain model using JPA annotations will look like the following:

```
@Data
@NoArgsConstructor
@AllArgsConstructor
@Entity
public class Tweet {
    @Id
    @GeneratedValue(strategy = GenerationType.IDENTITY)
    private Integer id;

    @CreationTimestamp
    private Timestamp postTime;

    @ManyToOne
    private User tweetUser;

    @NotNull
    private String content;

}
```

In the preceding code, `@Entity` is used to mark the `Tweet` class as a JPA entity. The `@Id` annotation marks the `id` property as the identity field of the document. The `@Data` annotation is from the Lombok library and is used to mark a POJO as a class that will hold data. This means that `getters`, `setters`, the `equals` method, the `hashCode` method, and the `toString` method will be generated for that class. `@AllArgsConstructor`, which will generate a constructor with all the properties, and `@NoArgsConstructor`, which will generate a default constructor.

Implementing the User domain model using JPA annotations will look like the following code:

```
@Data
@NoArgsConstructor
@AllArgsConstructor
@Entity
public class User {

    @Id
    @NotNull
    private String userId;

    @JsonIgnore
    @NotNull
    private String password;

    @NotNull
    @Column(unique = true)
    private String screenName;

    @NotNull
    private Role role;

    private String bio;

    private String profileImage;

    @ElementCollection
    private Set<String> following;

}
```

In the preceding code, `@Entity` is used to mark the `Tweet` class as a JPA entity. `@AllArgsConstructor` will generate a constructor with all the properties and `@NoArgsConstructor` will generate a default constructor. `@ElementCollection` is used to persist a `Set` collection.

Implementing the `Role` enum will look like the following code:

```
public enum Role {
    ADMIN, USER
}
```

Implementing Spring Data JPA repositories

With the domain model implemented successfully, `JpaRepository` for it can be implemented using the Spring Data JPA. The specialty of this is that there is no need to implement anything. Just writing an interface that extends from the `JpaRepository` interface would be sufficient to expose methods to find one, find all, save, delete, and so on. The following code shows `TweetRepository`:

```java
public interface TweetRepository extends JpaRepository<Tweet, Integer> {

    List<Tweet> findByTweetUser_ScreenNameOrContentContains(String
    screenName, String mention);

}
```

Since tweets need to be listed for a particular logged in user or any tweets that mention them (with the @ symbol in front of the name), the `findByTweetUser_ScreenNameOrContentContains` method is implemented, which will generate the appropriate query to search the tweets. Apart from this, all the default `findAll`, `findById`, `delete`, and `save` methods will be available.

The following code shows `UserRepository`:

```java
public interface UserRepository extends JpaRepository<User, String> {
    User findByScreenName(String screenName);
}
```

In the preceding code, there is a method by the name of `findByScreenName`, where `screenName` is a property of the `User` class.

Caveat for going reactive with blocking JDBC

Java Database Connectivity (JDBC) API is still blocking and synchronous. There are proposals to make it fully non-blocking and asynchronous, but that work is still in progress. This means, as of writing this book, there is no way to do reactive programming if you persist to a database using JDBC.

But there is a small caveat that can be used to mimic reactive behavior, you can use a pool of threads to execute synchronous tasks asynchronously.

The following `DbConfig` class is used to do just that:

```
@Configuration
public class DbConfig {

    private Integer connectionPoolSize;

    public DbConfig(@Value("${spring.datasource.maximum-pool-size:10}")
    Integer connectionPoolSize) {
        this.connectionPoolSize = connectionPoolSize;
    }

    @Bean
    public Scheduler dbScheduler() {
        return Schedulers.fromExecutor(Executors.newFixedThreadPool
        (connectionPoolSize));
    }
}
```

The `dbScheduler()` method creates a `Scheduler` bean, which encapsulates a standard Java fixed-size thread pool for executive tasks. This bean will be used in the service layer, as explained in the next section.

Using Service to encapsulate business logic

It is a good practice to encapsulate business logic inside `Service` methods so that controllers and repositories are loosely coupled. The following is a `Service` written to encapsulate the business logic for `Tweet`:

```
@Service
@Transactional(readOnly = true)
public class TweetService {

    private final TweetRepository tweetRepository;
    private final Scheduler dbScheduler;

    public TweetService(TweetRepository tweetRepository, Scheduler
    dbScheduler) {
        this.tweetRepository = tweetRepository;
        this.dbScheduler = dbScheduler;
    }

    @Transactional(rollbackFor = Exception.class)
    public Mono<Tweet> save(Tweet tweet) {
        return Mono.fromCallable(() ->
```

```
        tweetRepository.save(tweet)).publishOn(dbScheduler);
    }

    public Flux<Tweet> getTweets() {
        return Flux.fromIterable(tweetRepository.findAll()).
        publishOn(dbScheduler);
    }

    public Flux<Tweet> getRelevantTweets(String screenName) {
        return Flux.fromIterable(tweetRepository.
        findByTweetUser_ScreenNameOrContentContains(screenName,
        "@"+screenName)).publishOn(dbScheduler);
    }
}
```

The `save` method saves `Tweet` in the database. The `getTweets` method retrieves all `Tweets` from the database. `getRelevantTweets` will retrieve tweets intended for a user identified by a particular `screenName`.

The following is the `Service` written to encapsulate the business logic for the `User`:

```
@Service
@Transactional(readOnly = true)
public class UserService implements UserDetailsService {

    private final UserRepository userRepository;
    private final Scheduler dbScheduler;

    public UserService(UserRepository userRepository, Scheduler dbScheduler) {
        this.userRepository = userRepository;
        this.dbScheduler = dbScheduler;
    }

    @Transactional(rollbackFor = Exception.class)
    public Mono<User> save(User user) {
        return Mono.fromCallable(() ->
         userRepository.save(user)).publishOn(dbScheduler);
    }

    public Mono<User> getUserByScreenName(String screeName) {
        return Mono.fromCallable(() ->
        userRepository.findByScreenName(screeName)).
        publishOn(dbScheduler);
    }

    public Mono<User> getByUserId(String userId) {
        return Mono.fromCallable(() ->
```

```
            userRepository.findById(userId).get()).
            publishOn(dbScheduler);
    }

    @Override
    public UserDetails loadUserByUsername(String screename) throws
    UsernameNotFoundException {
        User user = userRepository.findByScreenName(screename);

        if (user == null) {
            throw new UsernameNotFoundException(screename);
        }

        return new org.springframework.security.core.
            userdetails.User(user.getScreenName(), user.getPassword(),
            Arrays.asList(new SimpleGrantedAuthority
            (user.getRole().toString())));
    }
}
```

The `save` method saves the `User` in the database. The `getUserByScreenName` method retrieves a user by the `screenName`. The `getUserById` method retrieves a user by ID. The `UserDetailsService.loadUserByUsername` method is implemented in this service as well, to support Spring Security.

In these services, the `DbConfig.dbScheduler` bean is used to delegate the execution of synchronous tasks asynchronously, using a thread pool. The `Mono` and `Flux` constructs have a `publishOn` method, which can be used to achieve this delegation.

Using Angular 5 for the frontend

In this section, how to use Angular 5 to implement the frontend will be explained in detail.

Getting started with Angular 5 application development

This section expects Node.js and npm to have been already installed using the *Technical requirements* section. We will be using the Angular CLI to simplify the development because it helps to create new Angular projects, generate code, and so on.

The Angular CLI can be installed using the following command, and more information about it can be found at https://cli.angular.io:

```
npm install -g @angular/cli
```

Now, the Angular client `stub` project can be created by issuing the following command:

```
ng new frontend
```

Now, the `stub` project is created and all the necessary source code and configuration files will be available inside a directory named `frontend`, which will have roughly the following structure:

```
frontend/
├── src/
│       ├── app/
│       ├── assets/
│       ├── environments/
│       └── index.html
└── package.json
```

Also, Angular Material will be used to simplify layout design and to provide themes that can be installed using the following command, after going into the `frontend` generated directory:

```
npm install --save-exact @angular/material@5.2.4 @angular/cdk@5.2.4
```

Angular Material helps to develop applications that look good on any device, and it has very detailed documentation at https://material.angular.io.

Generating Angular services

Angular uses services to communicate with backend APIs, so it is important to understand this and use Angular CLI to generate code for this. There are two main backend APIs that need to be accessed via Angular services in our application. One is `Tweets` and the other is `Users`. So, we shall generate those using the following commands:

```
ng g s tweets
```

This will generate a `tweets.service.ts` file under the `/src/app` directory, but for simplicity of development, it should be moved to a new directory under `/src/app/shared/tweets` for better grouping and structure.

The `tweets.service.ts` file looks like the following after modifying the `stub` code:

```
import { Injectable } from '@angular/core';
import { HttpClient } from '@angular/common/http';
import { HttpHeaders } from '@angular/common/http';
import { Observable } from 'rxjs/Observable';
import { AuthService } from '../../auth.service';

@Injectable()
export class TweetsService {
  public API = '//localhost:8080';
  public TWEETS_API = this.API + '/tweets';
  private authService;

  constructor(private http: HttpClient, authService: AuthService) {
    this.authService = authService;
  }

  getAll(): Observable<any> {
    let headers = new HttpHeaders().set('Authorization', 'Bearer '+this.authService.getToken());
    return this.http.get(this.TWEETS_API, {headers: headers});
  }

  save(tweet: any): Observable<any> {
    let headers = new HttpHeaders().set('Authorization', 'Bearer '+this.authService.getToken());
    let result: Observable<Object>;
    result = this.http.post(this.TWEETS_API, tweet, {headers: headers});
    return result;
  }

}
```

`TweetsService` will use `HttpClient` to retrieve tweets and save tweets using the backend API, with the standard REST `GET` and `POST` methods.

Generating the users service

This will generate a `users.service.ts` file under the `/src/app` directory, but for simplicity of development, it should be moved to a new directory under `/src/app/shared/users` for better grouping and structure:

```
ng g s users
```

The `users.service.ts` file looks like the following after modifying the `stub` code:

```
import { Injectable } from '@angular/core';
import { HttpClient, HttpHeaders } from '@angular/common/http';
import 'rxjs/add/operator/map';
import { AuthService } from '../../auth.service';
import { Observable } from 'rxjs/Observable';

@Injectable()
export class UsersService {

  public API = '//localhost:8080';
  public USERS_API = this.API + '/users';

  constructor(public http: HttpClient, private authService:
   AuthService) {
  }

  getByScreenName(screenName): Observable<any> {
    const apiLink = this.USERS_API + '/' + screenName;
    let headers = new HttpHeaders().set('Authorization', 'Bearer
    '+this.authService.getToken());
    return this.http.get(apiLink, {headers: headers});
  }

  follow(userId): Observable<any> {
    const apiLink = this.USERS_API + '/' + userId + '/follow';
    let headers = new HttpHeaders().set('Authorization', 'Bearer
    '+this.authService.getToken());
    return this.http.put(apiLink, {}, {headers: headers});
  }
}
```

`UsersService` will use `HttpClient` to retrieve the user by `screenName`, follow a user, and so on, using the backend API with the standard REST `GET` and `PUT` methods.

These two services need to be registered as providers in `/src/app/app.module.ts`:

```
import { BrowserModule } from '@angular/platform-browser';
import { NgModule } from '@angular/core';
import { TweetsService } from './shared/tweets/tweets.service';
import { UsersService } from './shared/users/users.service';
...

@NgModule({
  ...
  providers: [TweetsService, UsersService, ...],
  bootstrap: [AppComponent]
```

```
})
export class AppModule { }
```

Generating Angular page components

Since now there is a means to retrieve data from the backend, there needs to be ways to display that data. There are three main pages that need to be created, which are the **Tweets List** page, the **Tweets Add** page, and the **User Profile** page. So, we shall generate those using the following command:

ng g c tweets-list

This will generate the `tweets-list.component.css`, `tweets-list.component.html`, `tweets-list.component.spec.ts`, and `tweets-list.component.ts` files under the `/src/app/tweets-list` directory.

The `tweets-list.component.ts` file will look like the following after modifying the stub code:

```
import { Component, OnInit } from '@angular/core';
import { TweetsService } from '../shared/tweets/tweets.service';
import { AuthService } from '../auth.service'

@Component({
  selector: 'app-tweets-list',
  templateUrl: './tweets-list.component.html',
  styleUrls: ['./tweets-list.component.css']
})
export class TweetsListComponent implements OnInit {

  tweets: Array<any>;

  constructor(private tweetsService: TweetsService, private authService: AuthService) { }

  ngOnInit() {
    this.authService.checkCredentials();
    this.tweetsService.getAll().subscribe(data => {
      this.tweets = data;
    });
  }

}
```

`TweetsListComponent` will use an injected `TweetsService` to get all tweets for a particular user from the backend and store them in an array variable named `tweets` so that they can be used in the HTML to be rendered.

`tweets-list.component.html` will look like the following after modifying the `stub` code:

```html
<mat-card>
  <mat-card-header>Tweets</mat-card-header>
  <mat-card-content>
    <mat-list>
      <mat-list-item *ngFor="let tweet of tweets">
        <a mat-list-avatar
          href="/profile/{{tweet.tweetUser.screenName}}">
          <img mat-list-avatar src="{{tweet.tweetUser.profileImage}}"
          alt="{{tweet.tweetUser.profileImage}}"/></a>
        <h3 mat-line>{{tweet.content}}</h3>
      </mat-list-item>
    </mat-list>
  </mat-card-content>

  <button mat-fab color="primary" [routerLink]="['/tweets-add']">Tweet</button>
</mat-card>
```

The preceding source code uses `mat-*` elements to structure the layout of the **Tweets List** page and the `mat-list-item` element will use the `tweets` array from the `TweetsListComponent` class to display `tweet` content, a user profile image, and a link to the user profile. Also, it will have a button to redirect to the **Tweets Add** page, which will be explained later. This will act as the main page. Routing for this is also defined in the `/src/app/app.module.ts` file:

```typescript
const appRoutes: Routes = [
  { path: '', redirectTo: '/tweets-list', pathMatch: 'full' },
  {
    path: 'tweets-list',
    component: TweetsListComponent
  }
  ...
];

@NgModule({
  ...
  imports: [
    ...
    RouterModule.forRoot(appRoutes)
```

```
    ],
    ...
})
export class AppModule { }
```

Generating the Tweets Add page

To generate the **Tweets Add** page, we use the following code:

```
ng g c tweets-add
```

This will generate the `tweets-add.component.css`, `tweets-add.component.html`, `tweets-add.component.spec.ts`, and `tweets-add.component.ts` files under the `/src/app/tweets-add` directory.

`tweets-add.component.ts` will look like the following after modifying the `stub` code:

```
import { Component, OnInit } from '@angular/core';
import { Subscription } from 'rxjs/Subscription';
import { ActivatedRoute, Router } from '@angular/router';
import { TweetsService } from '../shared/tweets/tweets.service';
import { NgForm } from '@angular/forms';
import { AuthService } from '../auth.service'

@Component({
  selector: 'app-tweets-add',
  templateUrl: './tweets-add.component.html',
  styleUrls: ['./tweets-add.component.css']
})
export class TweetsAddComponent implements OnInit {

  tweet: any = {};

  constructor(private route: ActivatedRoute,
              private router: Router,
              private tweetsService: TweetsService,
              private authService: AuthService) { }

  ngOnInit() {
  }

  gotoList() {
    this.authService.checkCredentials();
    this.router.navigate(['/tweets-list']);
  }
```

```
  save(form: NgForm) {
    this.authService.checkCredentials();
    this.tweetsService.save(form).subscribe(result => {
      this.gotoList();
    }, error => console.error(error));
  }

}
```

`TweetsAddComponent` will use an injected `TweetsService` to save a `tweet` submitted by a logged in `User`. On success, it will redirect to the **Tweets List**.

`tweets-add.component.html` will look like the following after modifying the `stub` code:

```
<mat-card>
  <form #tweetsForm="ngForm" (ngSubmit)="save(tweetsForm.value)">
    <mat-card-header>
      <mat-card-title><h2>Add Tweet</h2></mat-card-title>
    </mat-card-header>
    <mat-card-content>
      <mat-form-field>
        <textarea matInput placeholder="Tweet"
          [(ngModel)]="tweet.content" required name="content"
          #content cols="50" rows="10"></textarea>
      </mat-form-field>
    </mat-card-content>
    <mat-card-actions>
      <button mat-raised-button color="primary" type="submit"
              [disabled]="!tweetsForm.form.valid">Save</button>
      <a mat-button routerLink="/tweets-list">Cancel</a>
    </mat-card-actions>
    <mat-card-footer>
    </mat-card-footer>
  </form>
</mat-card>
```

The preceding source code uses `mat-*` elements to structure the layout of the **Tweets Add** page. It also has a `ngForm`, which uses the `TweetsAddComponent.save` method to submit a `tweet` to the backend by invoking the API.

Generating the User Profile page

To generate the **User Profile** page, we use the following code:

```
ng g c user-profile
```

This will generate the `user-profile.component.css`, `user-profile.component.html`, `user-profile.component.spec.ts`, and `user-profile.component.ts` files under the `/src/app/user-profile` directory.

`user-profile.component.ts` will look like the following after modifying the `stub` code:

```
import { Component, OnDestroy, OnInit } from '@angular/core';
import { Subscription } from 'rxjs/Subscription';
import { ActivatedRoute, Router } from '@angular/router';
import { AuthService } from '../auth.service';
import { UsersService } from '../shared/users/users.service';
import { NgForm } from '@angular/forms';

@Component({
  selector: 'app-user-profile',
  templateUrl: './user-profile.component.html',
  styleUrls: ['./user-profile.component.css']
})
export class UserProfileComponent implements OnInit, OnDestroy {

  subscription: Subscription;

  user: any;

  constructor(private route: ActivatedRoute,
              private router: Router,
              private usersService: UsersService,
              private authService: AuthService) { }

  ngOnInit() {
    this.authService.checkCredentials();
    this.subscription = this.route.params.subscribe(params => {
      const screenName = params['screenName'];
      this.usersService.getByScreenName(screenName).subscribe(data => {
        console.log(data);
        this.user = data;
      });
    });
  }

  follow(userId) {
    this.usersService.follow(userId).subscribe(data => {
```

```
      console.log(data);
    }, err => console.log("Error "+err));
  }

  ngOnDestroy() {
    this.subscription.unsubscribe();
  }

}
```

`UserProfileComponent` will use an injected `UserService` to follow a user by submitting to the user ID of a logged in user.

`tweets-add.component.html` will look like the following after modifying the `stub` code:

```
<mat-list>
  <h2>{{user.screenName}}</h2>
  <mat-divider></mat-divider>
  <img mat-list-avatar src="{{user.profileImage}}"
alt="{{user.profileImage}}" width="200" height="200"/>
  <mat-divider></mat-divider>
  {{user.bio}}
  <mat-divider></mat-divider>
  <form #followForm="ngForm" (ngSubmit)="follow(user.userId)">
    <button mat-raised-button color="primary" type="submit">Follow</button>
  </form>
</mat-list>
```

The preceding source code uses `mat-*` elements to structure the layout of the **User Profile** page. It also has a `ngForm`, which uses the `UserProfileComponent.save` method to follow a user in the backend by invoking the API.

Using Spring Web Flux for the REST controller

Controllers are the integration point between the model and resources in an Application. They act like the glue that binds everything together while taking care of business logic execution and response. The following Maven starter `dependency` needs to be added to enable Spring WebFlux:

```
<dependencies>
    ...
  <dependency>
      <groupId>org.springframework.boot</groupId>
```

```
            <artifactId>spring-boot-starter-webflux</artifactId>
        </dependency>
        <dependency>
            <groupId>org.springframework.boot</groupId>
            <artifactId>spring-boot-starter-tomcat</artifactId>
        </dependency>
    </dependencies>
```

The preceding `dependency` will import Asynchronous Servlets, Spring, and Tomcat dependencies to enable the successful writing of reactive web applications using Spring.

Implementing controllers

The following code is for `TweetController`, which caters for retrieving and saving tweets:

```
@RestController
@RequestMapping("/tweets")
public class TweetController {

    private final TweetService tweetService;
    private final UserService userService;

    public TweetController(TweetService tweetService, UserService userService) {
        this.tweetService = tweetService;
        this.userService = userService;
    }

    @PostMapping
    public Mono<Tweet> save(Principal principal, @RequestBody Tweet tweet) {
        Mono<User> user =
        userService.getUserByScreenName(principal.getName());
        return user.flatMap(u -> {
                              tweet.setTweetUser(u);
                              return tweetService.save(tweet);
                           });
    }

    @GetMapping
    public Flux<Tweet> getAll(Principal principal) {
        return tweetService.getRelevantTweets(principal.getName());
    }

}
```

From the preceding code, we can see that the `save` method uses `Principal`, which has information about the logged in user, to save a `Tweet` object sent as the request body of a `POST` method.

The `getAll` method uses `Principal`, which has information about the logged in user, to retrieve all the tweets relevant to that user.

The following code is for `UserController`, which caters for retrieving the user by `screenName` and following a user by user ID:

```
@RestController
@RequestMapping("/users")
public class UserController {

    private final UserService userService;

    public UserController(UserService userService) {
        this.userService = userService;
    }

    @GetMapping("/{screenName}")
    public Mono<User> getUserByScreenName(@PathVariable String
    screenName) {
        return userService.getUserByScreenName(screenName);
    }

    @PutMapping("/{userId}/follow")
    @ResponseStatus(code = HttpStatus.OK)
    public void followUser(Principal principal, @PathVariable String
     userId) {
        Mono<User> user =
        userService.getUserByScreenName(principal.getName());
        user.subscribe(u -> {
            if (!u.getUserId().equalsIgnoreCase(userId)) {
                u.getFollowing().add(userId);
                userService.save(u);
            }
        });
    }
}
```

The `getUserByScreenName` method will use `screenName` sent as part of the URL to retrieve the matching user.

The `followUser` method will use the `Principal` object and the user ID submitted as part of the URL to follow a user.

Enabling Angular frontend access to controllers

The backend REST controllers will eventually run on their own web server and the Angular frontend will run on its own server. This means each runs with different origins (domain, protocol, port) and they need to communicate with each other. This is where **cross-origin resource sharing** (**CORS**) comes in.

When client code like the Angular frontend tries to access an endpoint that is not residing in the same place as itself, the browser will send an `HTTP OPTIONS` request to the same endpoint to check whether the Angular frontend's origin is allowed. It will decide this by the response headers it receives from the `OPTIONS` request, such as `ACCESS-CONTROL-ALLOW-ORIGIN`, `ACCESS-CONTROL-ALLOW-METHODS`, and so on.

In order to support this, the following `CorsFilter` configuration needs to be done in the REST API backend:

```
@Bean
public FilterRegistrationBean corsFilter() {
    UrlBasedCorsConfigurationSource source = new
    UrlBasedCorsConfigurationSource();
    CorsConfiguration config = new CorsConfiguration();
    config.setAllowCredentials(true);
    config.addAllowedOrigin("*");
    config.addAllowedHeader("*");
    config.addAllowedMethod("*");
    source.registerCorsConfiguration("/**", config);
    FilterRegistrationBean bean = new FilterRegistrationBean(new
    CorsFilter(source));
    bean.setOrder(Ordered.HIGHEST_PRECEDENCE);
    return bean;
}
```

The preceding filter allows all origins, all headers, and all methods for any endpoint.

Using Spring Security for authentication and authorization

Spring Security is a widely used project to enable authentication and authorization using many different mechanisms, such as form-based logic, header-based login (Basic), and so on. But, there are more complex scenarios, such as JWT, SSO, and OAuth2, that can also be enabled using Spring Security. In this section, we will look at how to use Spring Security with OAuth2 to configure an authentication and authorization mechanism for the Tweety application.

Understanding OAuth2

OAuth2 is an authorization contract that enables applications to be secured by providing limited access to user accounts that are available an on an HTTP service. Parties involved in an OAuth2 authorization are as follows:

- **Resource**: The protected artifact in the Resource Server
- **Resource Owner**: The owner of the resource being requested
- **Resource Server**: The server that has the resource being requested
- **Authorization Server**: The server that has the responsibility to authorize the request
- **Client**: The application that is trying to access a resource

Let's look at the orchestration flow between these parties in the following flow diagram:

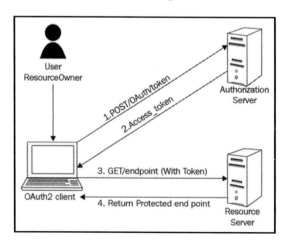

From the preceding diagram, we infer the following:

1. The first step will initiate when the **User** tries to access a resource using an **OAuth2 client**, such as an Angular application in our case.
2. The OAuth2 client will send a **POST /oauth/token** request to the **Authorization Server** with the `grant_type` and credentials.
3. The **Authorization Server** will validate the `grant_type` and credentials, generate an **Access_token**, and return it to the **OAuth2 client**.
4. Then, with the **Access_token** in hand, the **OAuth2 client** can access the protected resource endpoint by sending it as a header to the **Resource Server**.
5. Finally, the **Resource Server** will return the response from the protected resource endpoint.

Setting up dependencies and configuration

Initially, before enabling Spring Security OAuth2, the `dependency` and `configuration` classes need to be specified. The following Maven starter `dependency` needs to be included:

```xml
<dependencies>
    ...
    <dependency>
        <groupId>org.springframework.boot</groupId>
        <artifactId>spring-boot-starter-security</artifactId>
    </dependency>
    ...
    <dependency>
        <groupId>org.springframework.security.oauth</groupId>
        <artifactId>spring-security-oauth2</artifactId>
        <version>2.3.3.RELEASE</version>
    </dependency>
</dependencies>
```

The preceding entries will import all `dependencies` related to Spring Security and Spring Security OAuth2. Now, let's look at the configuration.

Configuring the Resource Server

The following `OAuth2ResourceServerConfigurer` will configure all the necessary filters required to run a Resource Server:

```
@Configuration
@EnableResourceServer
public class OAuth2ResourceServerConfigurer extends
ResourceServerConfigurerAdapter {

}
```

The preceding configuration class extends from `ResourceServerConfigurerAdapter` and is annotated with `@EnableResourceServer` to set up all the necessary filters.

Configuring the Authorization Server

The following `OAuth2AuthorizationServerConfigurer` will configure all the necessary filters required to run an Authorization Server:

```
@Configuration
@EnableAuthorizationServer
public class OAuth2AuthorizationServerConfigurer extends
AuthorizationServerConfigurerAdapter {

    @Autowired
    private AuthenticationManager authenticationManagerBean;

    @Override
    public void configure(ClientDetailsServiceConfigurer clients)
    throws Exception {
        clients.inMemory().withClient("angularjsapp").secret("
        {noop}angularjs123").authorizedGrantTypes("password").
         scopes("read,write");
    }

    @Override
    public void configure(AuthorizationServerEndpointsConfigurer
    endpoints) throws Exception {
        endpoints.authenticationManager(authenticationManagerBean);
    }
}
```

The preceding configuration class extends from
`AuthorizationServerConfigurerAdapter` and is annotated with
`@EnableAuthorizationServer` to set up all the necessary filters. Also, in
the `configure(ClientDetailsServiceConfigurer clients)` method, it configures
in-memory OAuth2 client credentials for accessing the protected `/oauth/token` endpoint,
and in the `configure(AuthorizationServerEndpointsConfigurer endpoints)`
method, it configures `AuthenticationManager`, which is injected.

Configuring web security

The following `WebSecurityConfig` will configure all the necessary filters required to
protect the resource endpoints:

```
@Configuration
@EnableWebSecurity
public class WebSecurityConfig extends WebSecurityConfigurerAdapter {

    @Autowired
    private UserDetailsService userDetailsService;

    @Override
    protected void configure(AuthenticationManagerBuilder auth) throws
     Exception {
        auth.userDetailsService(userDetailsService);
    }

    @Override
    @Bean
    public AuthenticationManager authenticationManagerBean() throws
     Exception {
        return super.authenticationManagerBean();
    }

}
```

In the `configure(AuthenticationManagerBuilder auth)` method, it has
`UserDetailsService` configured using an injected bean `UserDetailsService`, which is
injected. As our `UserService` already implements this interface, it will be injected into
this.

Using an Angular service for OAuth2 authentication and authorization

OAuth2-based security is enabled in the backend API now. Angular can be modified to include code to generate and retrieve an `access_token`, use it to access protected resource endpoints. For this particular reason, an `AuthService` like the following one is used:

```typescript
import {Injectable} from '@angular/core';
import {Router} from '@angular/router';
import { Cookie } from 'ng2-cookies';
import { Http, Response, Headers, RequestOptions } from '@angular/http';
import { Observable } from 'rxjs/Observable';
import 'rxjs/add/operator/catch';
import 'rxjs/add/operator/map';

@Injectable()
export class AuthService {
  constructor(
    private router: Router, private http: Http){}

  getAndSaveAccessToken(loginData){
    let params = new URLSearchParams();
    params.append('username',loginData.username);
    params.append('password',loginData.password);
    params.append('grant_type','password');

    let headers = new Headers({'Content-type': 'application/x-www-form-
      urlencoded; charset=utf-8',
                               'Authorization': 'Basic
    '+btoa("angularjsapp:angularjs123")});
    let options = new RequestOptions({ headers: headers });
     this.http.post('http://localhost:8080/oauth/token',
      params.toString(), options)
    .map(res => res.json())
    .subscribe(
      data => this.saveToken(data),
      err => console.log(err.body)
    );
  }
```

The preceding getAndSaveAccessToken method will access the /oauth/token endpoint with an authorization header with the value 'Basic '+base64encode("angularjsapp:angularjs123"). This will pass the grant_type parameter with the value's password, username, and the password of the user trying to log in. In return, the endpoint will return a JSON with access_token, refresh_token, expires_in, and others. This is depicted in the following code:

```
saveToken(token){
  var expireDate = new Date().getTime() + (1000 * token.expires_in);
  Cookie.set("access_token", token.access_token, expireDate);
  this.router.navigate(['/']);
}
```

The preceding saveToken method will save the retrieved access_token from the preceding method into a browser cookie for later use. Consider the following code:

```
getToken() {
  return Cookie.get('access_token');
}
```

The preceding getToken will return the access_token that's stored as a browser cookie:

```
checkCredentials(){
  if (!Cookie.check('access_token')){
    this.router.navigate(['/login']);
  } else {
   let headers = new Headers({'Content-type': 'application/x-www-form-
   urlencoded; charset=utf-8',
     'Authorization': 'Bearer '+Cookie.get('access_token')});
   let options = new RequestOptions({ headers: headers });
    this.http.get('http://localhost:8080/tweets', options)
        .map(res => res.json())
        .subscribe(
          data => console.log(data),
          err => {
            console.log(err);
            this.router.navigate(['/login']); }
      );
  }
}
```

The preceding `checkCredentials` method will first check whether a browser cookie for the `access_token` is already available; if found, it will check whether it is still valid by sending a dummy request. If either the `access_token` is not found or it is invalid, it will redirect to the login page. This is shown with the following code:

```
logout() {
  Cookie.delete('access_token');
  this.router.navigate(['/login']);
}
```

The preceding `logout` method deletes the `access_token` cookie and navigates to the login page.

In order to use this `AuthService`, there needs to be a login page defined. That is why `/src/app/login.component.ts` and `/src/app/login.component.html` have been created.

The following `LoginComponent` will use it as follows:

```
import { Component } from '@angular/core';
import { AuthService } from './auth.service';
import { NgForm } from '@angular/forms';

@Component({
  selector: 'login-form',
  providers: [AuthService],
  templateUrl: './login.component.html'
})
export class LoginComponent {
    public loginData = {username: "", password: ""};

    constructor(private authService:AuthService) {}

    login(ngForm: NgForm) {
      this.authService.getAndSaveAccessToken(ngForm);
    }
}
```

Use `AuthService` to get and save the access token with the username and password extracted from the following form:

```
<mat-card>
  <form #loginForm="ngForm" (ngSubmit)="login(loginForm.value)">
    <mat-card-header>
      <mat-card-title><h2>Login</h2></mat-card-title>
    </mat-card-header>
    <mat-card-content>
```

```
        <mat-form-field>
          <input matInput placeholder="Username"
          [(ngModel)]="loginData.username" required name="username"
          #username/>
        </mat-form-field>
        <mat-form-field>
          <input type="password" matInput placeholder="Password"
          [(ngModel)]="loginData.password" required name="password"
          #password/>
        </mat-form-field>
      </mat-card-content>
      <mat-card-actions>
        <button mat-raised-button color="primary" type="submit"
            [disabled]="!loginForm.form.valid">Login</button>
      </mat-card-actions>
      <mat-card-footer>
      </mat-card-footer>
    </form>
</mat-card>
```

The form is submitted to the `LoginComponent.login` method, and in `TweetsService` and `UsersService`, the `AuthService.getToken` method is used to submit the `access_token` as a header before sending requests to protected resource endpoints.

Demonstrating Tweety

When everything is built and run, and run, the backend will be able to be accessed using the `http://localhost:8080` URL.

There are several ways to run a Spring Boot application; some of them are mentioned here:

- Running the Spring Boot application main class using an IDE.
- Building a JAR or WAR file using the following Maven command and then running:

```
$ cd backend
$ mvn clean install
$ java -jar target/<package-name>.[jar|war]
```

- Running Tweety using the Spring Boot Maven plugin:

    `$ mvn clean spring-boot:run`

- Building the frontend using the following command:

    `$ npm install`

- Running the frontend using the Angular CLI command that will start the frontend application in `http://localhost:4200`:

    `$ ng serve`

Accessing the login page

Before anything can be done on Tweety, users need to log in. The following is the login page, which will be presented when a user tries to access `http://localhost:4200` initially:

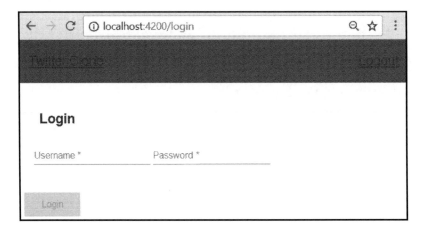

There are two users available by default in the system. One has the username `shazin` and the password `abc123`. The other has the username `shahim` with the password `abc123`.

Accessing the List Tweets page

When logged in as user `shazin`, the following is the page listing tweets:

Accessing the Send Tweet page

Sending `Tweet` can be done using the following page, by clicking the **Tweet** button from the **List Tweets** page:

Building a Twitter Clone with Spring Boot

The `Tweet` body mentions that starting with the @ symbol is possible. This sort of tweet will be visible to the mentioned user. After sending a tweet, it will redirect back to the **List Tweets** page with a newly added tweet:

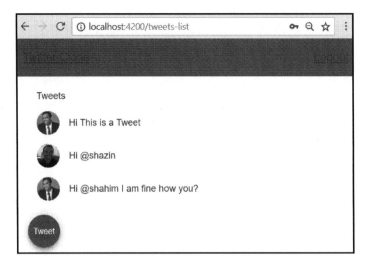

Accessing the User Profile page

By clicking the avatar image in of a tweet, that user's profile page can be accessed as follows:

Finally, logging in as the user shahim lists his tweets and mentions as follows:

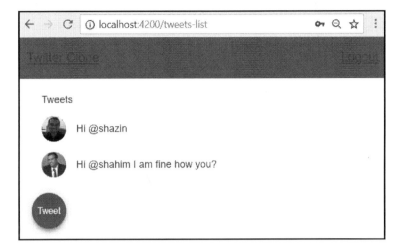

Summary

Congratulations on completing this chapter, where the skills and knowledge required to build a Twitter clone, nicknamed Tweety, were discussed in detail. This chapter started off by explaining what an Angular frontend application is and how the MVVM pattern can benefit both in terms of development and maintenance. We talked about the requirements for the backend and frontend to be developed and used a **Unified Modeling Language** (**UML**) use case diagram to explain the requirements visually.

This chapter also talked about how to understand the domain model of an application, based on requirements (Tweety), and how to use Spring Data JPA to convert those domain models into entities in an H2 database. A UML class diagram was used to explain the domain model in detail.

Furthermore, this chapter explained how to write data repositories for documents using the Spring Data JPA with minimum effort using common CRUD operations. Next, we explained how to write custom query methods in data repositories. We also explained how to encapsulate business logic inside Spring Service components, and some caveats to provide reactive capabilities with non-reactive data layers.

Subsequently, this chapter talked about how to write presentation views to list tweets and create a tweet using the Angular Framework. We also explained how to use Angular Material syntax to develop pages.

Near the end of this chapter, we talked about how to use Spring WebFlux controllers to provide routing and coordinating for different services. Furthermore, we talked about how to protect controller endpoints using Spring Security OAuth2 to allow the proper authentication and authorization of users. This chapter also demonstrated the use of Tweety in detail. Let's learn more about some interesting features of Spring Boot 2.0 in the following chapters.

Questions

Please answer the following questions to see whether you have successfully mastered this chapter:

1. What is MVVM?
2. What is Angular?
3. What is the Angular CLI?
4. What is Angular Material?
5. What is CORS?
6. What is OAuth2?
7. Which parties are involved in OAuth2?

Further reading

In order to improve your knowledge of Angular and Spring Security OAuth2, the following books are recommended, which will be helpful in the coming chapters:

- *Learning Angular, Second Edition*: https://www.packtpub.com/web-development/learning-angular-second-edition
- *OAuth 2.0 Cookbook*: https://www.packtpub.com/virtualization-and-cloud/oauth-20-cookbook

8
Introducing Spring Boot 2.0 Asynchronous

This chapter will introduce the reader to asynchronous application development with Spring Boot 2.0 and explain how it can be used to develop decoupled, scalable application pipelines. We will begin by explaining what asynchronous application development is, and how to achieve asynchronous capabilities. Later, we will explain what Apache Kafka is and how to use Apache Kafka as a middle tier to achieve decoupling and scalability. Furthermore, we will explain what the Quartz Scheduler is and how to use it to achieve scheduled executions. Finally, we will demonstrate an image-resizing application that runs asynchronously and can be scaled.

The following topics will be covered in this chapter:

- Using Spring Kafka for communication
- Using Quartz for scheduling
- Demonstrating Image Resizer

Technical requirements

In order to implement the web application using Spring Boot, the following build tools need to be downloaded and installed:

- To install **Java Development Kit (JDK)** 8, download it from its official page at http://www.oracle.com/technetwork/java/javase/downloads/jdk8-downloads-2133151.html
- To install Maven 3, download it from its official page at https://maven.apache.org/download.cgi

- To install IntelliJ IDEA, download it from its official page at `https://www.jetbrains.com/idea/download/`
- To install Apache Kafka, download it from its official page at `https://kafka.apache.org/downloads`

The source code for this chapter can be found at `https://github.com/PacktPublishing/Spring-Boot-2.0-Projects-Fundamentals-of-Spring-Boot-2.0`, under the `Chapter08` directory.

Getting started

In this section, readers will get an overview of asynchronous applications. The requirements, design, and implementation details will be discussed in brief.

Synchronous applications

Synchronous applications are programs that can process events, requests, and tasks sequentially with an order, and where one needs to finish in order for another to begin:

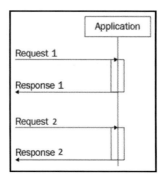

As shown in the preceding diagram, an asynchronous application will process one request after another, meaning any requests coming simultaneously will be forced to wait until the initially received request has finished processing. These sort of applications have their pros and cons, for example, in GUI frameworks such as Java Swing.

Asynchronous applications

Asynchronous applications are programs that can process events, requests, and tasks with time slicing so that one request can be active and run while another one is also but not running:

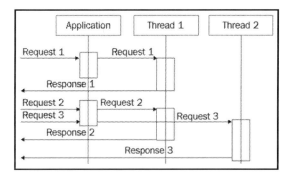

Modern web servers, As shown in the preceding diagram, an asynchronous application can accept and delegate multiple requests threads/processes to keep accepting requests for a certain level. While doing this, the application will usually have a queue to hold received yet unprocessed requests up until threads to process them become available.

The requirement of asynchronous applications

The requirement is to build two asynchronous, decoupled applications that will communicate using a message queue to resize images that are uploaded into a system. This resizing is done so that the same images can be viewed from different devices without a problem.

The use case diagram

The following use case diagram shows the requirements for the Image Resizer:

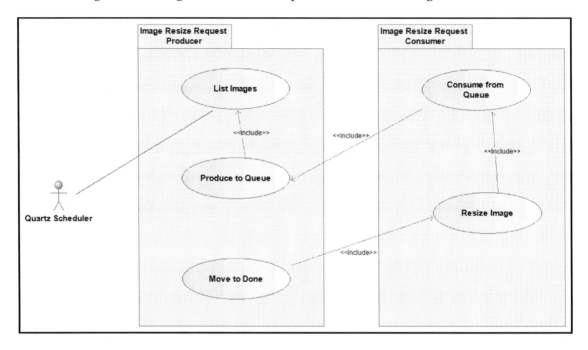

The actor is **Quartz Scheduler** as this application doesn't allow user interactions. It has the following use cases:

- **List Images**: This use case is where images that need to be resized are identified and listed.
- **Produce to Queue**: This use case is where images that need resizing are produced to the message queue to be consumed.
- **Consumer from Queue**: This use case is where an Image Resize Request is consumed from the queue.
- **Resize Image**: This use case is where the actual resizing of an image is taking place. A new image with the given width and height will be created.
- **Move to Done**: This use case is where an original image that was used for resizing is moved to a `Done` location to avoid redoing the resizing on the same image.

The architecture of an image resizing application

The architecture for the image resizing application is as follows:

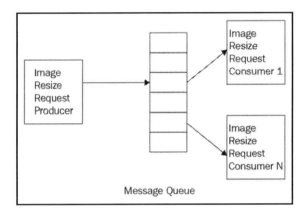

There are three main components involved in image resizing:

- **Image Resize Request Producer**: This component is responsible for finding out which images need to be resized and delegating the image resizing to **Image Resize Request Consumer** by submitting the request to a **Message Queue**. This allows decoupling and scalability.
- **Message Queue**: This component is responsible for queuing Image Resize Requests until they are consumed and processed by the **Image Resize Request Consumer**.
- **Image Resize Request Consumer**: This component is responsible for consuming requests from the **Message Queue** and actually resizing the images based on the width and height specified in the request. There can be more than one consumer.

Using Spring Kafka for communication

As explained in the previous section, an asynchronous application will use some kind of queue to hold received yet unprocessed requests till those requests are processed. For this purpose, an in-memory data structure, such as a Java `ConcurrentLinkedQueue`, can be used. But clearly, this method has limitations, as the queue exists only until the process exists and there is no reliability, durability, fault tolerance, and scalability. This is where message queues come in handy.

There are so many widely used message queues available in both free and open source form as well as proprietary form. The online website of Queues (http://queues.io/) lists many of these widely used queues and can be used as a reference guide to decide the perfect queue for an application.

In the application being developed, however, Apache Kafka will be used as the messaging queue. Let's have a look at what it is and how it benefits as a middle tier for the asynchronous application being developed.

Understanding Apache Kafka

Apache Kafka is a production grade, high performing, scalable, fault-tolerant messaging platform that enables the following three features:

- Publishing and subscribing streams of records similar to a message queue
- Storing streams of records in a fault tolerant, durable way
- Processing streams of records

Apache Kafka consists of the following key concepts:

- Kafka is run on clusters, which span over multiple servers across different data centers
- Kafka cluster stores stream of records categorized into topics
- Each record consists of a key, a value, and a timestamp

A topic in Apache Kafka is the core abstraction of the stream of records. It is multi-subscriber, meaning it can have zero, one, or many subscribers listening for data written to it. Each topic is represented as a partitioned immutable commit log, which is appended and has a unique ID number known as the offset, used to uniquely identify each record in the partition.

Apache Kafka can be used both as a message queue and a publish-subscribe using the same topic concept. When a topic is used as a message queue, even when multiple consumers listen to that topic, only one would be able to consume a message, wherein publish-subscribe models messages can be broadcast to multiple consumers.

In this application, however, we will be using an Apache Kafka topic as a message queue. Also, the Spring Kafka library will be used to enable easy communication with Apache Kafka. Spring Kafka provides templates and listeners to both produce to and consume from Apache Kafka topics easily.

Setting up dependencies and configuration

Initially, before using Apache Kafka for message queue dependency and configuration, a class needs to be specified. The following Maven starter dependency classes need to be included:

```
<dependencies>
    <dependency>
        <groupId>org.springframework.kafka</groupId>
        <artifactId>spring-kafka</artifactId>
        <version>2.1.7.RELEASE</version>
    </dependency>
</dependencies>
```

The preceding entries will import all the dependencies of Spring Kafka, which can be used to produce and consume from Apache Kafka topics.

Configuration for the Image Resize Request Producer

The Image Resize Request Producer is responsible for listing images that need to be resized and submitting those to the Apache Kafka topic. The following is the configuration for the producer:

```
@SpringBootApplication
public class SpringBootAsyncProducerApplication {

    ...

    @Bean
    public ReplyingKafkaTemplate<String, String, String> kafkaTemplate(
    ProducerFactory<String, String> pf,
    KafkaMessageListenerContainer<String, String> replyContainer) {
    return new ReplyingKafkaTemplate<>(pf, replyContainer);
    }

    @Bean
    public KafkaMessageListenerContainer<String, String> replyContainer(
    ConsumerFactory<String, String> cf) {
    ContainerProperties containerProperties = new
  ContainerProperties("asyncReplies");
    containerProperties.setGroupId("async");
    return new KafkaMessageListenerContainer<>(cf, containerProperties);
    }
```

```
@Bean
public NewTopic asyncRequests() {
return new NewTopic("asyncRequests", 10, (short) 2);
}

@Bean
public NewTopic asyncReplies() {
return new NewTopic("asyncReplies", 10, (short) 2);
}

}
```

In the preceding configuration, two Apache Kafka topics by the names `asyncRequests` and `asyncReplies` are created as Spring Beans with a number of replications 10 and replication factor of 2. The `asyncRequests` topic is responsible for sending the message to the consumer and the `asyncReplies` topic is used to get a response back from the consumer as an acknowledgment.

The `kafkaTemplate` Spring Bean is created with an instance of `ReplyingKafkaTemplate` to enable a request-response style of communication.

The `replyContainer` Spring Bean is created to configure the reply received from the `asyncReplies` topic.

Furthermore, the following `ScheduledImageResizeRequestSubmitter` is used to list images and submit those to the Apache Kafka topic to be consumed and processed:

```
@Component
public class ScheduledImageResizeRequestSubmitter {

    private static final Logger LOGGER =
LoggerFactory.getLogger(ScheduledImageResizeRequestSubmitter.class);

    private final ReplyingKafkaTemplate<String, String, String> template;
    private final ObjectMapper objectMapper;
    private final String imagesDirectory;

    public
ScheduledImageResizeRequestSubmitter(ReplyingKafkaTemplate<String, String, String> template, ObjectMapper objectMapper,
@Value("${images.input.directory}") String imagesInputDirectory) {
        this.template = template;
        this.objectMapper = objectMapper;
        this.imagesDirectory = imagesInputDirectory;
    }
```

The preceding constructor injects and initializes `ReplyingKafkaTemplate`, `ObjectMapper`, and the image's input directory path.

The following code uses two reactor `Flux` objects:

```
public void scheduleTaskWithCronExpression() {
 Flux.just(new
File(imagesDirectory).listFiles()).filter(File::isFile).subscribe(
 f -> {
 Flux.just(new Dimension(800, 600), new Dimension(180, 180), new
Dimension(1200, 630)).subscribe(d -> {
 try {
 ImageResizeRequest imageResizeRequest = new ImageResizeRequest((int)
d.getWidth(), (int) d.getHeight(), f.getAbsolutePath());
 ProducerRecord<String, String> record = new
ProducerRecord<>("asyncRequests",
objectMapper.writeValueAsString(imageResizeRequest));
 record.headers().add(new RecordHeader(KafkaHeaders.REPLY_TOPIC,
"asyncReplies".getBytes()));
 RequestReplyFuture<String, String, String> replyFuture =
template.sendAndReceive(record);
 ConsumerRecord<String, String> consumerRecord = replyFuture.get();
 } catch (Exception e) {
 LOGGER.error("Error while sending message", e);
 }
 },
 e -> LOGGER.error("Error while running lambda"),
 () -> f.renameTo(new File(f.getParent() + "/Done", f.getName())));
 }
 );
 }

}
```

The initial one is to list files that are not directories inside of the directory specified by the variable `imagesDirectory`. The value for this variable is configurable and loaded from the `application.properties` file, as follows:

```
images.input.directory=C:\\Users\\Images
```

Then, it will create another `Flux` object to send dimensions so that image resizing can take place. So, it will be one image converted into multiple dimensions. For this scenario, the 800 x 600, 180 x 180, and 1,200 x 630 dimensions are used.

Introducing Spring Boot 2.0 Asynchronous

It will send `ImageResizeRequest` serialized into a JSON so that the consumers can deserialize and use it. `ImageResizeRequest` is shown as follows:

```
@Data
@NoArgsConstructor
@AllArgsConstructor
public class ImageResizeRequest {

    private Integer width;

    private Integer height;

    private String inputFile;

}
```

Finally, the `ImageResizeRequest` JSON will be sent to the `asyncRequests` topic with the `REPLY_TOPIC` header set to `asyncReplies` and sent to the Apache Kafka using the `ReplyingKafkaTemplate` bean.

Configuration for Image Resize Request Consumer

The Image Resize Request Consumer is responsible for listening for messages coming from Apache Kafka topic and doing the actual resizing of the images. Consider the following code:

```
@SpringBootApplication
public class SpringBootAsyncConsumerApplication {

    ...

    @KafkaListener(id="server", topics = "asyncRequests")
    @SendTo
    public String listen(String input) {
        try {
            ImageResizeRequest imageResizeRequest = objectMapper().readValue(input, ImageResizeRequest.class);
            File imageFile = new File(imageResizeRequest.getInputFile());
            String[] nameParts = imageFile.getName().split("\\.");
            BufferedImage image = ImageIO.read(imageFile);
            ImageIO.write(resize(image, imageResizeRequest.getWidth(),
imageResizeRequest.getHeight()), "png", new File(imageFile.getParent() +
"/Done", imageResizeRequest.getWidth() + "x" +
```

```
        imageResizeRequest.getHeight() + "-" + nameParts[0] + ".png"));
        } catch (IOException e) {
            LOGGER.error("Error while processing input {}", input, e);
        }
        return input;
    }

    @Bean
    public NewTopic asyncRequests() {
        return new NewTopic("asyncRequests", 10, (short) 2);
    }

}
```

In the preceding configuration, two Apache Kafka topics by the name `asyncRequests` are created as a Spring Bean with a number of replications `10` and replication factor of `2`. The `listen` method is responsible for consuming requests sent by the producer via the Apache Kafka topic `ayncRequests`. This method is annotated with `@KafkaListener`, which points to the `asyncRequests` topic and also has the `@SendTo` annotation to send a reply back to the `asyncReplies` topic.

Starting Spring Boot applications in a non-web mode

Since both Image Resize Request Producer and Image Resize Request Consumer need to run as console applications, which shouldn't run inside a web container, such as Tomcat, Jetty, a slightly different bootstrapping code, is used in the main methods, as follows:

```
public static void main(String... args) {
    new SpringApplicationBuilder(ConfigClass.class).web(WebApplicationType.NONE).build().run(args);
}
```

In the preceding code, the `SpringApplicationBuilder` builder class is used to non-web the Spring Boot application. `ConfigClass.class` needs to be replaced with the actual configuration class that defines the beans. Finally, it is built and run.

Using Quartz for scheduling

As explained in the previous sections, the Image Resize Request Producer is supposed to run on schedule so that the Image Resize Request Consumers can do the actual work of resizing. In order to achieve this, Quartz Scheduler is used.

Understanding Quartz

Quartz is a fully open source, high-performing scheduling framework that can be easily integrated with Java applications of any sort. Quartz can be used to schedule simple as well as complex jobs, which may be scaled to hundreds if not thousands of jobs. The specialty of Quartz is that it also supports enterprise-level features, such as transactional jobs and clustering.

Setting up dependencies and configuration

The Image Resize Request Producer is responsible for listing images and submitting to Apache Kafka periodically. For this reason, `spring-boot-starter-quartz` is used as follows:

```
<dependencies>
    ...
    <dependency>
        <groupId>org.springframework.boot</groupId>
        <artifactId>spring-boot-starter-quartz</artifactId>
    </dependency>
</dependencies>
```

The preceding Maven `dependency` will import all the required dependencies for Quartz as well as auto-configuration.

Configuration for Quartz scheduling

In order to periodically submit an Image Resize Request, the Image Resize Request Producer must be able to run at any given interval. For this purpose, CRON expressions are used, which can be specified in a variety of ways (for example, run every Monday at 12.00 a.m., run every day at 2.00 p.m, and so on). The following CRON expression to run every minute is configured as a property in the `application.properties` file:

```
images.cron=0 * * * * ?
```

In the preceding CRON expression 0 represents seconds, first * represents minutes, second * represents hours, third * represents day of month, fourth * represents month, fifth * represents day of week and ? represents the year. CRON expressions can be very simple of very complex so use Oracle Documentation of CRON to learn more. The following configuration is used in the `SpringBootAsyncProducerApplication` class to enable Quartz scheduling:

```
@Bean MethodInvokingJobDetailFactoryBean
methodInvokingJobDetailFactoryBean(ScheduledImageResizeRequestSubmitter
scheduledImageResizeRequestSubmitter) {
    MethodInvokingJobDetailFactoryBean methodInvokingJobDetailFactoryBean =
new MethodInvokingJobDetailFactoryBean();
methodInvokingJobDetailFactoryBean.setTargetObject(scheduledImageResizeRequ
estSubmitter);
methodInvokingJobDetailFactoryBean.setTargetMethod("scheduleTaskWithCronExp
ression");

    return methodInvokingJobDetailFactoryBean;
}

@Bean
public CronTriggerFactoryBean trigger(JobDetail job,
@Value("${images.cron}") String imagesCron) {
    CronTriggerFactoryBean cronTriggerFactoryBean = new
CronTriggerFactoryBean();
    cronTriggerFactoryBean.setCronExpression(imagesCron);
    cronTriggerFactoryBean.setJobDetail(job);
    return cronTriggerFactoryBean;
}
```

The `methodInvokingJobDetailFactoryBean` **bean defines** `JobDetail`, **which uses** `ScheduledImageResizeRequestSubmitter`, **which are defined earlier, to specify** `targetObject` **as well as the** `targetMethod` **with the** `scheduleTaskWithCronExpression` **method, which needs to run when the CRON expression triggers.**

The `trigger` **bean defines** `CronTrigger` **using** `CronTriggerFactoryBean`, **which takes in the property** `images.cron` **from** `application.properties` **to configure it. The** `JobDetail` **created inside** `methodInvokingJobDetailFactoryBean` **will be invoked when this CRON trigger is fired.**

Demonstrating Image Resizer

When everything is put together, the following commands can be used to start Apache Kafka, Image Resize Request Producer, and Image Resize Request Consumer.

There are several ways to run a Spring Boot application, and some of them are mentioned here:

- Running the Spring Boot application main class using an IDE
- Building a JAR or WAR file using the following Maven command and then running

Building all dependencies

The following command can be used to build all the dependencies from the root directory `spring-boot-2-async`:

```
$ mvn clean install
```

Running Apache Kafka

Apache Kafka needs to be running before producers and consumers can start communicating using it. Apache Kafka makes use of Apache ZooKeeper for maintaining configuration information, naming, providing distributed synchronization, and providing group services in a decentralized manner. The default Apache Kafka packaging downloaded in the technical requirements section will have Apache ZooKeeper bundled with it. The following command can be used to start Apache ZooKeeper with its default configuration.

To run Apache ZooKeeper on Linux/Unix, we use the following command:

```
$ <Absolute Path To Kafka>/bin/zookeeper-server-start.sh ../config/zookeeper.properties
```

Running Apache ZooKeeper on Windows

To run Apache ZooKeeper on Windows, we use the following commands:

```
$ <Absolute Path To Kafka>/bin/windows/zookeeper-server-start.sh ../../config/zookeeper.properties
```

Running Apache Kafka on Linux/Unix

To run Apache Kafka on Linux/Unix, we use the following commands:

```
$ <Absolute Path To Kafka>/bin/kafka-server-start.sh
../config/server.properties
```

Running Apache Kafka on Windows

To run Apache Kafka on Windows, we use the following commands:

```
$ <Absolute Path To Kafka>/bin/windows/kafka-server-start.sh
../../config/server.properties
```

Running Image Resize Request Consumer

After building everything, the following commands can be used to run the Image Resize Request Consumer:

```
$ cd spring-boot-2-async-consumer
$ mvn spring-boot:run
```

Running Image Resize Request Producer

Before running, the producer `src/main/resources/application.properties` will need to be edited to point to a directory in the file system where images will be placed. This is done with the following code:

```
images.input.directory=<Absolute Path To Images Directory>
```

Also, a directory by the name `Done` needs to created inside that directory:

```
$ cd <Absolute Path To Images Directory>
$ mkdir Done
```

After building everything, the following commands can be used to run the Image Resize Request Producer:

```
$ cd ../spring-boot-2-async-consumer
$ mvn spring-boot:run
```

Introducing Spring Boot 2.0 Asynchronous

The following screenshot shows an image in the directory configured by `images.input.directory` in the `application.properties` file:

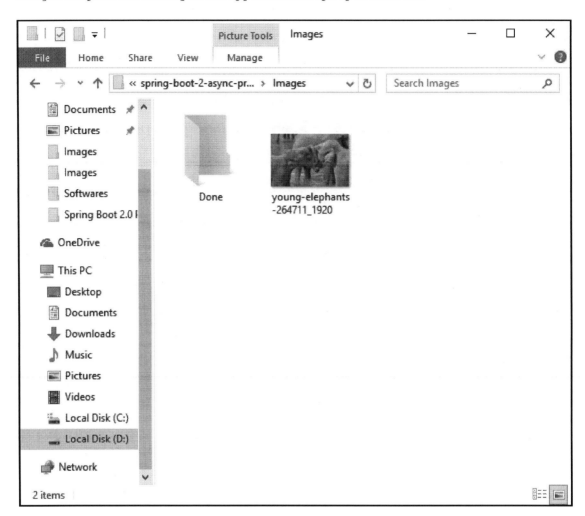

Chapter 8

The following screenshot shows resized images in the `Done` directory, which is inside the same directory specified in `images.input.directory`, along with the original image also:

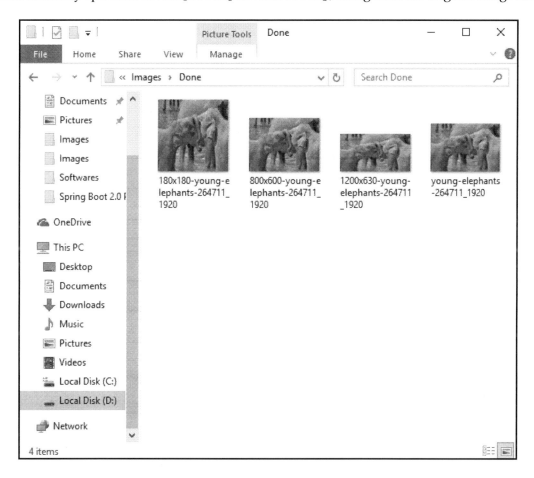

The dimensions are prefixed for easier identification of the images. The original image is the courtesy of https://pixabay.com/en/young-elephants-baby-elephants-264711/.

Summary

Congratulations on completing this chapter, where the skills and knowledge required to build an asynchronous, scalable producer-consumer application were discussed. This chapter started off by explaining what a synchronous application is and what an asynchronous application is.

This chapter also talked about how asynchronous applications can enable decoupling and scalability by using an intermediate queue. We discussed in-memory queues provided out of the box by Java as well as advanced queues such as Apache Kafka that enable fault tolerance, clustering, and scalability while giving high performance.

Furthermore, we explained how to write producers and consumers for Apache Kafka using the Spring Kafka library, which enables acknowledgment of message sending via replies. Spring Kafka does a lot of heavy lifting with auto-configuration so that it is easier to develop.

Subsequently, this chapter talked about Quartz and how to use it schedule Image Resize Request Producer to run periodically to pick up images that need to be resized and queue those in the Apache Kafka topic.

Eventually, this chapter talked about how to run Zookeeper and Apache Kafka and then demonstrated the use of Image Resize Request Producer and Image Resize Request Consumer running periodically and resizing images. We'll learn more on some interesting features of Spring Boot 2.0 in the upcoming chapters.

Questions

Please answer the following questions to see whether you have successfully mastered this chapter:

1. How do you start a Spring Boot application in non-web mode?
2. What is a synchronous application?
3. What is an asynchronous application?
4. What is a message queue?
5. What is Apache Kafka?
6. What is Spring Kafka?
7. What is Quartz?

Further reading

In order to improve your knowledge of Apache Kafka and Spring Boot 2.0, the following books are recommended to be read, as they will be helpful in the coming chapters:

- *Apache Kafka 1.0 Cookbook* - `https://www.packtpub.com/big-data-and-business-intelligence/apache-kafka-10-cookbook`
- *Mastering Spring Boot 2.0* - `https://www.packtpub.com/application-development/mastering-spring-boot-20`

9
Building an Asynchronous Email Formatter

This chapter will introduce the reader to the details of how to build an Asynchronous Email Formatter, using Spring Boot 2 as the backend development framework and Apache Kafka as a message queue. We will explain how to use JPA as the persistence layer, which is a widely used data source. Subsequently, we will use Apache FreeMarker to create the email templates and show you how to use placeholders to provide dynamic data to email templates. Furthermore, we will use Spring Web MVC and Spring Security to implement controllers and provide authentication and authorization.

The following topics will be covered in this chapter:

- Using Spring Data JPA for persistence
- Using Apache FreeMarker for templates
- Using Spring Kafka for communication
- Using Spring Web MVC for REST controller
- Using Spring Security for authentication and authorization
- Demonstrating the Email Formatter

Technical requirements

In order to implement the web application using Spring Boot, the following build tools need to be downloaded and installed:

- To install **Java Development Kit (JDK)** 8, download it from its official page at http://www.oracle.com/technetwork/java/javase/downloads/jdk8-downloads-2133151.html

Building an Asynchronous Email Formatter

- To install Maven 3, download it from its official page at `https://maven.apache.org/download.cgi`
- To install IntelliJ IDEA, download it from its official page at `https://www.jetbrains.com/idea/download/`
- To install **Spring Tool Suite (STS)**, download it from its official page at `https://spring.io/tools`
- To install Apache Kafka, download it from its official page at `https://kafka.apache.org/downloads`

The source code for this chapter can be found at `https://github.com/PacktPublishing/Spring-Boot-2.0-Projects-Fundamentals-of-Spring-Boot-2.0`, under the `Chapter09` directory.

Getting started

In this section, the readers will get an overview of the Asynchronous Email Formatter being developed. The requirements, design, and implementation details will be discussed in brief.

Why Email Formatter is useful

Email formatting is required whenever we need to send emails to users based on an event such as User Registration, User Password Reset, and so on. This means that Email Formatter should be able to work independently of the main application, as email sending is a blocking task that may take a long time to execute. This is where the asynchronous nature of using a message queue comes in handy. In this chapter, however, we will be looking at a User Password Reset workflow that sends an auto-generated password on request by a user. But any other workflow, such as User Registration, can also be implemented with minor changes.

The use case diagram

The following use case diagram shows the requirement for Email Formatter:

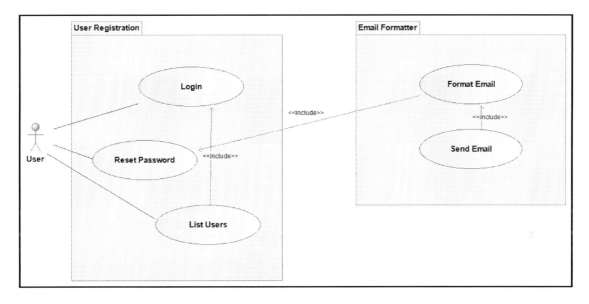

The actor is the **User** of the Tweety. It has the following use cases:

- **Login**: This use case is required to authenticate users so that each user can be uniquely identified to allow only authenticated users to perform actions.
- **List Users**: This use case is where a user can list all the usernames of available users. It requires the user to be authenticated.
- **Reset Password**: This use case is where a user can request to reset his/her password.
- **Format Email**: This use case is where, based on a **Reset Password** request, an email will be formatted and filled with the relevant user details.
- **Send Email**: This use case is where an actual **Reset Password** email is sent to the user's email address.

The architecture of the Email Formatter application

The architecture for the Email Formatter application is as follows:

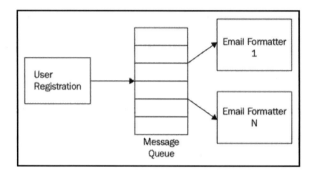

There are three main components involved in image resizing:

- **User Registration**: This component is responsible for accepting reset password requests from users and submitting the request to a **Message Queue**. This allows decoupling and scalability.
- **Message Queue**: This component is responsible for queuing reset password requests until they are consumed and processed by the Email Formatter consumers.
- **Email Formatter Consumer**: This component is responsible for consuming requests from the **Message Queue** and actually doing the formatting and sending of the emails to the recipient. There can be more than one consumer.

Using Spring Data JPA for persistence

This section will introduce JPA and how to use Spring Data JPA repositories to provide **Create, Retrieve, Update, and Delete (CRUD)** operations on JPA easily.

Class diagram for the domain model

Since the domain model is the most important component of an application, this section will go over designing it before we go any further. The following is the simple class diagram for this web service:

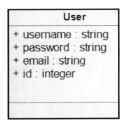

There is only one main domain model, as shown in the preceding diagram. This is explained as follows:

User: This is the main domain model, which will store user details such as **username**, **password**, **email**, and **id**.

Implementation of the domain model using JPA annotations

This section will explain the details of how to configure and use Spring Data JPA with an embedded database with the domain model designed in the previous section.

Setting up dependencies and the configuration class

Initially, before implementing the domain model, the `dependencies` and `configuration` classes need to be specified. The following Maven starter `dependency` and H2 database dependency need to be included:

```
<dependencies>
    ...
    <dependency>
        <groupId>org.springframework.boot</groupId>
        <artifactId>spring-boot-starter-data-jpa</artifactId>
    </dependency>

    <dependency>
        <groupId>com.h2database</groupId>
```

[279]

```
        <artifactId>h2</artifactId>
        <version>1.4.196</version>
    </dependency>
</dependencies>
```

The following `RepoConfig` is used:

```
@Configuration
@EnableJpaRepositories(basePackages =
"com.packtpub.spring.boot.email.formatter.model")
@EnableTransactionManagement
@EntityScan(basePackages =
"com.packtpub.spring.boot.email.formatter.model.domain")
public class RepoConfig {
}
```

The `@EnableJpaRepositories` annotation is used to set the base package where repositories are available. `@EnableTransactionManagement` is used to enable the Spring JPA Transaction Manager. The `@EntityScan` annotation is used to set the base package where domain entities are available.

Implementing the domain model

Implementing the domain model `User` using JPA annotations will look like the following:

```
@Entity
@Data
@NoArgsConstructor
@AllArgsConstructor
public class User {

    @Id
    @GeneratedValue
    private Integer id;

    @Column(unique = true)
    private String username;

    @Column(unique = true)
    private String email;

    private String password;

}
```

In the preceding code, the `@Entity` annotation is used to mark the `User` class as a JPA entity so that it will be eligible to be used in the JPA persistence environment. The `@Data` annotation is from the Lombok library and is used to mark a POJO as a class that will hold data. This means `getters`, `setters`, the `equals` method, the `hashCode` method, and the `toString` method will be generated for that class.

The `@Id` annotation marks the ID property as the identity field of the entity, whereas `@GeneratedValue` marks it as an auto-generated value. The newly added annotations, which are also from the Lombok library, are `@AllArgsConstructor`, which will generate a constructor with the `id`, `username`, `password`, properties, and `@NoArgsConstructor`, which will generate a default constructor.

Implementation of Spring Data JPA repositories

With the domain model implemented successfully, `JpaRepository` for those can be implemented using Spring Data JPA. The specialty here is that there is no need to implement anything. Just writing an interface that extends from the `JpaRepository` interface will be sufficient to expose methods to find one, find all, save, delete, and so on. The following code shows `UserRepository`:

```
public interface UserRepository extends JpaRepository<User, Integer> {

    User findByEmail(String email);

    User findByUsername(String username);

}
```

In the preceding code, there are methods named `findByUsername` and `findByEmail` where `username` and `email` are properties of the `User` class.

Using Services to encapsulate business logic

It is a good practice to encapsulate business logic inside `Service` methods so that controllers and repositories are loosely coupled. The following `Service` is written to encapsulate the business logic for `User`:

```
Service
@Transactional(readOnly = true)
public class UserService implements UserDetailsService {
```

```java
        private final UserRepository userRepository;

        public UserService(UserRepository userRepository) {
            this.userRepository = userRepository;
        }

        public User getByEmail(String email) {
            return userRepository.findByEmail(email);
        }

        @Override
        public UserDetails loadUserByUsername(String username) throws
    UsernameNotFoundException {
            User user = userRepository.findByUsername(username);

            if (user == null) {
                throw new UsernameNotFoundException(username);
            }

            return new
    org.springframework.security.core.userdetails.User(username,
    user.getPassword(), Arrays.asList(new
    SimpleGrantedAuthority("ROLE_USER")));
        }

        @Transactional(rollbackFor = Exception.class)
        public User save(User user) {
            return userRepository.save(user);
        }

        public List<User> getAll() {
            return userRepository.findAll();
        }
    }
```

`UserService` also implements the Spring Security `UserDetailsService` interface in addition to supporting `User` detail loading. The `save` method saves a `User` instance in the database, `getByEmail` retrieves the `User` by email, and the `getAll` method retrieves all the users. More on this will be discussed in the *Using Spring Security for authentication and authorization* section of this chapter.

Using Apache FreeMarker for templates

Apache FreeMarker is used to generate the HTML body that will be embedded in the body of the email that will be sent when reset password requests are received. The following template, `src/resources/templates/reset_password_en.html`, is used:

```html
<!doctype html>
<html>
<head>
    <meta name="viewport" content="width=device-width" />
    <meta http-equiv="Content-Type" content="text/html; charset=UTF-8" />
    <title>Reset Password</title>
    <style>
        /** Styling Code **/
    </style>
</head>
<body class="">
<table border="0" cellpadding="0" cellspacing="0" class="body">
    <tr>
        <td> </td>
        <td class="container">
            <div class="content">

                <!-- START CENTERED WHITE CONTAINER -->
                <span class="preheader">This email is sent to reset the password of ${USERNAME}.</span>
                <table class="main">

                    <!-- START MAIN CONTENT AREA -->
                    <tr>
                        <td class="wrapper">
                            <table border="0" cellpadding="0" cellspacing="0">
                                <tr>
                                    <td>
                                        <p>Hi ${USERNAME},</p>
                                        <p>Your password has been reset. Your new password is following.</p>
                                        <table border="0" cellpadding="0" cellspacing="0" class="btn btn-primary">
                                            <tbody>
                                            <tr>
                                                <td align="left">
                                                    <table border="0" cellpadding="0" cellspacing="0">
                                                        <tbody>
                                                        <tr>
```

```html
                    <td>${NEW_PASSWORD}</td>
                                                                        </tr>
                                                                    </tbody>
                                                                </table>
                                                            </td>
                                                        </tr>
                                                    </tbody>
                                                </table>
                                                <p>Please re-login and change the
password so that it will be your secret.</p>
                                                <p>Good luck! Hope it works.</p>
                                            </td>
                                        </tr>
                                    </table>
                                </td>
                            </tr>

                            <!-- END MAIN CONTENT AREA -->
                        </table>

                        <!-- START FOOTER -->
                        <div class="footer">
                            <table border="0" cellpadding="0" cellspacing="0">
                                <tr>
                                    <td class="content-block">
                                        <span class="apple-
link">Packtpub.com</span>
                                    </td>
                                </tr>
                                <tr>
                                    <td class="content-block powered-by">
                                        Powered by Shazin Sadakath.
                                    </td>
                                </tr>
                            </table>
                        </div>
                        <!-- END FOOTER -->

                        <!-- END CENTERED WHITE CONTAINER -->
                    </div>
                </td>
                <td> </td>
            </tr>
        </table>
    </body>
</html>
```

This is a standard HTML page with the custom placeholders `${USERNAME}` and `${NEW_PASSWORD}`, which will be populated by the following `EmailTemplateService`:

```
@Service
public class EmailTemplateService {

    private final Configuration configuration;

    public EmailTemplateService(Configuration configuration) {
        this.configuration = configuration;
    }

    public String getResetPasswordEmail(Map<String, Object> data, String templateName) throws IOException, TemplateException {
        Template template = configuration.getTemplate(templateName);
        return FreeMarkerTemplateUtils.processTemplateIntoString(template, data);
    }

}
```

When the `getResetPasswordEmail` method is called with `Map` of data and a template name, it will load the template and replace the placeholders with the actual value from `Map`. The template is derived from https://github.com/leemunroe/responsive-html-email-template.

Using Spring Kafka for communication

Apache Kafka is a production grade, high performing, scalable, fault-tolerant messaging platform. In the application, however, we will be using the Apache Kafka topic as a message queue. Also, the Spring Kafka library will be used to enable easy communication with Apache Kafka. Spring Kafka provides the ability for templates and listeners to both produce to and consumes from Apache Kafka topics easily.

Setting up dependencies and the configuration class

Initially, before using Apache Kafka for message queue dependency and configuration, the class needs to be specified. The following Maven starter `dependency` needs to be included:

```xml
<dependencies>
   <dependency>
      <groupId>org.springframework.kafka</groupId>
      <artifactId>spring-kafka</artifactId>
      <version>2.1.7.RELEASE</version>
   </dependency>
</dependencies>
```

The preceding entries will import all the `dependencies` of Spring Kafka, which can be used to produce to and consume from Apache Kafka topics.

Configuration for User Registration

The configuration for User Registration is as follows:

```java
@SpringBootApplication
@Import(RepoConfig.class)
public class SpringBootUserRegistrationApplication {
    ...

    @Bean
    public KafkaTemplate<String, String> kafkaTemplate(
            ProducerFactory<String, String> pf) {
        return new KafkaTemplate<>(pf);
    }

    @Bean
    public NewTopic resetPasswordRequests() {
        return new NewTopic("resetPasswordRequests", 10, (short) 2);
    }

}
```

In the preceding configuration, an Apache Kafka topic by the name `resetPasswordRequests` is created as a Spring Bean with a number of replications `10` and replication factor of `2`. The `resetPasswordRequests` topic is responsible for sending the message to the consumer.

The kafkaTemplate Spring Bean is created with an instance of KafkaTemplate to enable communication.

Furthermore, the following AsyncService is used to produce reset password requests:

```
@Service
@Transactional(readOnly = true)
public class AsyncService {

    private final KafkaTemplate<String, String> kafkaTemplate;
    private final UserService userService;
    private final ObjectMapper objectMapper;
    private final PasswordEncoder passwordEncoder;


    public AsyncService(KafkaTemplate<String, String> kafkaTemplate, UserService userService, ObjectMapper objectMapper, PasswordEncoder passwordEncoder) {
        this.kafkaTemplate = kafkaTemplate;
        this.userService = userService;
        this.objectMapper = objectMapper;
        this.passwordEncoder = passwordEncoder;
    }

    @Transactional(rollbackFor = Exception.class)
    public void sendResetPassword(String email) throws IOException {
        User user = userService.getByEmail(email);

        if (user != null) {
            ResetPasswordRequest resetPasswordRequest = new ResetPasswordRequest();
            resetPasswordRequest.setEmail(user.getEmail());

            RandomStringGenerator generator = new RandomStringGenerator.Builder()
                    .withinRange('a', 'z').build();
            String newPassword = generator.generate(10);
            resetPasswordRequest.setNewPassword(newPassword);
            resetPasswordRequest.setUsername(user.getUsername());
            ProducerRecord<String, String> record = new ProducerRecord<>("resetPasswordRequests", objectMapper.writeValueAsString(resetPasswordRequest));
            kafkaTemplate.send(record);

            user.setPassword(passwordEncoder.encode(newPassword));
            userService.save(user);
```

```
            }
        }
    }
```

The `sendResetPassword` method will find the `User` by email, and if found will generate a `10` digit random password, send a JSON message to the `resetPasswordRequests` Apache Kafka topic, and update the user password with the generated password before saving `User`.

Configuration for the Email Formatter consumer

The Email Formatter consumer is responsible for listening for messages coming from the Apache Kafka topic and doing the actual formatting and sending of emails. Consider the following code:

```
@SpringBootApplication
public class SpringBootEmailFormatter {

    private static final Logger LOGGER =
LoggerFactory.getLogger(SpringBootEmailFormatterConsumerApplication.class);

    @Autowired
    private EmailSenderService emailSenderService;

    @KafkaListener(id="resetPasswordRequests", topics =
"resetPasswordRequests")
    public String listen(String in) {
        try {
            ResetPasswordRequest resetPasswordRequest =
objectMapper().readValue(in, ResetPasswordRequest.class);
emailSenderService.sendResetPasswordEmail(resetPasswordRequest);
        } catch (IOException e) {
            LOGGER.error("Error while sending Reset Password Email", e);
        }
        return in;
    }

    @Bean
    public NewTopic resetPasswordRequests() {
        return new NewTopic("resetPasswordRequests", 10, (short) 2);
    }

}
```

Chapter 9

In the preceding configuration, one Apache Kafka topic by the name of `resetPasswordRequests` is created as a Spring Bean with a number of replications `10` and replication factor of `2`. The `listen` method is responsible for consuming requests sent by the producer via the Apache Kafka topic `resetPasswordRequests`. This method is annotated with `@KafkaListener`, which points to the `resetPasswordRequests` topic.

Furthermore, the following `EmailSenderService` is used to format and send actual emails:

```
@Service
public class EmailSenderService {

    private static final Logger LOGGER = 
LoggerFactory.getLogger(EmailTemplateService.class);

    public static final String RESET_PASSWORD_EN_HTML = 
"reset_password_en.html";

    private final EmailTemplateService emailTemplateService;
    private final JavaMailSender javaMailSender;

    public EmailSenderService(EmailTemplateService emailTemplateService, 
JavaMailSender javaMailSender) {
        this.emailTemplateService = emailTemplateService;
        this.javaMailSender = javaMailSender;
    }

    public boolean sendResetPasswordEmail(ResetPasswordRequest 
resetPasswordRequest) {
        boolean sent = false;
        try {
            Map<String, Object> data = new LinkedHashMap<>();
            data.put("USERNAME", resetPasswordRequest.getUsername());
            data.put("NEW_PASSWORD", 
resetPasswordRequest.getNewPassword());

            String resetPasswordEmailContent = 
emailTemplateService.getResetPasswordEmail(data, RESET_PASSWORD_EN_HTML);

            MimeMessage mimeMessage = javaMailSender.createMimeMessage();
            MimeMessageHelper mimeMessageHelper = new 
MimeMessageHelper(mimeMessage);

            mimeMessageHelper.setTo(resetPasswordRequest.getEmail());
            mimeMessageHelper.setText(resetPasswordEmailContent, true);
            mimeMessageHelper.setSubject("Password Reset");
```

```
            javaMailSender.send(mimeMessage);
            sent = true;
        } catch (Exception e) {
            LOGGER.error("Error while sending email", e);
        }
        return sent;
    }
}
```

`sendResetPasswordEmail` first retrieves the required data for email formatting from `ResetPasswordRequest` and will create a `Map` of the data to be submitted to `EmailTemplateService.getResetPasswordEmail`, along with the template file named `reset_password_en.html`, which is available inside the `src/resources/templates` directory. Then, it will use `JavaMailSender` to actually send the email.

Configuring Java Mail

Initially, before using the Java Mail queue, the `dependency` and `configuration` classes need to be specified. The following Maven starter `dependency` needs to be included:

```
<dependencies>
    ...
    <dependency>
        <groupId>org.springframework.boot</groupId>
        <artifactId>spring-boot-starter-mail</artifactId>
    </dependency>
</dependencies>
```

The following configuration properties also need to be added to the `application.properties` file:

```
spring.mail.host=localhost
spring.mail.port=25
spring.mail.username=
spring.mail.password=
```

The `spring.mail.host` property will point to `localhost`, while `spring.mail.port` will point to the default SMTP port 25. The `spring.mail.username` and `spring.mail.password` are intentionally left blank because there won't be any authentication for SMTP server. These can be filled, if there are credentials for the SMTP server.

Using Spring Web MVC for the REST controller

Controllers are the integration point between the model and view in the MVC paradigm. They act like the glue that binds together everything while taking care of business logic execution and routing. The following Maven starter `dependency` needs to be added to enable Spring Web MVC:

```
<dependencies>
    ...
    <dependency>
        <groupId>org.springframework.boot</groupId>
        <artifactId>spring-boot-starter-web</artifactId>
    </dependency>
</dependencies>
```

The preceding `dependency` will import the servlet, Spring, and Tomcat dependencies to enable the successful writing of servlet-based web applications using Spring.

Implementation of controller annotations

The following is `UserController`, which enables reset password for `User` and the listing of users in the `User Registration` module:

```
@RestController
@RequestMapping("/users")
public class UserController {

    private final AsyncService asyncService;
    private final UserService userService;

    public UserController(AsyncService asyncService, UserService
userService) {
        this.asyncService = asyncService;
        this.userService = userService;
    }

    @GetMapping
    public List<String> listUsers() {
        return userService.getAll().stream().map(u ->
u.getEmail()).collect(Collectors.toList());
    }

    @RequestMapping("/reset-password/{email}")
```

```
    @ResponseStatus(HttpStatus.OK)
    public void resetPassword(@PathVariable("email") String email) throws Exception {
        asyncService.sendResetPassword(email);
    }

}
```

The preceding controller is mapped to the URL `"/users"` and injects `AsyncService` and `UserService`. The `listUsers` method is mapped to the `GET` request, which will call the `UserService.getAll()` method to return all the users and then use the Stream API to list the email addresses of users returned.

The `resetPassword` method is mapped to the URL `"/users/reset-password/{email}"` with the `GET` request, which will call the `AsyncService.sendResetPassword` method with the passed in an email address.

Using Spring Security for authentication and authorization

Spring Security is widely used to enable authentication and authorization, using many different mechanisms such as form-based logic, header-based login (Basic), and so on. In this application, we will be protecting the `User Registration` microservice. Consider the following code:

```
<dependencies>
    ...
    <dependency>
        <groupId>org.springframework.boot</groupId>
        <artifactId>spring-boot-starter-security</artifactId>
    </dependency>
    ...
</dependencies>
```

The preceding entries will import all the `dependencies` related to Spring Security. Now, let's look at the configuration:

```
@Configuration
@EnableWebSecurity
public class SecurityConfig extends WebSecurityConfigurerAdapter {

    @Bean
    public PasswordEncoder passwordEncoder() {
```

```
        return new SCryptPasswordEncoder();
    }

    @Override
    public void configure(WebSecurity web) throws Exception {
        web.ignoring().antMatchers("/users/reset-password/**");
    }

    @Override
    protected void configure(HttpSecurity http) throws Exception {
http.csrf().disable().authorizeRequests().antMatchers("/users**").hasRole("
USER").and().formLogin().permitAll();
    }
}
```

In the `configure(WebSecurity web)` method, it configures the ignore `"/users/reset-password"` from Spring Security. In the `configure(HttpSecurity http)` method, it configures a `formLogin()` method and protects the `"/users"` URL to have the role `USER` to access it. `@EnableWebSecurity` will enable all the other configurations required for Spring Security. Also, it creates `ScryptPasswordEncoder` as the `passwordEncoder` bean so that it will be used to encode passwords.

Demonstrating Email Formatter

When everything is put together, the following commands can be used to start Apache Kafka, the `User Registration` microservice, and the Email Formatter consumers.

There are several ways to run a Spring Boot application, and some of them are mentioned here:

- Running the Spring Boot application main class using an IDE
- Building a JAR or WAR file using the following Maven command and then running it

Building all dependencies

The following command can be used to build all the dependencies from the root directory `spring-boot-2-email-formatter`:

```
$ mvn clean install
```

Running Apache Kafka

Apache Kafka needs to be running before producers and consumers can start communicating using it. Apache Kafka makes use of Apache ZooKeeper for maintaining configuration information, naming, providing distributed synchronization, and providing group services in a decentralized manner. The default Apache Kafka packaging downloaded in the technical requirements section will have Apache ZooKeeper bundled with it. The following command can be used to start Apache ZooKeeper with its default configuration.

To run Apache ZooKeeper on Linux/Unix, we use the following command:

```
$ <Absolute Path To Kafka>/bin/zookeeper-server-start.sh
../config/zookeeper.properties
```

Running Apache ZooKeeper on Windows

To run Apache ZooKeeper on Windows, we use the following commands:

```
$ <Absolute Path To Kafka>/bin/windows/zookeeper-server-start.sh
../../config/zookeeper.properties
```

Running Apache Kafka on Linux/Unix

To run Apache Kafka on Linux/Unix, we use the following commands:

```
$ <Absolute Path To Kafka>/bin/kafka-server-start.sh
../config/server.properties
```

Running Apache Kafka on Windows

To run Apache Kafka on Windows, we use the following commands:

```
$ <Absolute Path To Kafka>/bin/windows/kafka-server-start.sh
../../config/server.properties
```

Running SMTP server

Since the Email Formatter consumer is supposed to format and send emails, we will be using a dummy **Simple Mail Transfer Protocol** (**SMTP**) server, as it is just for demonstration purposes. For this, fakeSMTP is used, which can be downloaded from http://nilhcem.com/FakeSMTP/download.html. After downloading and unzipping it, the following command can be used to run fakeSMTP:

```
$ java -jar fakeSMTP-<version>.jar
```

This will open the following window:

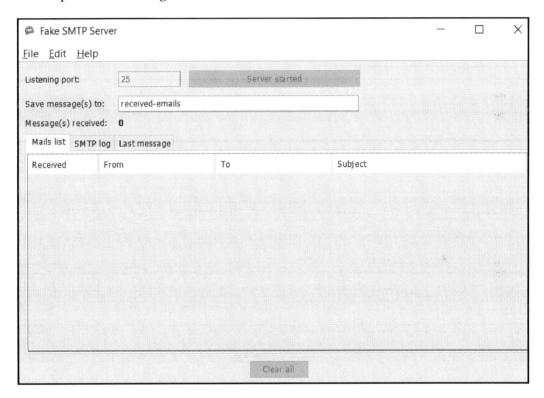

Clicking on the **Start Server** button will make it start to listen for SMTP requests.

Running the Email Formatter consumer

After building everything, the following commands can be used to run the Email Formatter consumer:

```
$ cd spring-boot-2-email-formatter-consumer
$ mvn spring-boot:run
```

Running the User Registration microservice

After building everything, the following commands can be used to run the `User Registration` microservice:

```
$ cd spring-boot-2-user-registration
$ mvn spring-boot:run
```

After starting the `User Registration` microservice, an HTTP `GET` request can be sent to the `http://localhost:8080/users/reset-password` URL with the email as follows:

Chapter 9

This will return a status `200` and a reset password request to the `resetPasswordRequests` Apache Kafka topic, which will be consumed by the Email Formatter consumer to format and send the email to the SMTP server.

After some time, the `fakeSMTP` server window will show the email sent by the Email Formatter, as follows:

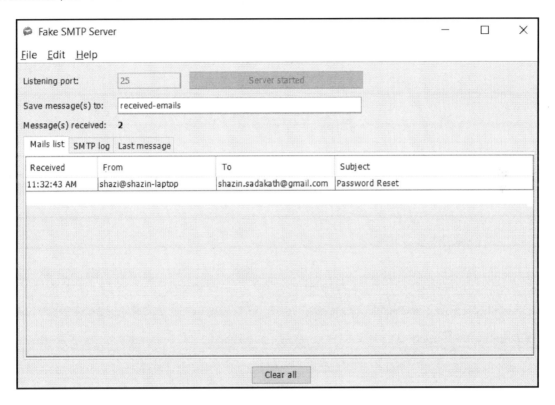

Building an Asynchronous Email Formatter

Double-clicking on the email in the **Mails list** tab will open the email in your default email client (in this case **Mozilla Thunderbird**), seen as follows:

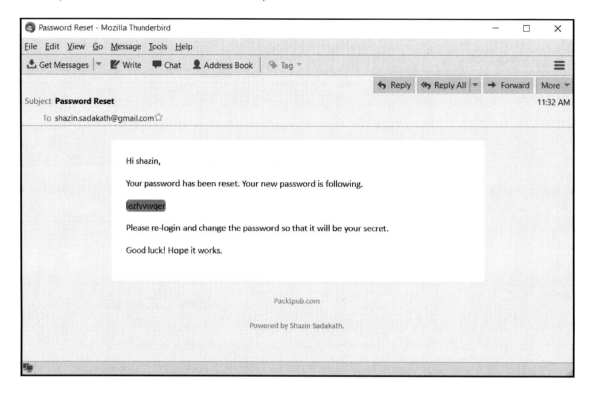

Now, when trying to access the URL `http://localhost:8080/users`, **users will be redirected to the login page as follows:**

For the username, shazin can be used, while for **password**, the new password in the reset password email can be used. Then, this will successfully redirect to the URL http://localhost:8080/users and will show the correct response:

Summary

Congratulations on completing this chapter, where the skills and knowledge required to build an asynchronous, scalable Email Formatter application were discussed.

This chapter showed you how to use Spring Data JPA for creating entities and repositories to store data in a **relational database management system (RDBMS)**. An in-memory database named H2 was used for demonstration.

Next, we explained how to use Apache FreeMarker to format emails by replacing placeholders with actual values and generating HTML content dynamically.

Furthermore, we explained how to write producers and consumers for Apache Kafka using Spring Kafka library. Spring Kafka does a lot of the heavy lifting with auto-configuration so that it is easier to develop.

We explained how to use Spring Web MVC REST controllers to accept reset password requests from users and also how to protect endpoints using Spring Security form-based authentication and authorization.

Subsequently, this chapter talked about Java Mail and how to use it to send emails from the Email Formatter consumer.

Eventually, this chapter talked about how to run ZooKeeper and Apache Kafka, and then demonstrated the use of the Email Formatter consumer and the `User Registration` microservice to accept reset password requests from users, queue the Apache Kafka topic and format, and send emails via consumers. This concludes an exciting learning journey of Spring Boot 2.0 with hands-on examples. Hopefully, this book provided a greater deal of understanding of Spring Boot, Spring Boot 2.0, Spring Web Flux, Spring Security, Spring Data JPA, Spring Data MongoDB, Spring Data Redis and many more frameworks. Happy learning!

Questions

Please answer the following questions to see whether you have successfully mastered this chapter:

1. What are the uses for the `@EnableJpaRepositories` annotation and the `@EnableTransactionManagement` annotation in Spring Data JPA?
2. What is Apache Kafka?
3. What is Apache FreeMarker?
4. What is SMTP?
5. What is Spring Security?
6. What is the use of `PasswordEncoder`?
7. What is `fakeSMTP`?

Further reading

In order to improve your knowledge of Apache Kafka and Spring Boot 2.0, the following books are recommended to be read, as they will be helpful in the coming chapters:

- *Apache Kafka 1.0 Cookbook* - https://www.packtpub.com/big-data-and-business-intelligence/apache-kafka-10-cookbook
- *Mastering Spring Boot 2.0* - https://www.packtpub.com/application-development/mastering-spring-boot-20

Assessments

Chapter 1, Introduction

1. Spring Boot is a standalone, production-grade, flexible, and extensible application development framework for building enterprise-grade Spring applications with minimum code and configurations.
2. A class annotated with the `@SpringBootApplication` annotation and a Java `main` method that calls the `SpringApplication.run` method with the class annotated with `@SpringBootApplication` and the `main` method arguments:

   ```
   @SpringBootApplication
   public class SpringBootIntroApplication {

       public static void main(String[] args) {
           SpringApplication.run(SpringBootIntroApplication.class,
           args);
       }
   }
   ```

3. Spring Boot 2.0 requires at least Java 8 to develop and run applications.
4. HTTP/2 is an improved version of HTTP that has introduced support for multiplexing, push, and header compression from the ground up to enable efficient communication between client and server.
5. The default dispatcher type for a Spring Boot 2.0 Servlet Filter is `DispatcherType.REQUEST`.
6. The next minor release version of Spring Boot 2.0, which is in milestone plan, is Spring Boot 2.1.0.
7. A Spring Boot 2.0 application with JPA starter will by default use HikariCP, which is the fastest and most efficient connection pooling framework available at the moment.

Chapter 2, Building a Basic Web Application

1. A web application is an application that is exposed through a private or public network that allows multiple concurrent users to connect to and use the application.

2. MVC pattern is a multi-tiered application development pattern used in web application development to enable separation of concerns and support ease of development and maintenance.

3. A relational database is a data store that uses relations (tables with columns, rows, and relationships between them) to maintain data while guaranteeing **ACID (Atomicity, Consistency, Independent, Durable)** properties.

4. JPA provides object/relation mapping capabilities to enable mapping between relational database tables and Java objects in order to ease persistence in Java applications.

5. `@Entity` annotation in JPA is used mark a POJO in Java to be used for object-relational mapping.

6. A Template engine is used to enable separation of concerns when developing presentation views. By using a Template engine-specific templates, UI engineers who are experts in frontend development can work independently.

7. Spring Security is a framework that enables authentication and authorization for an application, mostly web applications while covering most of the commonly known web security vulnerability.

Chapter 3, Building a Simple Blog Management System

1. Elasticsearch is an open source search and analytics engine that can run in a distributed environment. It provides RESTful APIs to ingest and retrieve high volume, velocity data. Elasticsearch is used for log analytics, full-text search, and so on.

2. Apache Freemarker is a popular template engine that can generate text output based on template and variable data. Apache Freemarker templates use a custom programming language named **Freemarker Template Language (FTL)**, which is used to write programming constructs in presentation views.

3. A Flux that can be used to send *0..N* number of data and a Mono that can be used to send `0..1` data.
4. A Blog Management System is a system that must be publicly accessible via the internet and registered users must be able to write, edit, and delete content. There must be capabilities for administrators to curate the Blog Management System.
5. A Controller Advice is used to hold `@ExceptionHandler`, `@InitBinder`, or `@ModelAttribute` methods, which are meant to be shared across multiple `@Controller` classes.
6. A Password Encoder is used to secure a password using a one-way hashing algorithm (SHA-256, MD5, BCrypt, and more) for storing so that it cannot be reversed to find the original password.
7. This can be done by returning a `UserDetailsRepositoryReactiveAuthenticationManager` as a bean, which is configured to have a `ReactiveUserDetailsService` implementation and a `PasswordEncoder` implementation.

Chapter 4, Introduction to Kotlin

1. Yes, variables and expressions can be used inside string literals beginning with a $ sign.
2. A nullable variable/argument can be assigned null at any point of code. However, before using, defensive code must be used to check for null safety. Kotlin has reduced the chances of `NullPointerException` using a nullable variable/argument. An example of a nullable variable/argument is `var no : Int? = 0`, which uses `?` at the end of the data type.
3. Explicit casting in Kotlin is where when a type checking is done using the is a keyword. Within the block of code that follows, there is no need to do a type casting to the destination type. Here is the following code:

```
var s : Any = "Shazin";
if (s is String) {
 // No need to cast s of type Any to type String inside this block of code like java does using ((String) s)
 // All properties and functions of String class can be used without type casting
 println(s.length);
}
```

4. Object expressions and object declarations can be used to create and use objects without creating a class declaration. Object expressions can be used to create objects and assign them to variables, function arguments without a class. Object declarations have a name and can be used to create singleton objects that cannot be assigned to variables or arguments, but whose functions can be called using the name.
5. A companion object is an object declaration that begins with a `companion` keyword inside of a class. Functions inside the companion object can be called just as if they are functions of the enclosing class.
6. Infix functions are a special type of functions that can be used with two operands similar to the `1 + 2` expression. An Infix function can be defined using the `infix` keyword.
7. No, variables defined inside a local function are out of scope for enclosing function, but it works the other way round.

Chapter 5, Building a Reactive Movie Rating API Using Kotlin

1. **Representational State Transfer (REST)** is an architectural style that defines a set of good practices, standards, and properties that can be implemented on top of **Hypertext Transfer Protocol (HTTP)**. A web service that conforms to REST standards enables easy interoperability between devices on the internet.
2. MongoDB is a free and open source document store that stores data in a schema-less JSON format, which is highly flexible, and each individual document can have different fields. MongoDB allows ad-hoc querying, indexing, and aggregation out of the box.
3. Kotlin is a programming language for the JVM that has concise syntax, is interoperable, safe, and tool friendly.
4. The `data` keyword in Kotlin can be used to mark classes whose sole purpose is to hold and transfer data. Classes with this keyword will get the `equals()`, `hashCode()`, `toString()`, `copy()` functions autogenerated by the compiler.
5. Basic Authentication is HTTP header-based authentication where a header named `Authorization` is used with the `"Basic "+base64Encode(username:password)` value to authenticate and authorize users.

6. Integration Testing is an end-to-end functionality testing of an application to verify whether all components are functioning together correctly.
7. Postman is a GUI-based tool to invoke and test RESTful APIs.

Chapter 6, Building an API with Reactive Microservices

1. A Maven module is a way to modularize large projects into smaller subprojects so that build and deployment can be sped up.
2. Redis is an in-memory, key/value store that provides high availability, performance, and scalability.
3. Microservices architecture is a way of designing and implementing software as a collection of independently deployable services that are highly coherent and loosely coupled.
4. Independent isolated teams, domain-specific laying, ability to automate deployments, fault tolerance, and the ability to scale individual features.
5. Containerization is the process of deploying applications in a portable and predictable manner by packaging components along with their dependencies into isolated, standard process environments called containers.
6. Docker is a very popular container platform. It is used by many developers and IT operations staff to provide independence from the underlying infrastructure and applications they run. Docker can be run on-premise hardware, in the cloud, or in a hybrid setup as well. Docker containers are lightweight and ideal for Microservices development.
7. Nginx is a load balancer/proxy server to create clusters of web servers.

Chapter 7, Building a Twitter Clone with Spring Boot

1. **Model-view-viewmodel (MVVM)** is a design pattern used to enable two-way data binding between view and model so that one changes when the other does.
2. Angular is a very famous framework that conforms to MVVM design pattern, which allows highly responsive frontend applications that update efficiently when data from server changes or when a user interacts with the application. Apart from this, Angular provides routing, dependency injection, components, templates, and such to enable flexible, modular development.

3. Angular CLI is a tool to ease the development of Angular applications because it helps create new Angular projects, generate codes, and more.
4. Angular Material is a framework that can be used to ease layout design and to provide themes.
5. CORS is a mechanism that uses HTTP headers to inform the browser to allow a web application running on one origin to have permission to access resources from a different origin.
6. OAuth2 is an authorization contract that enables applications to be secured by providing limited access to user accounts available on an HTTP service.
7. Resource, Resource Owner, Resource Server, Authorization Server, Client.

Chapter 8, Introducing Spring Boot 2.0 Asynchronous

1. The `SpringApplicationBuilder` can be used to start a Spring Boot application in a non-web mode like this:

    ```
    new SpringApplicationBuilder(ConfigClass.class).
      web(WebApplicationType.NONE).build().run(args);
    ```

2. Synchronous applications are programs that can process events, requests, and tasks sequentially in an order, and one needs to finish in order for another to begin.
3. Asynchronous applications are programs that can process events, requests, and tasks with time slicing so that one request can be active and can run while another one is also active but not running.
4. A message queue is a software layer that can be used to communicate between two applications with reliability, durability, fault tolerance, and scalability.
5. Apache Kafka is a production-grade, high performing, scalable, fault-tolerant messaging platform.
6. Spring Kafka library will be used to enable easy communication with Apache Kafka. Spring Kafka provides templates and listeners to both produce to and consume from Apache Kafka topics easily.
7. Quartz is a fully open source, high-performing scheduling framework that can be easily integrated with Java applications of any sort.

Chapter 9, Building an Asynchronous Email Formatter

1. The `@EnableJpaRepositories` annotation is to the set the base package where repositories are available. `@EnableTransactionManagement` is used to enable Spring JPA Transaction manager.
2. Apache Kafka is a production grade, high-performing, scalable, fault-tolerant messaging platform. In the application, however, we will be using Apache Kafka topic as a message queue. Also, Spring Kafka library will be used to enable easy communication with Apache Kafka. Spring Kafka provides templates and listeners to both produce to and consumes from Apache Kafka topics easily.
3. Apache Freemarker is used to generate the HTML body that will be embedded into the body of the email that will be sent when reset password requests are received.
4. SMTP stands for Simple Mail Transfer Protocol. SMTP is used to send emails from one server to another.
5. Spring Security is a widely-used project that enables authentication and authorization using many different mechanisms such as form-based logic, header-based login (Basic), and more.
6. A `PasswordEncoder` is used to encode passwords using popular algorithms such as BCrypt, SCrypt, SHA-256, etc for protection.
7. fakeSMTP is a dummy SMTP server that can be used for testing purposes. This SMTP will not send an email to the actual recipient.

Other Books You May Enjoy

If you enjoyed this book, you may be interested in these other books by Packt:

Spring Boot 2.0 Cookbook - Second Edition
Alex Antonov

ISBN: 9781787129825

- Get to know Spring Boot Starters and create custom auto-configurations
- Work with custom annotations that enable bean activation
- Use DevTools to easily develop and debug applications
- Learn the effective testing techniques by integrating Cucumber and Spock
- Observe an eternal application configuration using Consul
- Move your existing Spring Boot applications to the cloud
- Use Hashicorp Consul and Netflix Eureka for dynamic Service Discovery
- Understand the various mechanisms that Spring Boot provides to examine an application's health

Mastering Spring Boot 2.0
Dinesh Rajput

ISBN: 9781787127562

- Build logically structured and highly maintainable Spring Boot applications
- Configure RESTful microservices using Spring Boot
- Make the application production and operation-friendly with Spring Actuator
- Build modern, high-performance distributed applications using cloud patterns
- Manage and deploy your Spring Boot application to the cloud (AWS)
- Monitor distributed applications using log aggregation and ELK

Leave a review - let other readers know what you think

Please share your thoughts on this book with others by leaving a review on the site that you bought it from. If you purchased the book from Amazon, please leave us an honest review on this book's Amazon page. This is vital so that other potential readers can see and use your unbiased opinion to make purchasing decisions, we can understand what our customers think about our products, and our authors can see your feedback on the title that they have worked with Packt to create. It will only take a few minutes of your time, but is valuable to other potential customers, our authors, and Packt. Thank you!

Index

A

advanced programming, with Kotlin
  about 141
  functions 142
Angular 5
  page components, generating 233, 234
  reference 230
  services, generating 230, 231
  Tweets Add page, generating 235, 236
  used, for developing frontend for Tweety 229
  User Profile page, generating 237, 238
  users service, generating 231, 232
  using 230
Angular Material
  reference 230
Apache Cassandra drivers
  limitations 34
Apache FreeMarker
  about 91
  Create Article page, implementing 101
  error page, implementing 105
  List Articles page, implementing 98
  Show Article page, implementing 103
  template engines 90
  UI design, for Bloggest 92
  URL 92
  used, for Bloggest UI implementation 94
  used, for implementing layout 95
  using, for view 90
  using, templates 283
Apache Kafka
  about 260
  configuration, setting up 261
  dependencies, setting up 261
  executing 268
  executing, on Linux/Unix 269, 294
  executing, on Windows 269, 294
  features 260
  Image Resize Request Consumer, configuring 264, 265
  Image Resize Request Producer, configuring 261, 262, 263
  key concepts 260
  reference 256
  Spring Boot applications, starting in non-web mode 265
Apache ZooKeeper
  executing, on Windows 268, 294
application programming interface (API) 17
ApplicationContextInitializer
  used, for registering Spring Bean 18
asynchronous applications
  about 257
  overview 256
asynchronous data transfer
  Redis, using 197
  using, for cross-microservice communication 197
Asynchronous Email Formatter
  architecture 278
  building, technical requisites 275
  requirements 276

B

basic data types, Kotlin 127, 128, 129
blog management system
  Bloggest system, prerequisites 83
  Spring WebFlux, workflow 83
  web application architecture 82
Bloggest system
  about 83
  prerequisites 83
  use case diagram 84

Bloggest
  demonstrating 114, 119, 122
Bootstrap
  about 67
  URL 68

C

CommentType enumeration 52
components, image resizing
  Email Formatter Consumer 278
  Message Queue 278
  User Registration 278
conditional statements, Kotlin
  if statement 131
  when statement 132
configuration properties
  binding 19
  environment variables, with indices 22
  property origin 21
  property type java.time.Duration, direct binding in ISO-8601 form 22
  tightened rules, for governing relaxed property binding 21
containers 199
controller
  implementing 106, 110, 194, 197
  Spring WebFlux, using 106, 193
Create, Retrieve, Update, Delete (CRUD)
  operations 51, 85, 150, 183, 184
cross-microservice communication
  asynchronous data transfer, using 197
cross-origin resource sharing (CORS) 241
Cross-Site Request Forgery (CSRF) 68
custom health indicator 27, 28
custom Spring Boot Actuator endpoint
  connecting, with management tools 24
  connecting, with monitoring tools 24
  exposing 23
  extending, with specialized implementation for web 24

D

Data Definition Language (DDL) 53
Docker
  about 199
  features for microservices 199
  images, building with Maven 200, 202
  used, for building of microsevice system 202, 205
  used, for deploying microservices 206, 207
  used, for supporting microservices 199
domain model, implementing with Spring Data Redis annotations
  about 185, 186
  dependencies and configuration, setting up 185
domain model
  class diagram 279
  comment 52
  configuration 52
  dependencies and configuration, setting up 279
  dependencies, setting up 52
  implementation, JPA notation used 52, 279
  implementing 54, 280
  user 52

E

Email Formatter Consumer
  Apache Kafka, executing 294
  configuration 288
  demonstrating 293
  dependencies, building 293
  executing 296
  Java Mail, configuration 290
  SMTP server, executing 295
  User Registration microservice, executing 296, 299

F

features, Kotlin
  concise syntax 126
  developer friendliness 126
  interoperability 126
  safe coding and runtime 126
Font Awesome 67
for loop, Kotlin
  with array 133
  with collection 133
  with value range 134
Freemarker Template Language (FTL) 91
functions, Kotlin advanced programming

default arguments 143
generics 144
infix notation 142
local functions 142
named arguments 143
variable number of arguments (vararg) 144

H

HTTP/2 protocol
  using, by Spring Boot 2.0 28, 30
HyperText Transfer Protocol (HTTP) 148

I

IDEA IntelliJ
  downloading link 8
  reference 148
Image Resizer, components
  Image Resize Request Consumer 259
  Image Resize Request Producer 259
  Message Queue 259
Image Resizer
  Apache Kafka, executing 268
  architecture 259
  demonstrating 268
  dependencies, building 268
  Image Resize Request Consumer, executing 269
  Image Resize Request Producer, executing 269, 271
  Quartz Scheduler, use cases 258
  requisites 257
  use case diagram 258
IntelliJ IDEA
  download link 125
  reference 256
IntelliJ
  used, for opening Spring Boot Project 9

J

Jakarta Enterprise Edition (Jakarta EE)
    applications 90
Java 9
  correct AspectJ version, using 34
  JAXBException, tackling 33
  Spring Boot 2.0, executing 33

Java Archive (JAR) 13
Java Database Connectivity (JDBC) 226
Java Development Kit (JDK) 8
  download link 7, 125
  reference 147, 255
  URL 81
Java Enterprise Edition (Java EE) 65
Java Persistence API (JPA) 50
Java Server Pages (JSP) 47
Java Server Tag Library (JSTL) elements 65, 90
Java Server Template Library (JSTL) 47
Java virtual machine (JVM) 13
JSP Standard Tag Library (JSTL) 35

K

Kotlin codes
  syntax 129
Kotlin
  about 126
  advanced programming 141
  automatic casting 132
  basic data types 127
  compile-time null safety 132
  conditional statements 131
  default imports 126
  enums 139
  extensions 138
  for loop 133
  functions 130
  generic types 139
  interfaces 137
  nullable values 132
  objects 140
  packages 129
  string interpolation 130
  type checking 132
  variables 131
  while loop 134

L

Lambda expression
  reference 19
Linux/Unix
  Apache Kafka, executing 269, 294

M

Maven 3
  download link 7, 125
  reference 147, 255
Maven Surefire Plugin
  issues 34
Micrometer
  used for customising metrics 26
migration guide
  reference link 33
migration
  JVM, using 33
Model-view-controller (MVC) pattern 46
model-view-viewmodel (MVVM) 220
MongoDB
  about 151
  features 151
Moviee API
  demonstrating 168
  integration test, performing 168, 170
  Postman, using 171
  REST architecture, requisites 149
  Spring Security, using for authorization 166, 167
  use case diagram 150
  User, use cases 150

O

OAuth2
  about 242
  configuration, setting up 243
  dependencies, setting up 243
object-oriented programming (OOP), with Kotlin
  about 135
  abstract classes 136
  classes 136
  concrete classes 137
  visibility modifiers 135
objects, Kotlin
  companion objects 141
  declarations 140
  object expressions 140

P

Plain Old Java Object (POJO) 20
Postman
  GET available Taxis endpoint, accessing 212
  Get Movie endpoint, accessing 172
  Get Movie endpoint, accessing with invalid Movie ID 173
  Get Taxi Status endpoint, accessing 211
  List Movies endpoint, accessing 171
  location, submitting to update Taxi Location endpoint 209
  submitting, for canceling Taxi Booking endpoint 215
  submitting, for registering Taxi endpoint 207
  submitting, to Accept Taxi Booking endpoint 214
  submitting, to Book Taxi endpoint 213
  submitting, to update Taxi Status endpoint 210
  Taxi Bookings endpoint, accessing 216
  using 171
prerequisites, reactive microservices
  project structure 182
  use case diagram 181
  use cases, of Taxi Microservice 182
property binding API 20

Q

Quartz
  about 266
  configuration, setting up 266
  dependencies, setting up 266
  scheduling, configuration 266
  used, for scheduling 266

R

Rapid application development (RAD) 13
reactive microservices
  architecture 178
  developing, technical requisites 178
  features 179
  overview 178
  requisites 180
Representational State Transfer (REST)
  architecture 148, 149
requisites, for Asynchronous Email Formatter

use case diagram 277
REST controller
   annotations, implementation 291
   Spring Web MVC, using 291
Retro Board
   demonstrating 77, 78
   UI implementation, with Spring Thymeleaf 67
revised Spring Security, Spring Boot 2.0
   changed default security auto-configuration strategy, using 42

S

Saber 207
search engine optimization (SEO) 116
Secure Socket Layer (SSL) 30
Service Provider Interfaces (SPI) 14
Simple Mail Transfer Protocol (SMTP) server
   executing 295
Spring Boot 1.x
   changes 17, 18
   configuration properties, binding 19
   property binding API 20
   Spring Bean, registering with ApplicationContextInitializer 18
Spring Boot 2.0
   AuthenticationManager bean, using 42
   changed actuator base path, using 37
   changed actuator configuration properties, using 37
   changed database schema creation strategy, using 41
   changed default behavior for path mapping, using 38
   changed default database initialization strategy, using 41
   changed Embedded Container Configuration, using 38
   changed HikariCP default connection pool, for JPA using 41
   changed Jackson support, using 40
   changed JSON support, using 40
   changed servlet-specific server properties, using 36
   changed Spring Boot Actuator security, using 40
   changed testing support, using 42
   dispatcher types for the servlet filter, using 39
   executing, on Java 9 33
   HTTP/2 protocol, using 28, 30
   JDK, using 33
   migrating 33
   modified configuration location strategy, using 40
   modified template engine extension handling, using 36
   modified transitive dependency to spring-boot-web-starter, using 39
   proxying strategy, using 40
   removed features 43
   renamed actuator endpoints, using 37
   revised Spring Security, using 42
   Spring Security OAuth2, migrating to Spring Security core 42
   Spring Security, used for securing applications 31
   updated configuration properties, using 36
Spring Boot Actuator
   custom endpoints, using annotations 22
   custom health indicator 27, 28
   metrics, customising with Micrometer 26
Spring Boot application
   anatomy 14, 15
Spring Boot Project
   initiating 8
   opening, with IntelliJ 9
   opening, with Spring Tool Suite (STS) 11
Spring Boot
   about 13
   features 13, 32
   initiating 13
   Spring Framework ecosystem, supporting 16
Spring Data Elasticsearch
   about 86
   configuration class, setting up 87
   dependencies, setting up 87
   domain model implementation, with annotations 87
   domain model, class diagram 86
   domain model, implementing 88
   Elasticsearch 85
   repositories, implementation 89
   using, for persistence 85

Spring Data JPA
  about 51
  business logic, encapsulating with Services 227, 229, 281
  class diagram, for domain model 222
  dependencies, setting up 223
  domain model, class diagram 51, 279
  domain model, implementation with JPA annotations 52
  domain model, implementing 223, 224, 225
  Java Database Connectivity (JDBC), using 226
  Java Persistence API (JPA) 50
  repositories, implementing 56, 226, 281
  repositories, testing 56
  services, testing 62
  services, used for encapsulating business logic 61
  Spring Boot Devtools, using for database visualization 59
  URL 56
  using 222
  using, for persistence 50, 278
Spring Data MongoDB
  about 151
  business logic, encapsulating with service 155, 157
  configuration classes, setting up 153
  dependencies, setting up 153
  domain model 152
  domain model, class diagram 152
  domain model, implementing 153, 154
  repositories, implementing 155
  services, testing 157, 158, 159, 161
  using 150
Spring Data Redis
  class diagram, for domain model 184
  domain model, implementing with annotations 185
  repositories, implementing 187
  Service, used for encapsulating business logic 187, 191, 193
  using, for persistence 183
Spring Framework 5.0
  using 34
Spring Framework ecosystem
  supporting, in Spring Boot 16

Spring Kafka
  dependencies and configuration, setting up 286
  Email Formatter Consumer, configuration 288
  used, for communication 259, 285
  User Registration, configuration 286
Spring Security
  Angular service, used for OAuth2 authentication and authorization 246, 247, 248
  Authorization Server, configuring 244
  OAuth2 242
  Resource Server, configuring 244
  used, for authentication and authorization of Tweety 242
  using, for authentication 74, 111
  using, for authentication and authorization 292
  using, for authorization 74, 111
  using, for authorization of Moviee API 166, 167
  web security, configuring 245
Spring Thymeleaf
  about 66
  template engines 65
  UI design, using for Retro Board 66
  used, for Retro Board UI implementation 67
  using, for view 65
Spring Tool Suite (STS)
  download link 125
  downloading link 8
  reference 148
  URL 82
  used, for opening Spring Boot Project 11
Spring Web Flux
  Angular frontend access, enabling to controllers 241
  ControllerAdvice, implementation 110
  TweetController, implementing 239, 240, 241
  using, for controller 106
  using, for REST controller 238
Spring Web MVC
  Controllers annotations, implementation 70
  controllers, testing 71
  using, for REST controller 291
  using, with servlet 3.x for controller 69
  workflow 47
Spring WebFlux
  MovieController, implementing 162, 163

[320]

MovieController, testing 163, 164, 166
  using, for controller 193
  using, for MovieController 161
synchronous applications 256
synchronous data transfer
  Redis, using 199

T

templates
  Apache Freemarker, using 283
  reference 285
Tweety
  architecture 220
  authentication, with Spring Security 242
  authorization, with Spring Security 242
  demonstrating 249
  frontend, developing with Angular 5 229
  List Tweets page, accessing 251
  login page, accessing 250
  requisites 221
  Send Tweet page, accessing 251
  use case diagram 221
  User, use cases 222

U

Uniform Resource Identifier (URI) 149
Uniform Resource Locator (URL) 148
upgraded Spring Framework 5.0
  dropped support, for frameworks 35
  modified CORS support behavior 35
  removed classes 35
  removed methods 35
  removed packages 35
  using 34
user interface (UI) 46, 82

W

web application architecture
  about 46
  prerequisites 49
  Spring Web MVC, workflow 47
  use case diagram 49
Web Archive (WAR) 13
Windows
  Apache Kafka, executing 269
  Apache ZooKeeper, executing 268, 294
World Wide Web (WWW) 148

Made in the USA
Middletown, DE
04 October 2018